Also available at all good book stores

9781785315466

9781785313929

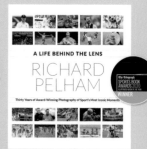

9781785315466

9781785315381

9781785316838

9781785316869

9781785316906

9781785317262

9781785317286

THE
UNDISPUTED
CHAMPIONS OF EUROPE

THE
UNDISPUTED
CHAMPIONS OF EUROPE

How the Gods of Football
Became European Royalty

STEVEN SCRAGG

First published by Pitch Publishing, 2021

Pitch Publishing
A2 Yeoman Gate
Yeoman Way
Worthing
Sussex
BN13 3QZ
www.pitchpublishing.co.uk
info@pitchpublishing.co.uk

A CIP catalogue record is available for this book
from the British Library.

ISBN 978 1 80150 005 0

Typesetting and origination by Pitch Publishing
Printed and bound in the UK by TJ Books Ltd

Contents

For my dad. The person who gave me both my love for my team of choice, but also my appreciation for the wider game.

Acknowledgements

WRITE A book, he said. Well the book eventually became a trilogy, and for that I have my *These Football Times* colleague Will Sharp to thank. I will not rest until I have set you off on a long overdue book of your own. Beyond that, none of this would have been possible without the support of Omar Saleem, Hyder Jawád, Stuart Horsfield, Gary Thacker, and Aidan Williams. Endless podcasts and online chats have stirred the footballing soul. I'd also like to say thank you for the trust shown by Jane and Paul at Pitch Publishing, plus Duncan Olner for turning an image in my head into a glorious book cover. At home, Bev, Sam, Elsie, and Florence have all saved the day on various occasions. My dad, Alison, and David have all offered encouragement and support. Much needed distractions have been supplied by the magnificent Hayley Coleman, along with Andy, and Carrie Knott. A big thank you, too, to all who have taken the time to both purchase one, two, or all three of these books, and to all who have interacted on social media.

Introduction

GLINTING AND glistening under the glaring spotlight, usually presented to the winning captain in a European city of immense stature, the Coupe des Clubs Champions Européens was the most visually reflective of the three major European prizes on offer in the month of May. As the flashbulbs popped away and the floodlights shone bright, the European Cup absorbed all light and bounced it straight back into the eyes of a captivated and increasingly global audience.

While the European Cup Winners' Cup offered an eclectic and random form of footballing entertainment, and the UEFA Cup boasted a list of teams that would put its older and more vaunted siblings to shame on a regular basis, resplendent also with the final that owned the best atmosphere, in riposte the European Cup Final felt like the centre of the footballing universe. It was an event that permeated an enchanting sense of occasion matched by no other club game.

There was always something that little bit more reverential about the European Cup Final. A game that would be broadcast live in the UK far more often than not, irrespective of the two teams taking part, while in comparison many British successes in the Cup Winners' Cup, Inter-Cities Fairs Cup and its successor the UEFA Cup were only followed live on the radio, by supporters, and interested observers who would be made to wait for late-night highlights instead.

For instance, while the less intrepid Liverpool supporters who opted not to travel to West Germany for the second leg of the 1973 UEFA Cup Final weren't able to watch live coverage of their team's success against Borussia Mönchengladbach, a week later they were spoilt for broadcasting choice, as both the BBC and ITV covered the European Cup Final live, a game contested by opponents from the Netherlands and Italy.

It was with a sense of awe that I would sit in front of the television, transfixed by an occasion that didn't require hype, that didn't need an accompanying soundtrack of 'Zadok the Priest'. In 1983, when Hamburger SV faced the might of Juventus, on a night in Athens when La Vecchia Signora were expected to belatedly come of age as the champions of Europe, only to be denied, an evening that marked the first European Cup Final not to have an English presence for seven years, it was the wonderful Barry Davies who set the pre-match tone when he spoke to the nation.

Davies effused with consummate class of a stadium that was entirely in keeping with an ancient yet modern city and its iconic ruins, going on to run his audience through all they needed to know prior to kick-off, informing them of how Athens had been alive to the sound of song, fine wine, and beautiful food, and how the Juventus supporters heavily outnumbered their HSV counterparts. He talked of the thoroughly Latin atmosphere, and of the slight breeze that the players would appreciate, on an evening when the temperature was still '73 degrees Fahrenheit, with a humidity of 48 per cent'.

No hyperbole from Davies, and from here he took us through to the start of the game via a barely concealed lament at the state of the pitch at Wembley compared to that of the

Olympic Stadium, followed by his approval of the flares and firecrackers that were being set off, and the 6.2 ratio of Italian to West German players having taken part in the 1982 World Cup Final.

As the whistle was blown to begin the 1983 European Cup Final, Davies offered up what was in one part a pair of rhetorical questions, and on the other hand a prayer to Olympus, for a game to match the beauty of the surroundings, when he proclaimed, 'Can we hope for an Olympic spirit, in such a stadium? Are we to see the jaws of Gentile, or the expression of Platini,' before tempering it with the disclaimer, 'Maybe we'll have the first, before the freedom of the second?'

It was with such marvellous scene-setting that Davies transported you from your living room to these stadiums, and these finals. It mattered not that so many of them seemed to end 1-0.

Two years later, it was Davies again who described the scenes prior to a European Cup Final that Juventus had reached, this time in Brussels and with an infinitely more sombre note as 39 souls needlessly died at the dilapidated Heysel Stadium. Over 35 years on from the Heysel disaster, with a combination of sadness and acceptance, his voice tilts to the perfectly weighted tone, when his mind's eye drifts to the topic.

For me, Davies was the voice of the European Cup Final, something he delightedly laughs out loud about when suggested to him. It was a gig that was blessed by his commentary every other year, in days when the BBC would alternate annually with ITV in broadcasting the biggest night on the European club football calendar. On the BBC and ITVs off years, the compensation was that they would cover the Cup Winners' Cup Final instead.

In between the 1983 and 1985 European Cup Finals, Davies also covered Juventus when they defeated FC Porto in the 1984 Cup Winners' Cup Final. He must have felt a kinship to them by the time he arrived in Brussels.

The European Cup Final represented a footballing plateau; there was a rarefied air that required an authoritative voice behind the microphone, as these were peaks where the teams who reached the summit had been compelled to win their domestic league titles to gain entry to the tournament in the first place. This was heavyweight football, a VIP section for those who had earned the right to be there.

Once in the European Cup, however, you would have to skate across thin ice to reach the final. One false move, one off night, and it would be over. Sent back to square one to win your domestic league once again, in order to be permitted another attempt at landing 'Old Big Ears'.

High jeopardy would then come into play in the final. To reach a European Cup Final both teams had endured an odyssey like no other, via domestic success of great magnitude, followed by a tightrope walk all the way to the last hurdle. Imagine going through all of that, only to lose. An event that was akin to playing Snakes and Ladders, only to hit that last snake up in the 90s on the board.

Within this environment, there was a footballing socialism at play. Qualification was open to any team who had won their domestic league title the previous season, while should the holders of the European Cup not have simultaneously won their own league championship, that was fine too. If you won the European Cup you automatically had the right to defend it.

A classic and simple format. No sleight of hand, no partitioning and protection of the great and the good of the game, no backs scratched, no shepherding away of the less fashionable clubs who arrived by winning a league title in a perceived backwater; even the draw was an unseeded one. Every team was classed as equal in the European Cup before a ball was kicked in anger, upon which the men and boys separated themselves not in the boardrooms of UEFA and their commercial partners but out on the football pitches of the north, east, south, and west of the continent.

A fair chance for all to prevail and despite an English club reaching the 1979 final, it was an occasion contested by two teams that the contemporary game would be loaded against today. The Swedish champions, FF Malmö, were beaten by a Nottingham Forest side who two years earlier had nervously edged over the Second Division finish line, marginally ahead of Bolton Wanderers, to gain promotion back to the First Division after a five-year exile.

Between 1955/56 and 1991/92, it made for a heady concoction where at one end of the spectrum it wasn't an outlandish dream for 1. FC Saarbrücken to win at the San Siro against AC Milan, when representing the protectorate of the Saarland, or at the other end for Hamrun Spartans of Malta to battle it out with Benfica, safely within the same boundaries of a tournament where the giants still satisfyingly collided too. It made for a magnificent contrast that while shared with the Cup Winners' Cup and the UEFA Cup was somehow brought into sharper focus in the European Cup, partly because of how brightly the big teams shone on European club football's biggest stage.

Conversely, if you saw a member of European football royalty among the runners and riders in the Cup Winners' Cup or UEFA Cup, after achieving immortality in the European Cup, it somehow jarred, as if they had let themselves down to a degree. Yet in the European Cup you would look at a Real Madrid, with the knowledge that to win La Liga they had had to finish above not only their big city rivals over at the Vicente Calderón, but also Barcelona, Valencia, Athletic Club, and Real Sociedad.

It was the same rule for Milan in Serie A, Liverpool in the First Division, Bayern Munich in the Bundesliga, and Ajax in the Eredivisie. The list of rivals they each had to defeat to win their respective league title to earn a crack at the European Cup was a who's who of impressive proportions. So, when the part-timers of HJK Helsinki were pitted against the might of Ajax, it was both a brutal and beautiful experience.

Yet, despite the heavy defeat, HJK, along with the likes of Stade Dudelange, Jeunesse Esch, Floriana, Crusaders, Oulun Palloseura, and Odense Boldklub, were glorious by association. Teams who had climbed their own domestic mountains to earn the right to cross paths with the biggest and best, they left indelible impressions of their own upon the European Cup, whereas in the Champions League era the hurdles have become too numerous and of such heights that they have long since bid farewell to the tournament before it has even begun for the elite clubs.

Within this, character has been lost, cashed in to create what is a European Super League in all but name. As successful a marketing concept as the Champions League has been, it has proved to be a marginalisation of football's perceived riffraff, which has ultimately taken the shine off the business end of the tournament. The extraordinary air of the European Cup has been replaced by a feeling of excess and homogenisation in the shape of its successor.

With the rough and undesirable edges knocked off, once the tournament was supersized certain elite teams wound up being pitted against one another with an almost indecent regularity. Real Madrid and Juventus, for instance, drawn together in the European Cup on two occasions for a sum of four games, have since walked on to a Champions League pitch together 16 times, while prior to them fading away from being a Champions League staple, Arsenal were paired with

Bayern Munich in four out of a five-season span. Familiarity invites contempt.

No matter how magnificent Lionel Messi and Cristiano Ronaldo are, they have almost played out careers where they have been as much a part of the family weekly ritual as the supermarket run or a Friday night takeaway. We have been able to chart their progress from the very beginning and marvel at how they developed, yet never have they offered the sense of mystery that their European Cup-winning counterparts did, the fewer sightings of which were embraced within an air of awe.

A place where the icons resided, the European Cup was where legends were created, or further enhanced. Di Stéfano, Gento, Puskás, Águas, Eusébio, Altafini, Rivera, Prati, Mazzola, Suárez, Jair, Gemmell, Johnstone, Chalmers, Best, Charlton, Moulijn, Kindvall, Israël, Cruyff, Neeskens, Rep, Beckenbauer, Müller, Breitner, Keegan, Dalglish, Souness, Francis, Robertson, Withe, Mortimer, Morley, Magath, Platini, Rossi, Boniek, Duckadam, Futre, Madjer, Van Breukelen, Koeman, Baresi, Maldini, Rijkaard, Gullit, Van Basten, Prosinečki, Pančev, Savićević, Stoichkov and Laudrup; all names that will echo through eternity, who could very easily be joined by page upon page of others.

These icons of the pitch were, of course, carrying out the strategic genius of Villalonga, Carniglia, Muñoz, Guttmann, Rocco, Herrera, Stein, Busby, Happel, Michels, Kovács, Lattek, Cramer, Paisley, Clough, Barton, Fagan, Trapattoni, Jenei, Jorge, Hiddink, Saachi, Petrović and Cruyff. Thirty-seven European Cups won by 19 different coaches. In the cases of Muñoz and Cruyff, their legends burned so brightly that they were both European Cup-winning captains and coaches.

Rather than an omnipresent shadow cast across huge swathes of the football season, as is the wont of the Champions

League, the European Cup represented an intermittent yet magical mirage, seen twice as autumn circumnavigated its way toward winter, and then again on three more occasions as spring entwined within the early notes of summer. Always lovingly cherished, and never taken for granted, the sense of occasion was palpable.

These are the fabled years of the European Cup.

1

Who Do You Think You Are?

IT WAS within the pages of the French sports weekly *Le Miroir des sports* in 1934 that Gabriel Hanot suggested football's future lay within the concept of a cross-border European club competition. Not a cup competition, but a league.

Hanot had put plenty of thought into his idea. Under his plan, the top two teams in each national league would advance to a pan-European league for the following season before returning to domestic duties 12 months later, replaced in Hanot's league by two more teams per nation from the previous various domestic campaigns.

Some 87 years later, football threatened to tear itself apart all in the name of a cross-border Super League. Nothing in the sport is as new as you might think it to be.

While there had been a series of other attempts to create compelling cross-border competitions before, the Mitropa Cup being the most cohesive entity, the concept of challenge games between teams from different nations can be traced back to a time before the inception of league systems.

Added to this, as soon as football had gained organised traction in most industrialised nations it did not take long before touring clubs set off to conquer others. Rather than love thy neighbour, it was a case of beat thy neighbour, while also enjoying the gracious hospitality on offer.

By 1887, Aston Villa and Hibernian were facing off in the self-proclaimed 'World Championship', the first of a cluster of games that was eventually contested by England and Scotland's respective league champions.

In the 20th century, 1909 and 1911 saw the playing of the Sir Thomas Lipton Trophy in Turin, which was comfortably won on both occasions by West Auckland, the second of these successes coming with a 6-1 victory against Juventus. Classed as an international tournament by some football historians, it was even dramatised by Tyne Tees Television in 1982, in a production entitled *The World Cup: A Captain's Tale*, starring Nigel Hawthorne, Dennis Waterman, and Tim Healy, among a list of other fine actors.

Interrupted by the Second World War, beyond his 1934 musings it would take 21 years before a heavily tinkered version of Hanot's vision was put into operation, inspired for launch by a series of high-profile floodlit friendlies during 1953 and 1954.

A game at Molineux particularly caught the imagination, between Wolverhampton Wanderers and Budapest Honvéd in December 1954, which was broadcast live by the BBC. It was the first of a hat-trick of such matches in as many days, the others being West Ham United vs Milan and Chelsea vs Vörös Lobogó, one of the many pseudonyms of the great MTK Budapest.

Wolves were no stranger to games against continental opposition, something they were embracing even before the arrival at the club of Stan Cullis, but the installation of floodlights in 1953 brought with it a new impetus. The evocative feel of a classical European night beneath artificial light was broadcast live to the nation, while 55,000 spectators clicked through the Molineux turnstiles to drink in the experience for themselves. A month earlier, the visitors had been Spartak Moscow. These were games which ensured the floodlights soon paid for themselves.

Put into context, in an era in which the FA Cup was of vital importance and enjoyed massive popularity, two months later, when Wolves welcomed Charlton Athletic to Molineux in the fifth round on a Saturday afternoon, there were 6,000 fewer paying customers than there had been for their friendly against Honvéd. Even the visit of Arsenal in the fourth round had attracted a smaller gate than the great Hungarians did.

Classed by many as an unofficial world championship match, Wolves' victory against a team which boasted the presence of six members of the Hungarian national team who had helped to defeat England 6-3 at Wembley a little under a year earlier, was used as irrefutable proof of English football's continued imperialism over the game.

Hanot and others were less convinced and renewed their calls for a Europe-wide cup competition, imploring that one game on a far from perfect English winter pitch was not representative of a footballing summer of pomposity. What Wolves really needed to do was to travel to Budapest, Moscow, and Milan, and show that they could do it there too.

What Honvéd brought with them was an air of mystique, these games coming eight years after Dynamo Moscow's magnificent British tour, during which they faced Chelsea, Cardiff City, Arsenal, and Rangers.

While the British public were certainly displaying an appetite for matches against mysterious continental opposition, the bureaucrats who ran the game had other ideas. The English and the Scottish, notorious when it came to bristling at new ideas, had only relented to re-joining FIFA in 1946, along with the Irish and Welsh associations, having been in exile since

1928. Nor had this been the first time the home nations had walked away from the world game's governing body.

Hanot had argued against this exile but it was with it in mind in 1934 that he would have his work cut out in obtaining the involvement of British clubs for his European league. A prickly yet visionary character, he had been a fine footballer in his own right then later the coach of the French national team, and turned his hand to journalism too, becoming the editor of the influential newspaper *L'Équipe*, where he anonymously lambasted his own management in print.

Finally the European Cup was born, proposed to the UEFA congress of March 1955 and ratified the following month. In Jacques Ferran, Hanot had found a kindred footballing spirit, and together they are credited as the founding fathers of the tournament, Hanot driven by his long-held vision and Ferran by the notion that South America had beaten Europe to the punch in creating a continental club competition of purpose.

For their knowledge, passion, commitment, and administrative skills, Hanot and Ferran would be at the forefront of *L'Équipe's* organisation of the first half-decade of the European Cup.

Up and running for the 1955/56 season, true to form, English football shunned the new venture, with the champions Chelsea being pressed not to take part. Not until the era of the Champions League would Stamford Bridge host games from Europe's premier tournament.

With the first five years of the European Cup operating on an invitational basis, when the Scottish champions Aberdeen followed the example of Chelsea in turning down their opportunity to take part, it eventually fell to fifth-placed Hibernian to accept the invitation.

Progressives in British football might have been in the minority, but those who were sold on the idea were in possession of great influence. At Wolves, Stan Cullis was under no illusions just how important the infant European competition was, and how combined with increasing television interest the future was plain to see. Manchester United's Matt Busby was another to be attracted to the challenge.

Up to this point, English football had been quite happy with its position as the givers of the game to the world, spreading the word as part of the industrial revolution and being the benevolent missionaries, drifting through all manner of global seaports, building railway systems and raiding the natural resources of countless nations, while leaving them the gift of football as recompense.

The problem came when many of those nations took to football with a skill, zeal, thirst and vision that often superseded the motherland. When it came to the Football Association, the British authorities were incensed by movements and inventions such as FIFA, UEFA, the World Cup, European club competition, and the European Championship.

There was an oft-repeated reticence to take part that was nothing short of damaging. As the footballing world turned, the English dug their heels in and refused to be party to these new and unsettling innovations. The FA was not for rocking the boat it felt it had constructed. It looked at the altering landscape and promptly took its ball home.

Difficulties in obtaining the involvement of teams for the inaugural European Cup was not solely confined to the British, however. Of the 16 teams to accept the first wave of invitations, only seven of them were their nation's reigning domestic champions.

Hibs were rewarded for their enthusiasm and would go on to become the first British team to contest a European Cup semi-final, where they were defeated by the enigmatic Stade de Reims.

Reims would contest the final in 1956, and again in 1959. A team frozen in time, by 1964 they had been shockingly relegated from the French First Division just two years beyond the last of their six league titles, from where they would sink into semi-obscurity. They have periodically returned to the top flight but also suffered a 33-year exile during which they almost ceased to exist, befalling liquidation and embracing rebirth in 1992.

In the formative years of the European Cup, however, Reims were the essence of French football, boasting the skills of Raymond Kopa, a player so impressive that Real Madrid would swoop for him beyond the 1956 European Cup Final.

After three glory-laden years at the Santiago Bernabéu Stadium, Kopa made the return transfer to Reims after the two teams had again faced one another in the 1959 European Cup Final. He would remain dedicated to the club for the remainder of his career, even sticking with them in relegation.

Kopa was not the only legendary figure to star for Reims. To cushion the blow of his transfer to Madrid, Just Fontaine arrived from Nice, while they were also served with distinction by Dominique Colonna, Roger Marche, Robert Jonquet, Armand Penverne, Jean Vincent, and Roger Piantoni. For a while, they also had the future French national team manager Michel Hidalgo.

One of the great enigmas of European football, these two European Cup Finals came within the eye of the Reims storm. Those six league titles were won within a 14-season span, between 1948/49 and 1961/62, a period in which they also won the Coupe de France twice.

Shining brightly for a decade and a half, the way they faded was stunning, but in 1956 they came desperately close to setting an alternative landscape to the one that Madrid sculpted. Twice leading the first European Cup Final, Reims disorientated Madrid in the opening ten minutes at the Parc des Princes, cutting a swathe through the Spanish side's defence.

Michel Leblond became the first European Cup Final goalscorer, catching out Juan Alonso at his near post with only six minutes on the clock, while it was a gift from the Madrid goalkeeper that handed Janusz Templin the second goal just four minutes later. By the half-hour mark the scores were level, Alfredo Di Stéfano slamming one in from close range after an intricate build-up, and Héctor Rial doing likewise 16 minutes later.

Hidalgo restored Reims's lead shortly after the hour, with a glancing header, yet within five minutes Marquitos had claimed a fortuitous equaliser. From there, Madrid ended the game the stronger of the two teams and it fell to Rial to strike the winning goal.

Madrid's success in the first European Cup Final came by the narrowest of margins, leading only after scoring the winning goal and having trailed for a third of the game. Fate smiled upon them and they used that momentum to take advantage for the next four years.

It had not been the only sliding door that Madrid had worked their way through in that inaugural European Cup campaign, as in the quarter-final against Partizan, a 4-0 first-leg victory was very nearly overturned in the second leg, when the Yugoslavs won 3-0. The two teams would later face one another again, in the 1966 final.

Another massive set of games were then played in the semi-final against AC Milan. There was almost 130,000 in attendance at the Santiago Bernabéu for the first leg in what should forever stand as the stadium's record attendance. A 4-2 victory for the hosts left much still to be played for in the return.

European Cup fever was running rampant in the Spanish capital, yet in Milan it was still to fully catch on in terms of enthusiasm. Only 30,000 turned up at the San Siro to see I Rossoneri claw back to within a goal of taking the tie to a play-off match, on an occasion when the Italian champions were awarded two penalties for the vaguest of infringements. A sizeable contingent of travelling Madrid supporters had been in attendance to see their team reach the final.

Three years later, it was less of a contest as Madrid eased to a sedate 2-0 victory over Reims at the Neckarstadion in Stuttgart. The French side never recovered after conceding to Mateos in the first minute, and it was the same player who won yet missed a penalty not long after.

Kopa, given no quarter by his former team-mates, was put out of proceedings for a spell before the interval, falling to an uncompromising challenge from Vincent but eventually returning to limp through the rest of the game.

With Di Stéfano hitting Madrid's second goal, via a low drive from outside the penalty area just two minutes after the restart, it was enough to deflate Reims, who were overrun by their opponents for the remainder.

Again there was a fork in the road on the way to the final, where Madrid could have been deflected away from their stranglehold on the tournament. A family affair, a neighbourhood spat. Atlético Madrid made a wonderful nuisance of themselves, taking the semi-final to a third game, at Real Zaragoza's La Romareda, where they were narrowly beaten 2-1. Reims, too, had diced with an earlier exit when forced to fight back from a 2-0 first-leg reversal against Standard Liège in the quarter-finals.

These formative years of the European Cup were undeniably monopolised by Madrid's successes. Between the two finals won by defeating Reims, they had beaten Fiorentina in the 1957 final, within the comfort of their own Santiago Bernabéu home, and Milan a year later in a classic final at the Heysel Stadium.

Fiorentina had been stubborn opponents, with their goalkeeper Giuliano Sarti in a determined mood. It took an erroneously awarded penalty to break his resistance midway through the second half, converted by Di Stéfano.

With the entire complexion of the game changing, the Italians were forced to go on the front foot and Alonso was made to work. Yet it was Madrid who struck a second goal, on the breakaway, as Paco Gento clipped the ball over the advancing Sarti when put clean through with 15 minutes left. The unfortunate Fiorentina goalkeeper would return to European Cup Finals and enjoy later success with Internazionale.

For Madrid, it meant the further growth of their burgeoning legend having beaten Manchester United in the semi-final, Matt Busby having ignored the suggestions of English football's rule-makers not to take part. It was where Di Stéfano and Bobby Charlton crossed paths for the first time and an enduring mutual respect was born, on the same pitches that the ethereal Duncan Edwards worked his monochrome and haunting magic.

A year later, at the same stage of the tournament, while Madrid were enjoying a formulaic run to yet another final Manchester United were paired with Milan. Along with seven of his team-mates, Edwards would not play a part, however, each of them victims in the Munich air disaster. The 21-year-old had hung on to life for 15 days until succumbing to his injuries on 21 February 1958.

Forever the committed pencil pushers, the Football Association denied Manchester United the services of Charlton for the semi-final games against Milan, instead insisting he be called to international duty during an era in which club games overlapped with internationals. After a spirited 2-1 win for United in the first leg at Old Trafford, the Serie A champions were too strong at the San Siro.

In Brussels, it was Madrid who prevailed once again, twice coming from behind to defeat the Milan of Cesare Maldini, Nils Liedholm, and Juan Alberto Schiaffino.

It was Schiaffino who opened the scoring just before the hour with a curled effort that evaded the despairing dive of Alonso. Di Stéfano was again seemingly Madrid's saviour with his 74th-minute equaliser, yet it was a goal that sparked a wild five minutes in which two more were scored.

First, Ernesto Grillo gave Milan the advantage once again from distance, before Rial looped in Madrid's second leveller. With Madrid utilising their greater experience in the big moments, it was left to Gento to roll in the winning goal in extra time.

As impressive as this all-encompassing domination of Madrid's was, the European Cup was already becoming a wonderfully layered competition and its first playing certainly turned heads and changed minds. In 1956/57, Bulgaria, Czechoslovakia, England, Luxembourg, Romania, and Turkey all joined the party. Madrid aside, who were granted entry as holders, all participants had indeed won their respective domestic league title, although Galatasaray's was more of a provincial Istanbul-based competition.

It was a marked contrast to the 1955/56 interest in participation. Suddenly, after the success of the inaugural playing of the tournament, no club seemed blasé enough to decline their invitation for the second event.

By 1957/58, Ireland, Northern Ireland, and East Germany were now on board. Turkey, however, fumbled their spot in the tournament, with the Turkish FA not being swift enough to register Beşiktaş in time for the draw.

Again, it was in the main domestic champions taking part, yet with Madrid having completed a European Cup and La Liga double, 1956/57 La Liga runners-up Sevilla were allowed entry, upon which they were ruthlessly beaten in the quarter-final by the holders.

Meanwhile, in Poland, Gwardia Warszawa did not win the Ekstraklasa but still took part in the European Cup. To offset the unease of their participation, Gwardia were then knocked out in a play-off, on the toss of a coin, against Wismut Karl Marx Stadt, when the second leg of their tie was abandoned at 100 minutes due to a floodlight failure. The East German team had procured their equaliser in the 90th minute to take the game into extra time.

Added to this, it was also the first time that Benfica and Ajax took part, while Milan required a play-off to progress past Rapid Wien, and when Shamrock Rovers faced Manchester United at a Dalymount Park without floodlights, the first leg of their first round tie did not have a half-time break. The players simply swapped ends and played on. A fatigued Rovers had held the visitors to only a 1-0 half-time advantage but they capitulated during the second half, eventually going down 6-0. In the second leg at Old Trafford, with floodlights and a half-time interval, Rovers put up strong resistance and Busby's side only managed to win 3-2.

In 1958/59, Greece and Finland took up their right to places in the tournament for the first time, although Olympiacos withdrew when drawn to face the Turkish champions Beşiktaş, who had gained entry by winning the second, and last, Federation Cup tournament. It was a success that went unrecognised as an official Turkish title until 2002.

Manchester United were given a special invite to take part as a gesture in support of the club in the wake of the tragic events in Munich. In typically draconian fashion, the

FA prevented them from taking up the offer, and unlike in 1956/57 this time the club did not ignore the will of their governing body.

Again, just as in 1956/57, Real Madrid completed a European Cup and La Liga double, thus Atlético Madrid, as runners-up in the league also represented Spain.

While most nations' league champions took up those precious European Cup berths, the Ekstraklasa continued to be something of a renegade, with Polonia Bytom taking Poland's place, from a sixth-place finish. This was also the season in which Juventus took part for the first time.

All the while, the European Cup was working its way into the soul of football, proving to be such a success that a secondary tournament by the name of the European Cup Winners' Cup was already on the drawing board, and the more cumbersome Inter-Cities Fairs Cup began to streamline itself.

European club football was here to stay. Even the British Isles had belatedly caught the bug, and Hampden Park was allotted the hosting rights for the 1960 European Cup Final. Now all it needed was for a history-defining game to take place and the deal would be sealed.

2

Hampden Park, 1960

ALL SELF-RESPECTING footballing empires eventually reach a zenith. That perfect performance which unwittingly marks, if not necessarily the end, then certainly the beginning of regression. They reach a peak from which they will subconsciously accept that in their current guise, there are no more mountains left to climb.

Before long, a new powerbase rises, hungry and talented enough to pick up the baton of success, from where the wheel turns slowly for the deposed kings, as if in stasis, to await their return to the top once again or alternatively forever drifting into the footnotes of the game.

Hampden Park was the location of the European Cup's first moment of zenith. Real Madrid were imperious in their deconstruction of Eintracht Frankfurt in the 1960 final, and while they would contest three further finals across the following six seasons, they were to win only the last of those. Los Blancos would be made to wait 32 years to be able to call themselves the European champions again.

Already three-times winners of the European Cup when they recruited him, it was in the summer of 1958 that Ferenc

Puskás arrived at Madrid. Christened in his Hungarian homeland as the 'Galloping Major', he had been effectively unemployed during what should have been the peak years of his career.

Banned from playing for two years by both FIFA and UEFA after his refusal to return to Hungary, when opting to stay away in the wake of the Soviet Union's crushing of his nation's 1956 designs upon revolution, Puskás and his family were effectively part of an exodus of 200,000 refugees who departed the country.

Having attracted the attention of Milan and Juventus until his career was mothballed, when Puskás's ban was finally lifted the great and the good of Serie A were no longer so sure of the benefits of signing the man who had been the beating heart of the legendary Mighty Magyars.

Concerns raged over Puskás's age and fitness, and incredulously, he had fallen into a situation where he was having to chase a game of football. Nomadic in his search for a new home, both in terms of his football and his family's future, he had settled in Austria for a short while, continuing to train with Weiner Sport-Club on top of the time he had spent in pursuit of a club in Italy.

Even England and the First Division had been a mooted option. When Manchester United were trying to put a team together in the weeks after the Munich air disaster in February 1958, Puskás was approached by the Old Trafford hierarchy only for the Football Association to close the door on the possibility.

Spain would open its arms to Puskás, however, and after flirtations with Español, it was at the stubborn insistence of Santiago Bernabéu himself that the player signed for Madrid. With the potency of Hungarian football still very fresh in mind, Zoltán Czibor and Sándor Kocsis would fall into the possession of Barcelona, persuaded by their compatriot László Kubala, a Catalonian resident since 1951.

In his first season with the club, having been the scorer of the goal that clinched Madrid their place in the 1959 European Cup Final, Puskás had missed the showpiece occasion through injury. Thus, by the time he walked on to the Hampden Park pitch 12 months later, he was in the mood to make up for lost time.

Netting eight goals on the way to the 1960 final, Puskás had added a hypnotic extra layer to an already unimpeachable Madrid team. A futuristic player who had absolutely everything – the vision, the close control, the precision, the tricks, the flicks, the eye for goal – he was other-worldly in his own right, but when deployed alongside Alfredo Di Stéfano it brought the European Cup its defining moment in Glasgow.

Madrid scored an astonishing 31 goals during their relentless run to a fifth successive European Cup. Puskás and Di Stéfano would account for 20 of them; this was a haul that was procured from only seven games. Between them the pair would score all seven goals in the final.

Luxembourg's champions, Jeunesse Esch, were given a sound thrashing in the first round, surely proud to have claimed two goals of their own in the second leg when twice having the temerity to take the lead early through Marcel Theis and Albert Schaak.

Madrid were then handed the unique challenge of overturning a first-leg deficit for the first time, in the quarter-final against OGC Nice. Exceedingly unlike Madrid, they threw away a 2-0 lead at the Stade Municipal du Rey, going down to a 3-2 loss, before a one-sided second leg saw them through.

This result created the European Cup's most incendiary collision course to date as in the semi-final, Madrid were paired with a Barcelona who had seen off Stan Cullis's Wolverhampton Wanderers in the previous round, and prior to that obliterated Milan.

Puskás, Di Stéfano, and Gento up against Luis Suárez, Evaristo, and Kocsis. Despite the Catalans being without the services of Kubala and Czibor, it should have made for two games that rested on the finest of knife edges. Madrid won both by the same 3-1 scoreline for a comfortable 6-2 aggregate win, results which precipitated the departure of the legendary Barcelona coach Helenio Herrera.

Herrera would swiftly resurface at Internazionale, bestowing upon the Milanese giants the levels of European Cup success that would be beyond Barcelona for another three decades. Going into the games against Madrid, Herrera had defied the will of the Barcelona board in refusing to field Kubala, the club's biggest star but also a man who had struggled with the demon drink. He had also sided with the players in a stand-off over expected bonuses.

So, with Barcelona having conspired against themselves almost as much as Madrid had toyed with them, it was to Hampden that the holders headed to face Eintracht Frankfurt.

Frankfurt had won what was to be their one and only West German championship in 1959. Still a competition that operated on a regional and nominally amateur basis, with a format that led to a championship final, by the time of the 1960 European Cup Final the Bundesliga was still another three years away from inception.

Confounding logic, Frankfurt were not one of West German football's heavy hitters. In defeating Kickers Offenbach in the 1959 championship decider, it was only the second time that the club had come to within such touching distance of the prize, having been beaten by Bayern Munich in 1932.

Armed with a relatively unremarkable set of players, it was the talented and adaptable Alfred Pfaff who was their most dangerous threat. Now 34, the Frankfurt legend had been part of West Germany's 1954 World Cup-winning squad, kept from an active role by the redoubtable figure of Fritz Walter.

Beyond Pfaff, Friedel Lutz would go on to make the West Germany squad for the 1966 World Cup, as back-up at right-back for Horst-Dieter Höttges. The rest of Paul Oßwald's team were largely made up of dependable rather than exceptional players, the pick of which were their captain Hans Weilbächer, the creative attacker Richard Kreß, and the prolific striker Erwin Stein, all of whom had flirtations with the national team.

Oßwald, in his third spell in charge of Frankfurt, had made his latest return from Offenbach in the summer of 1958. That 1959 championship fixture had been between Oßwald's past and present clubs and won the game the moniker of the 'Oßwald derby', with both teams taking to the pitch playing to the same system.

Handed a bye from the preliminary round, Frankfurt gained safe passage into the first round thanks to the Finnish champions Kuopion Palloseura pulling out of the tournament. BSC Young Boys were no match next, while Weiner Sport-Club – the team with which Puskás had trained while in limbo – did offer stubborn opposition in the last eight.

It was against Rangers in the semi-final that Frankfurt truly displayed what they were capable of. In the first leg at the Waldstadion, the Scottish champions were more than a match for Oßwald's side during the first half before completely capitulating in the second period. Having won 6-1, Frankfurt would score another half dozen goals in the return game at Ibrox Park.

Just over two weeks separated Frankfurt's trip to Glasgow for the second leg of the semi-final and their return journey for the final. After a domestic campaign of great frustration, they had failed to reach the season-ending championship round, hamstrung by the loss to injury of the impressive and unfortunate Erich Bäumler.

Madrid's concerns prior to the final rested not upon injury problems, but instead that with only 11 shirts available there would be a list of the great and good of football that would not even make their line-up.

Two years earlier, and again two years later, the Brazilian international Didi would play in World Cup-winning teams, yet there was no room for him within Miguel Muñoz's Madrid. He would be in good company, however, as he was kept company by Héctor Rial and Enrique Mateos, who both would have held hopes of taking part.

Frankfurt started the 1960 European Cup Final as the brighter of the two teams, testing Madrid's capabilities to deal with an aerial approach. Their goalkeeper, Rogelio Domínguez, was almost caught out early when forced to claw away a looping effort from beneath his crossbar.

By the 18th minute, Frankfurt had the lead. Kreß, stealing into space, was the first to a cross from the right by Stein, and the script had seemingly been torn apart by the first West German side to reach a European Cup Final.

Maintaining composure, Madrid soon played themselves into the game and would score the next six goals. Within five minutes of Frankfurt opening the scoring, Madrid had taken the lead; by half-time it was 3-1.

Di Stéfano found the bottom-right corner of Egon Loy's net, and he then converted after a Canário effort rebounded off the Frankfurt goalkeeper. Slightly hunched, and direct, there was something of the James Cagney, or even Peter Falk's depiction of Colombo, about the Argentine icon. Nothing too fancy, but generally unstoppable.

In line for a £625 bonus per player for winning the game, Madrid's incentive for victory was both historical and financial. Yet this was the type of verve that money cannot buy. Canário came close, and José María Vidal came even closer when hitting Loy's post. In response, Erich Meier was the hub of Frankfurt's best football.

Luis del Sol and Di Stéfano were testing Frankfurt's nerves, yet Puskás was the ultimate conductor, and it was the Hungarian who scored Madrid's third when powering past Loy shortly before half-time. By the interval the West German side were looking like an exhausted boxer sat on his stool, breathing heavily after being made an example of having unwisely landed the first punch.

Taking a physical approach to the restart, Kreß put in a late challenge on the Madrid captain José María Zárraga, which left him limping. While not an antagonistic game by any means, it was one where frustration would occasionally rise throughout the second half.

Ignoring the bait, Madrid continued to monopolise and move the ball around with ease. With Del Sol impressive, the holders had a reasonable shout for a penalty that was waved away. Soon enough, to the apparent displeasure of the Hampden Park crowd, Puskás had claimed his second and Madrid's fourth. Glaswegians were possibly just wanting a closer contest.

Six minutes later, a swift break from Gento was followed by Puskás clinching his hat-trick with a header from virtually on the goal line itself, and it was 5-1. The game had reached exhibition territory. Still, with a wonderful sense of misadventure, Frankfurt probed for goals of their own.

With just under 20 minutes remaining Puskás had scored his fourth, finding himself at the business end of a magnificent passing move that must have been disorientating for Frankfurt.

It was magical; there was absolutely no shame in being Frankfurt in this game, just as there was no shame in being Italy in either the 1970 World Cup Final or the 2012 European Championship Final.

This goal kicked off a wild five minutes during which Stein also pulled one back for Frankfurt, Di Stéfano completed his own hat-trick, and Stein struck again when taking advantage of a mistake by Vidal. No further goals were added but it was not for the want of trying. Puskás again came close, Gento hit the bar, and the post was struck once more.

Madrid's victory in the 1960 European Cup Final became the tournament's defining moment, the final by which all others would be measured. If some nations had remained sceptical about the European Cup, these notions had now been swept away. Now it was all about how to stop Los Blancos winning it for a sixth successive time, just as they seemed stronger than ever.

Stunningly, Madrid were made to wait for six years before they would get their hands on the trophy again, by which time Di Stéfano had departed for Español and Puskás had drifted from the team, towards retirement. Never losing that incredible skill, the end of his playing days did not come before scoring a glut of goals against Feyenoord in the 1965/66 preliminary round, performances that were the foundations for glory.

Gento aside, the only man to bridge all six of Madrid's European Cup successes, the 1966 Blancos vintage was a new generation, yet one which could not use this success as the springboard for more continental glory. It would be 19 years before they lifted their next major European trophy, and 32 years until they were to become the champions of Europe once again.

Yet for a team that was now within the safe hands of the likes of Pirri, Ignacio Zoco, Ramón Grosso, Amancio, Manuel

Velázquez, as well as the lingering presence of Gento, who would remain with Madrid until 1971, it should not have petered out the way it did in terms of continental endeavour. However, it was nothing that Madrid did wrong – it was simply the tilting of power to northern Europe.

While 1966 marked a line in the sand, 1960 set the lasting benchmark for all other European Cup Finals to measure themselves by. It became the legacy-defining club game as far as European football was concerned.

3

A Team of Light

LEGEND HAS it that within the afterglow of leading Benfica to a second successive European Cup glory in 1962, their visionary coach Béla Guttmann, had asked the club's directors for a well-deserved yet moderate pay rise in recognition of his achievements.

Reputedly, Benfica refused Guttmann's request, and upon his departure from the club he cursed them to 100 years without European glory. Almost 60 years later at the time of writing, they still await the curse to be lifted, having lost eight major European finals since Guttmann's 1962 exit.

Supernatural phenomena, or simply an unerring coincidence on the back of an impassioned fit of pique? Regardless, within a year of him taking his leave of Benfica, Guttmann was suggesting that they would win the 1963 European Cup Final as a club continuing to prosper without his input.

Benfica would, of course, lose. Just as they would in two further finals before the 1960s had drawn to a close. More final defeats would occur in 1988 and 1990, the last of those taking place in Vienna, where the great Eusébio had visited the grave of Guttmann prior to the game to ask for the curse to be lifted.

Added to this pain, Benfica lost the 1983 UEFA Cup Final, and back-to-back Europa League Finals in 2013 and 2014. During the last six decades they have also been beaten in four major European semi-finals. There may not be a curse at play, but there is certainly a seemingly insurmountable psychological barrier that they cannot clear.

This makes Guttmann's degree in psychology, which he picked up in Austria, a useful tool in further massaging the legend of the 'curse'. A master of mind games long before that branch of football management is credited to have kicked in, he was a footballing nomad who stretched the physical and mental boundaries of his players before swiftly moving on to pastures new. His 1959–62 spell at Benfica was the longest period he ever spent in any one appointment, during a career that spanned ten different nations.

Movement was everything for Guttmann, and while having emulated his parents in becoming a dance instructor as a teenager, he would not be the only coach to draw parallels between the dance floor and football pitch. A strong and powerful foundation could only prosper if grace, poise, and fine balance were standing upon the shoulders of physical giants.

Always open to new learning, the Hungarian-born Guttmann was a player of repute. Escaping the escalating anti-Semitism of his homeland, he made the move to Vienna, where he found no shortage of like-minded souls amid the burgeoning coffee house intellectualism that helped advance the tactical side of the game. It was a football thinker's utopia.

Guttmann's fruitful relationship with SC Hakoah Wien was punctuated by an eventful six-year stay in New York, so impressed was he by the city when on tour with the Austrian outfit. Upon his return to Europe, in 1932, he both played for Hakoah once more, and began his managerial odyssey with them.

Partly driven back to Europe by the Wall Street Crash, in which Guttmann almost lost everything he owned, by the end of the decade he was forced into hiding as war once again ravaged the continent and the Jewish community. Eventually captured and sent to a labour camp, Guttmann, along with the iconic Egri Erbstein, narrowly escaped the trains to Auschwitz.

There was no such escape for Guttmann's father, siblings, and many of his wider family; Erbstein, meanwhile, would perish along with his incredible Torino team in 1949 at the Superga air disaster.

Weaving his way to Portugal via coaching stop-offs beyond Austria, in the Netherlands, Hungary, Romania, Italy, Argentina, Cyprus, and Brazil, Guttmann's move to Benfica was made after spending a year in charge of the future European Cup winners, Porto, with whom he won the 1958/59 Primeira Divisão title.

While it had only been two years since Benfica's last domestic league success at the time of Guttmann's arrival, the 1950s had been an arduous decade compared to the domination they would enjoy throughout the 1960s. The 1950s had largely belonged to Sporting CP.

Inheriting a team with no shortage of talent, among other options, Guttmann could call upon the services of Portuguese internationals Costa Pereira, Ângelo Martins, Fernando Cruz, Joaquim Santana, Domiciano Cavém, Mário Coluna, and José Águas. To these gods of Benfica's history, he would add ingredients of his own, as in came Germano, José Augusto, António Simões, plus the cherry on the cake that was the incredible Eusébio.

It was with these players that Benfica could be vaguely accused of under-reaching in Europe. The natural heirs, perhaps, to the formative domination of Real Madrid, Benfica won the 1959/60 Primeira Divisão title with only one loss to set the club up with their second bite at the European Cup.

Benfica's 1954/55 domestic league success should have opened the door to the 1955/56 European Cup, only for Gabriel Hanot to instead invite Sporting, who had won the Primeira Divisão title for seven of the eight seasons prior to 1954/55. When then making their delayed debut in 1957/58, the club had fallen at the first hurdle to Sevilla.

With the tournament fully expected to be another procession to Madrid glory, Benfica were generally an unconsidered threat to lift the prize as the campaign got under way. Starting out with a trip to Edinburgh to take on the Scottish champions Heart of Midlothian, they breezed through to the final, scoring 23 goals along the way, during a run which evocatively took Guttmann back to both Budapest and Vienna.

With Eusébio still to be added to Benfica's arsenal, it was the prolific Águas who powered Guttmann's team to the 1961 European Cup Final, ably assisted by Augusto, Santana, Coluna, and Cavém. Águas was nothing short of a goalscoring phenomenon, scoring more goals than games he played in the Portuguese league.

Surprise finalist Benfica might have been, yet it was over on the other side of the draw where the seismic shock occurred. Barcelona ended Madrid's stranglehold on the European Cup in the first round, 4-3 on aggregate, amid much rancour and conjecture over disputed penalties and a glut of disallowed goals.

With the ties officiated by two English referees, the renowned Arthur Ellis had overseen the first leg at the Santiago Bernabéu. He had earlier presided over the infamous 'Battle of Bern' at the 1954 World Cup, between Hungary and Brazil. Ellis had also taken the whistle for the very first European Cup Final, the inaugural final of the European Championship, and the 1952 FA Cup Final.

For the return at the Camp Nou, Reg Leafe was handed the honours. Another referee of substance, Leafe had run the 1955 FA Cup Final, and taken games at both the 1950 and 1958 World Cups, alongside Ellis.

After pushing close to levelling the aggregate score, an incensed Madrid exited with Santiago Bernabéu himself throwing out claims of a potential UEFA conspiracy designed to prise the trophy out of Castilian hands for the first time.

Leafe would be involved in more controversy before the 1960/61 European Cup had run its course, when in loose control of the second leg of Benfica's semi-final against Rapid Wien. The game was to be abandoned shortly before its finish after he ruled that the Austrian international Robert Dienst had dived in his attempts to win a late penalty that would have had no more influence than winning his team the game, but not the place in the final. Even Guttmann suggested to Leafe that he might have saved a lot of chaos, had he just given the Austrians what they had wanted.

Barcelona, who would be cursed themselves in the European Cup until finally prevailing in 1992, almost threw away their place in the final. Saved by a last-gasp aggregate equalising goal by Sándor Kocsis against Hamburger SV at the Volksparkstadion, they would edge through in a tense play-off in Brussels to set up their date with Benfica at the Wankdorf Stadium in Bern.

With two attack-minded teams going up against one another, the 1961 European Cup Final would be a more than worthy successor to the legendary game that Madrid and Eintracht Frankfurt had served up, 12 months earlier at Hampden Park.

Águas, Coluna, Santana, Cavém, and Augusto vs Evaristo, Kocsis, Luis Suárez, Zoltán Czibor, and László Kubala, it was a straight shoot-out to see which team could be the most ruthless in front of goal.

A game played out in the very same city and venue where Kocsis and Czibor had suffered their shock defeat with Hungary against West Germany in the 1954 World Cup Final, it left Kocsis with an unsettling sense of foreboding about what was to come.

Kocsis was right to be concerned as another 90 minutes of the strangest of footballing voodoo soon unfolded, with defeat being met via the most outrageous of misfortunes. These were inclusive of a wild own goal which spun its way over the Barcelona goal line and back out again, plus claims of offside for what would prove to be Coluna's winning goal.

Barcelona endured a litany of near misses that tortured the Catalan soul, the most impressive being one incident where a shot from Kubala hit both posts before being possessively grasped to his chest by Pereira. This incredulous incident occurred after Barcelona had already hit the woodwork on three occasions.

With 15 minutes remaining, Czibor lashed in a wonderful strike from outside the penalty area, but it was to be frustration from there for Barcelona. Benfica were crowned champions of Europe for the first time, as a club that seemed anything other than cursed.

Witnessing all of this from the sidelines was Eusébio, having spent the majority of his first season with Benfica on a watching brief. With the talented Simões also set to make his breakthrough the following season, Guttmann's Benfica were in the rudest of health heading into their defence of the European Cup in 1961/62 and swept to a second successive final.

They were recipients of a bye in the preliminary round, and Guttmann was once again heading back to the Austrian capital in the first round, this time against Austria Wien. Percentage-playing away, ruthless at home, Benfica scored 11 goals in their combined home legs over the stretch of the first two hurdles of their defence of the trophy.

Against 1. FC Nürnberg, in the quarter-final, Benfica scored six without reply in response to losing the first leg 3-1 at the Städtisches Stadion. Increasingly sure-footed, Guttmann's team then found themselves up against Bill Nicholson's Tottenham Hotspur in the semi-final.

At the Estádio da Luz, the first leg went the way of the holders, although not perhaps within the style with which their supporters might have expected. Two vaguely untidy first-half goals were claimed by Simões and Augusto, against the run of play, with Tottenham playing the more refined football, including a well-worked Greaves effort that was disallowed for a marginal offside.

During the first 20 minutes of the second half, Tottenham imposed themselves wonderfully with Bobby Smith snatching a goal back within ten minutes of the restart. So impressive were they at the beginning of the second 45, the visitors created so many compelling chances that they would have deserved the lead, let alone an equaliser.

Like the first half, however, Augusto turned in the third Benfica goal against the run of play, albeit a beautifully crafted one, and Spurs had another goal disallowed, this time from Smith, who had also squandered a magnificent opportunity earlier on. A fascinating and shape-shifting evening, it set things up nicely for the return game a fortnight later at White Hart Lane.

Tottenham were on the front foot from the very start and Jimmy Greaves came close when forcing Pereira into a smart save, while Mário João was heroic with a last-ditch goal-line clearance a few minutes later. Counterpunching, however, it was Benfica who broke the fragile deadlock, the unstoppable

Águas turning the ball in at the back post after Simões split the home defence.

Unwilling to concede defeat, Dave Mackay hit the post only to see the rebound bounce straight into the arms of Pereira, while Greaves had a goal disallowed not much later, which could have killed off lesser teams, as the referee initially gave it only to be dissuaded by his linesman. In reply, Coluna struck Bill Brown's crossbar. It seemed only a matter of time before the ball found the back of one or the other team's net, and it was to be Benfica's, as Smith converted when the ball fell invitingly to him in the penalty area.

It had been level on the night at the interval, and when Danny Blanchflower planted an early second-half penalty past Pereira, nobody in White Hart Lane would surely have believed the goalscoring had come to an end. Yet it had.

This was not through any lack of endeavour, however. Wave, upon wave of Tottenham attacks were occasionally alleviated by Benfica breakaways. Simões had a goal of his own disallowed, Maurice Norman skimmed the Benfica post, and when Mackay looped a late header on to Pereira's crossbar, Nicholson's side had exhausted their last attempt to remain in the European Cup.

With the brutality of the European Cup demanding its participants to be their nation's domestic champions to obtain entry, given the First Division title would become an elusive prize to Tottenham in the decades to follow and they were never to return to the competition, at least not until the Champions League altered the European footballing landscape irrevocably.

Narrow margins; 12 months later Tottenham would be victorious in the 1963 European Cup Winners' Cup Final, something which poses the teasing hypothetical of just how they might have prospered had they reached the 1962 European Cup Final.

The holders, however, progressed, and Benfica handed the wonderful challenge of going head-to-head with the team they had succeeded as champions of Europe. Real Madrid, wounded by their 1960/61 abdication, were back, and the 1962 European Cup Final was to represent not only a fight for the trophy but a game to decide upon the undisputed best team in Europe.

Madrid, tested thoroughly by Juventus in the quarter-final when forced into a Paris play-off, had otherwise enjoyed a sedate stroll to their sixth final; Vasas SC, Boldklubben 1913, and Standard Liège had borne the brunt of 23 goals between them, with only one scored in return.

This was an altered version of Madrid, however, compared to the team who had so evocatively won the 1960 European Cup Final. They were still powered in attack by Ferenc Puskás, Alfredo Stéfano, and Paco Gento, José Santamaría was still the cornerstone of the defence, although while there were some familiar components of Miguel Muñoz's side there were also five players in his starting line-up who had never taken to the field for a European Cup Final.

In a game that marked a defined end to an era of exclusively attack-minded finals, Benfica and Madrid shared eight goals at Amsterdam's Olympisch Stadion on an evening when the holders showed the strength of body and mind to twice claw their way back into the reckoning.

Trailing 2-0 and then 3-2, left in arrears by the brilliance of a Puskás hat-trick, it would have been all too easy for Guttmann's side to fold. Yet Águas, Cavém, and Coluna had the fortitude to drag Benfica level, to provide Eusébio with the platform from which to score the last two goals of the evening, taking both the trophy and the status of European football's brightest talent from possession of Europe's first kings, Madrid.

There was something wonderfully tilting about the 1962 European Cup Final, offering elements of both the old world and the emerging new currency. Parts of the game are very much of its era, yet other aspects are ahead of its time. Benfica looked to be a revolutionary entity that might well have been set to clock up as many consecutive European Cups as Madrid had. Club and coach in perfect symbiosis, the moon seemed infinitely attainable.

Guttmann was soon gone, though, cursing Benfica as he went. He would return three years later for one season only, one of only two campaigns throughout the 1960s when Benfica did not win their domestic league title, narrowly denied by Sporting, while they fell at the quarter-final stage of the European Cup. It was as if Guttmann himself was not immune to his own curse.

While much beauty remained in European Cup Finals beyond the 1962 edition, they became noticeably more circumspect and much more balanced in just how many risks the competitors were willing to take in defence, when committing to attack. Gung-ho football was swiftly to fall out of fashion, something that was dictated to by the rise of not one, but two European Cup-winning teams from Milan.

It was a subtle sea change rather than an immediately glaringly obvious one, and Benfica would be present for the passing of the baton.

4

Milanese Magic

MILAN'S INTRODUCTION to European Cup football was an inauspicious one, beaten 4-3 at the San Siro by 1. FC Saarbrücken, Saarland's first and last representative in the tournament. Only 18,000 spectators had congregated to see the dawning of this new phenomenon. Among the names on the Milan team sheet on that cold Tuesday evening in November 1955 were Lorenzo Buffon, Nils Liedholm, and Cesare Maldini.

Buffon, a cousin of Gianluigi's grandfather, was locked within a legendary rivalry with his Internazionale counterpart Giorgio Ghezzi. Not only competing for footballing honours, and city bragging rights, the two also fought it out for the love of the Italian television personality Edy Campagnoli.

Eventually swapping tribes, Buffon would later represent Internazionale while Ghezzi ended his playing days keeping goal for Milan, both making these stunning switches via a season with Genoa rather than directly.

While Buffon would win the battle for the hand of Campagnoli, it would be Ghezzi who would star in a European Cup-winning Milan side, Buffon denied by the cruel hand of fate when injury ruled him out of the 1958 final against Real Madrid. Mocked by the footballing gods twice, Buffon also made way for Giuliano Sarti at Internazionale a year before I Nerazzurri won their first European Cup, in 1964.

Playing in front of Ghezzi in the 1963 final at Wembley, Maldini would go on to become Milan's first European Cup-winning captain, and father of the impossibly talented Paolo, setting in motion a Milan dynasty that is still making an impact to this very day at the sadly endangered San Siro, in the shape of Cesare's grandson Daniel, a playmaking midfielder at a club where his father Paolo is now the technical director.

As for Liedholm, a man whose association with Milan predated Nereo Rocco's by 12 years, the only member of the legendary Gre-No-Li triumvirate to grace the final of the European Cup would later take Roma to the 1984 final as coach, while the following season he handed the 16-year-old Paolo his Serie A debut, having returned to reclaim the reins at Milan.

Amid this swirl and churn of the great thinkers of the game, Giovanni Trapattoni was a receptive student, plying his defensive midfield trade for Milan under the iconic leadership of Rocco. As a city, Milan was suddenly the centre of the footballing universe with Helenio Herrera also pulling strings for Internazionale.

There is something utterly magnificent in the way the chapters of Italian football history interlink with one another, so often crossing multiple generations. Throw in the hypnotic style that went together with the compelling substance, and there was nowhere quite like Serie A during its peak years.

A league like no other, Serie A took place within a rarefied air. It attracted the great and the good of global footballing talent during the 1950s and early '60s before pulling up the drawbridge on foreign players not long after the Italian national team suffered an early elimination at the 1962 World Cup in Chile, four years beyond failing to even qualify for the 1958 tournament in Sweden.

Implemented from the summer of 1964, this cocooning of their domestic game offered early and encouraging results, albeit with an often-alleged sleight of hand, and the continued presence of those foreign players who had been recruited prior to the 1963/64 campaign as they were still allowed to transfer from one Italian club to another.

By 1970, on the international scene, Gli Azzurri were contesting the World Cup Final in Mexico, two years on from having won the European Championship on home soil, while their clubs, particularly the ones who resided at the San Siro, were making an impact in continental competitions.

It would be over a decade and a half before Serie A's ban on imports was lifted, with one foreign player initially permitted per team from the summer of 1980, edging up in number as the seasons passed. As the 1970s dawned, the remainder of the foreign players who had been inside the Italian game when the door clicked shut had dwindled. Those who did remain were ageing.

It's arguable, but the fact that no Serie A team contested a European Cup Final between 1973 and 1983, part of a 16-year gap between successes, could as easily be pinned on this form of footballing 'Itexit' as it could on the simple shifting sands of the sport.

Back on that night when European Cup football first descended upon the San Siro, Milan squandered a 3-1 lead to Saarbrücken. It was a seismic shock and certainly no indicator of the bright future which lay ahead for the club in the competition.

Even in turning the second leg around, Milan left it late to overpower their opponents as with 15 minutes to play at the

Ludwigsparkstadion the scoreline was 1-1, only for a Theodor Puff own goal to begin a swift capitulation to a 4-1 defeat for the home side.

With a lesson assimilated, in the first leg of the quarter-final Milan headed to the Austrian capital to take on Rapid Wien, where their measured approach earned them a 1-1 draw, before sweeping to a 7-2 victory back at the San Siro with Nordahl among the scorers.

This set up those first blockbuster clashes with Real Madrid in the semi-final, during which Milan's penalty-assisted late comeback in the second leg, fell only narrowly short after a wonderfully open and attacking first leg at the Santiago Bernabéu.

Having sat and witnessed Fiorentina become Italian football's first European Cup finalists the following season, it was with a slow-burning allure that Milan took to the 1957/58 playing of the tournament having reclaimed the Serie A title.

Thrown together with Rapid Wien once again, in the preliminary round, Milan made heavy weather out of progressing to the first round. After comfortably winning the first leg at home before surprisingly being turned over in the second leg, it was a tie that ended 6-6 on aggregate and in the days prior to the away goals rule, it meant a play-off game was required. So, off to Zürich the two teams went, where Milan prevailed, 4-2.

Sweeping past Rangers in the first round, Milan were simply too strong on their visit to Ibrox Park, not only cancelling out Max Murray's impressive opening goal but obliterating it when obtaining four goals in the last 15 minutes. The inspired Ernesto Grillo scored twice, the first when swerving past three Rangers defenders and his second from an almost impossible angle.

A fortnight later, in a game that was switched to the historic Arena Civica, Dario Baruffi scored shortly before the interval for Milan, and Giancarlo Galli swiftly after the restart on a saturated surface amid torrential rain, on an evening when abandonment was a very real possibility. Despite the game being way out of reach for Rangers, they dominated the second half and Buffon earned his clean sheet in his escalating duel with Don Kicthenbrand.

Having dealt with Borussia Dortmund convincingly in the quarter-final, in the semi-final Milan went up against a Manchester United side still struggling to cope within the aftermath of the Munich air disaster.

Without their manager, Matt Busby, and with a patchwork quilt of a team pulled together with a small band of survivors, fringe players and a couple of emergency signings, and despite going on to win only one of their last 14 league games after the tragedy in Munich, United seemed capable of superhuman feats in cup competitions.

A path was remarkably plotted to an FA Cup Final that would prove to be a bridge too far, when beaten by Bolton Wanderers, while when Milan headed to Old Trafford for the first leg of the European Cup semi-final five days later, the hosts pulled off a narrow 2-1 victory. It was a win which was decided by a disputed Eddie Taylor penalty, converted via the underside of Buffon's crossbar, with ten minutes left to play.

It was all a far cry from when Juan Alberto Schiaffiano, a World Cup winner with Uruguay in 1950 and the most expensive footballer in the world, opened the scoring having smartly advanced upon Harry Gregg to deftly ease the ball past the Manchester United goalkeeper midway through the first half. Milan then remained in control of the game until gifting an equaliser to Dennis Viollet.

On one hand, blessed to have come away with a win, United also had every reason to ponder what might have been possible had they been able to field Bobby Charlton, an option denied them after he had been named in the England side the previous day for a pre-World Cup friendly against Portugal at Wembley. He would again be missing for the second leg, when instead of travelling to Milan he would be with his national team on a tour behind the Iron Curtain that took in games against Yugoslavia and the Soviet Union.

Six days beyond Old Trafford, in front of 60,000 spectators at the San Siro, Milan were in a focused frame of mind against opponents who were vulnerable from the very start. Schiaffiano took just two minutes to level the aggregate scoreline when he got on the end of a beautifully crafted move in which Ernesto Cucchiaroni, and Liedholm played significant roles.

Pinned back for much of the first 20 minutes, with a huge amount of credit, United managed to hold on at 1-0 until the early exchanges of the second half when Liedholm sent Gregg the wrong way from the penalty spot after Ronnie Cope had handled on the goal line. Yet, led by Busby's assistant Jimmy Murphy, United had begun to impose themselves as the first half progressed, creating but squandering a few opportunities of their own.

With the mood on the terraces passionate, there were also sombre overtones and after half an hour the referee brought the game to a temporary halt, upon which a minute's silence was observed for those who lost their lives in Munich.

Liedholm's penalty seemed to deflate United, however, and Milan regained the upper hand, with Schiaffiano striking the post and Giancarlo Danova shooting straight at Gregg when well positioned.

One Manchester United goal would have levelled proceedings at this point but when Danova drifted in from the wing to place the ball home with the outside of his right foot for Milan's third goal, the visitors' task was now insurmountable.

More excellent work by Danova then set up Schiaffiano once more with just under 15 minutes to play. The 4-0 scoreline might not have flattered the fine football of Milan, yet neither did the determination and effort of Manchester United deserve to be on the end of a drubbing.

With Buffon missing for the final, at the Heysel Stadium in Brussels, Milan saw the chance to end Real Madrid's monopoly on the European Cup three years earlier than history would eventually decree almost literally slip through their fingers. In that closely contested final, Los Blancos' clinching goal was one that Buffon would have been incandescent to have conceded.

So close, yet so far in 1957/58, Milan came nowhere near in their next attempt at European Cup glory two seasons later. Twice torn asunder by the Barcelona of László Kubala, Luis Suárez, and Zoltán Czibor, it was a bitter disappointment to fanatical Rossoneri supporters, who had been offered a close-up glimpse of the promised land in the 1958 final.

With the exponential growth in popularity of the tournament, whereas the San Siro had been only half full when Madrid visited for the 1955/56 semi-final, when Barcelona were the first-round guests in November 1959, the iconic stadium had been packed. The combined attendance of both legs came close to 125,000, and European Cup interest had truly been piqued.

With the Serie A title eluding them again until the 1961/62 campaign, Milan were made to wait another three seasons for their next attempt at the European Cup. Madrid having finally been dethroned as European champions in 1960/61, and with Buffon, Schiaffiano, and Liedholm no longer in the Milan ranks as part of sweeping changes, the landscape had altered dramatically by 1962/63 both at the San Siro and within the tournament. Serie A was, however, still impatiently awaiting its first European Cup-winning team as Italy headed into a campaign that was fresh off the back of a short-lived yet incendiary trip to Chile for the national team at the World Cup.

Milan tore into their latest assault on the European Cup, running eight goals past Union Luxembourg in the first leg of the preliminary round as part of a 14-0 aggregate victory. Incredibly, eight of those goals were claimed by the insatiable José Altafini, a man who had been unlucky to sit out the 1958 World Cup Final with Brazil before going on to travel to the 1962 tournament with Italy, in what were days when the regulations over international borders and playing for more than one nation were considerably looser.

Altafini was emblematic of this new Milan. Signed from Palmeiras when still within the sweet and sour glow of the 1958 World Cup, by 1962/63 he was benefiting from the emergence a 19-year-old Gianni Rivera, the presence of his compatriot Dino Sani, the contributions of the gifted yet fragile Gino Pivatelli, and the addition to the team of Juventus's Bruno Mora.

Deposed as Serie A champions by their great rivals and San Siro bedfellows Internazionale, Milan compensated their devotees by finally cracking the European Cup code. After dismantling Union Luxembourg, they competently dealt with Alf Ramsey's surprise English champions Ipswich Town, defeating them 3-0 in the first leg on home soil, before slipping to a narrow defeat in the return at Portman Road a fortnight later, conceding a couple of goals late in the game when already leading 4-0 on aggregate.

Milan's hero against Ipswich had been Paolo Barison, scorer of their opening two goals in the first leg, and the man who grabbed the crucial strike in East Anglia. Barison was to be a doomed character, eventually losing his wife to his team-mate Altafini, in what was to become known as 'The Pink Scandal', an affair that caused reverberating shockwaves throughout Italy.

Tragically, Barison lost his life in April 1979 aged just 42 when travelling on the Autostrada dei Fiori, close to the Andorran border, with his former Milan team-mate Luigi Radice, who was by then the head coach of Torino. Barison, who had had a very short spell in charge of Milan, had been asked by Radice to take on a technical advisory role at the club, and the pair were very much in the wrong place at the wrong time when a lorry burst through the central reservation, veering from the opposite side of the carriageway, and into oncoming traffic. Radice, behind the wheel, miraculously survived.

Neither Barison nor Radice would play a part in the final. While Barison showed a knack of being the man to rely upon in the European Cup, scoring yet again in Istanbul against Galatasaray in the first leg of the quarter-final and twice more in the first leg of the semi-final against Bob Shankly's Dundee, he was the unlucky odd man out at Wembley. Radice, meanwhile, fell to a serious knee injury that would ultimately end his playing days prematurely, and would have otherwise been an automatic selection to face Benfica.

Two years prior to his more celebrated brother Bill taking Liverpool to the European Cup semi-finals, Bob's Dundee had cut a swathe through the tournament, 22 years ahead of their rivals from just a short stroll along Tannadice Street, Dundee United.

With the Scottish champions standing between Milan and their second European Cup Final, the first half of the first leg at the San Siro lived up to expectations. Despite taking the lead within three minutes through a Sani header, Dundee weathered the assault on their goalmouth and shocked the hosts when grabbing themselves an equaliser, via another headed goal, this time belonging to Alan Cousin.

Dundee did well to keep Milan to a 1-1 half-time scoreline but after the interval the game completely ran away from the Dens Park outfit as they slipped to a 5-1 defeat, yet not before they squandered a golden opportunity to take the lead when Doug Houston shot wide after breaking through on goal.

Added to this, ambiguities reigned over two of Milan's four second-half goals, with Dundee making loud claims that the ball went out of play in the build-up to Barison putting the home side ahead, while Altafini was undeniably in an offside position when Mora struck the third.

Uncharacteristically losing out in the aerial battles, Dundee had also been missing their captain, Bobby Cox. While they certainly had cause for complaint, Shankly's side were also fortunate not to concede further goals, and it was only thanks to some outstanding saves from Bert Slater and some desperate defending that Dundee restricted Milan to five.

A week later, Milan saw the job through with a stubbornly defensive performance at Dens Park. Breached only once, when Alan Gilzean scored just before the interval, Rocco's men redoubled their efforts after the restart, and any hopes of a late comeback for Dundee were ended five minutes from time when their goalscorer was sent off as he finally lost his composure in the face of some very physical treatment that went unpunished by the referee.

With Wembley handed its first European Cup Final as part of the Football Association's centenary celebrations, it was an occasion that also marked a swift about-face on English football authority's stance when it came to European club competitions. This was a game that was taking place less than eight years on from Chelsea being advised not to participate in the tournament's inaugural campaign.

One part of a trio of high-profile fixtures at the self-styled home of football prior to the 1963 European Cup Final, Brazil had visited for a friendly against England, while later in the year the national team would also take on a Rest of the World representative XI. This still did not stop the scheduling of Milan and Benfica's attractive clash for a Wednesday afternoon, which was played out in front of a stadium that was less than half full.

Apart from Barison being jettisoned in favour of Pivatelli, who was given the task of man-marking the Benfica captain Mário Coluna, the biggest absentee for the holders was Germano, a player considered to be among the very best central defenders in the world.

A beautifully balanced and technical game of football, just what any locals who clicked through the Wembley turnstiles will have thought of it is wide open to debate. Lacking in undirected speed, and with a blind dedication to go for goal at all costs, this was a brand of football that was much more considered, with the pace ebbing and flowing, and possession being everything. With the ball rarely going above head height, there was little in the way of percentage playing, and for those who had congregated for the game it was a rich feast of football.

Eusébio opened the scoring in the 19th minute when latching on to a flick from José Torres, the latter powering through on goal, outsprinting the Milan defence and finding the bottom-left corner when Ghezzi offered too much of a target to aim for instead guarding his near post a little too enthusiastically.

Unable to add to this goal, Benfica allowed Milan to work their way back into the game via the measured and intelligent passing of Rivera, a teenager with the thought processes of a player a decade older, while Pivatelli also began to gain the upper hand in his duel with Coluna, leaving Eusébio increasingly isolated.

Milan started the second half at a furious pace, with Altafini coming close to levelling the score three times within five minutes, eventually finding the equaliser shortly before the hour when taking advantage of a slip in the Benfica defence, to gain the space to drive the ball into Costa Pereira's bottom-right corner, much to the Portuguese international's disgust. It could have been so very different, however, as just moments earlier Torres had missed what seemed a simple headed opportunity to increase Benfica's lead.

This was simply the prelude to the five-minute span during which the 1963 European Cup Final was won and lost. Within two minutes of Milan having obtained their equaliser, Pivatelli had downed Coluna with a cynical tackle close to the halfway line. It was a challenge of his quarry which injured him enough to leave him largely a passenger for the remainder of the game, this during an era when substitutes were still not permitted.

Then, with just under 20 minutes left to play, Altafini struck again to give Milan a lead they would not relinquish. He had been sent through on goal after some Benfica indecision just inside the Milan half, but there were bitter and lasting recriminations on the legitimacy of the winning effort. One-on-one with Pereira, Altafini saw his initial effort parried by the goalkeeper only to make no mistake when the rebound fell kindly to him.

To Benfica players and followers alike, Altafini had been within the Benfica half when the ball was played forward, while Milan's response was that the ball had been played off a Benfica player. Regardless, when the footage is slowed down, while not irrefutable, it appears more likely than not that Altafini had been in his own half when the ball was played forward anyway.

Milan closed the game down with a consummate ease from this point, while Eusébio remained a potent danger; Benfica couldn't level the scoreline and as the final whistle was blown, the European Cup was at last prised from the vice-like grasp of the Iberian Peninsula.

Rocco, now the hottest coaching property in Serie A, accepted an offer to take over at Torino in the summer of 1963, to be succeeded by the former Real Madrid coach Luis Carniglia, a man with an impressive track record.

Along with one La Liga title, Carniglia had been at the helm at the Santiago Bernabéu when the club won the 1958 and 1959 European Cup Finals, the first of those two successes being against Milan. Either side of his spell in the Spanish capital, the Argentine had led Nice to the French league title in 1955/56 and Roma to Inter-Cities Fairs Cup glory in 1961.

Carniglia and Milan should have been the perfect match, yet by March 1964 he was gone, replaced by Liedholm, just over a fortnight after Milan's defence of their European Cup had floundered against their old Bête noire, Madrid.

Emboldened by the signing of the magnificent Amarildo, the man who had been forced to wear the unfillable boots of Pelé when Brazil's iconic number ten was injured at the 1962 World Cup, Milan had navigated their way past IFK Norrköping in the first round having received a bye in the preliminary round.

Yet their sedate start to the defence of their title was rudely punctured by a quarter-final draw that pitted them with Los Blancos. Only the fifth time that Milan had embarked upon a European Cup campaign up to this point, it is wild to consider that during three of those seasons, I Rossoneri had gone head-to-head with Madrid in what were steadily becoming the tournament's most eye-catching fixtures.

In the 1963/64 quarter-final, Milan were dissected in the first leg at the Santiago Bernabéu. Trailing 4-0 with over 25 minutes remaining, it must have been a sobering experience for Carniglia against his former club.

It took Amancio 17 minutes to break the deadlock when prodding a loose ball home from close range, the first player to react as a free kick rebounded off Milan goalkeeper Mario Barluzzi, who was covering for the injured Ghezzi.

What was the most surprising element of the evening was that Madrid were then made to wait until just before half-time for their second goal, when Ferenc Puskás was the penalty box opportunist after Milan had been carved open once again.

Milan's torture was compounded within a five-minute span either side of the hour when Alfredo Di Stéfano powered in a venomous free kick for 3-0, followed by Gento finding the top corner when the ball landed perfectly for him from a corner.

Taking their foot off the accelerator, Madrid allowed Giovanni Lodetti to snatch what appeared to be a well-worked consolation but would instead prove to be the springboard for providing Miguel Muñoz's Spanish champions with a significant second-leg scare at the San Siro.

Effortlessly collecting a through ball and taking advantage of a hesitant Madrid defence, Lodetti was the Milan hero again with just six minutes elapsed, giving the holders the perfect start in their bid to overturn their three-goal deficit.

When Altafini then struck swiftly after the interval, the impossible comeback seemed to be on. Yet with almost half the game with which to find the one goal that would level the aggregate scoreline, Milan found themselves frustrated in their efforts. Having trailed 4-0, Milan narrowly failed in their mission to fight back, losing out 4-3 on aggregate.

Milan passed the European Cup baton to Internazionale when Herrera's side won the 1962/63 Serie A title, their first

Scudetto in nine years and their first during the era of European club competition. Having not won the Coppa Italia since the 1930s, 1963/64 wasn't only I Nerrazzurri's first European Cup campaign, it was their first experience at all of this new dawning of continental club combat.

Thrown in at the deep end, into preliminary round games against Harry Catterick's Everton, Inter opted to swim rather than sink. They went to Goodison Park for the first leg where they took part in a goalless draw that offered up a performance that should not be judged by its cover.

The tie was all too easy to be presumed as the classic away Italian performance of bolting the defensive lock and strangulating the game until it yielded a valuable draw, but Herrera's side were instead always the more likely of the two teams to snatch a win.

From a crowd of 63,000, which generated the highest gate receipts of any football match played in England up to that point outside of the FA Cup Final, Everton's eager supporters went home unsatisfied, with their heroes made to look distinctly second best in all departments by a fluid and confident Inter.

Struggling to work openings, Catterick's side were drawn into a repetitive aerial approach which was easily dealt with by the visitors. When the alleys Everton ran into became increasingly blind, they swiftly ran out of ideas as Herrera opted for a man-to-man marking system.

It proved to be a frustrating night for the English champions, with Luis Suárez and Jair leading the best of an Inter offensive that often left the Everton defence off balance. While Suárez was clearly the best player on the pitch, Jair wouldn't have been flattered to have ended the game with a hat-trick.

Left with the unenviable task of avoiding defeat at the San Siro in order to retain their place in the tournament, Everton went to Milan in an aggressive mood. Shorn of the services of the influential midfielder Jimmy Gabriel, Catterick opted to hand a debut to the 18-year-old Colin Harvey.

In a physically demanding game, there were some understandable early nerves and an underhit back-pass by Harvey almost gifted Inter a goal. Yet the youngster who would go on to manage the club a quarter of a century later soon settled into the intimidating task handed to him, and despite Herrera's side being the more technically adroit unit, Inter were feeling the heat as the first half wore on without the breakthrough being made.

In a game that simmered without fully boiling over, a flurry of names went into the referee's notebook as Suárez and Jair were booked for Inter when reacting to strong challenges, while for Everton, Dennis Stevens and Brian Harris were also cautioned, all this in an era where you had to do some serious groundwork to earn your name being taken. The visitors, with frustration their most potent weapon, went in for the interval well positioned to pull off what had been billed as mission impossible.

Everton's first-half stifling of Inter was, however, undone within two minutes of the restart as Jair snatched what proved to be the only goal of the game. Continuing with an approach of containment, the visitors only really offered one serious counterpunch, which almost landed with 15 minutes remaining when Alex Scott came close to levelling the game.

In reply, Herrera's side were by far the more expansive and skilled, striking forth with subtlety and esoteric thought only to snatch at the chances they created, leaving them unable to build upon their narrow lead and Inter were nervy as they sneaked over the finish line.

On the same evening as Tom Finney was turning out for the Northern Irish outfit Distillery, helping procure an remarkable 3-3 draw against the mighty Benfica in Belfast,

Inter's clash with Everton had been one that should have graced the latter stages of the tournament rather than the first hurdle.

Inter's prize for progressing to the last 16 was another potentially tough draw, against an AS Monaco side captained by the future French national team manager Michel Hidalgo, who had been in the Stade de Reims team beaten in the very first European Cup Final in 1956.

Taking only a slender 1-0 lead into the second leg, a game that was moved from the original version of the Stade Louis II, 140 miles west to Olympique de Marseille's Stade Vélodrome, Inter would have been forgiven harbouring a sense of foreboding at having to face the French champions with little in the way of room for error.

Any nerves or hesitancy were swiftly eased thanks to two goals in four minutes from Sandro Mazzola with less than 20 minutes played. Despite Monaco clawing a second-half goal back with over half an hour to play, Herrera saw his team put the tie beyond doubt in the final few seconds when Suárez struck Inter's third.

On face value, FK Partizan must have felt like a kind draw in the quarter-final to Herrera, given the Yugoslav side had conceded four goals against Luxembourg's Jeunesse Esch in the previous round. They had even lost the first leg at the Stade Émile Mayrisch, a stadium that was far more used to seeing chastening defeats than stirring victories.

While Jair and Mazzola scored at the two extremes of the second half of the first leg in Belgrade, without reply, it wasn't until Herrera's side were 4-0 up on aggregate at the San Siro, and the tie was categorically over, that Partizan finally found a way past the commanding Sarti.

Ruthless in their brushing aside of Partizan, Inter were paired up in the semi-final with a Borussia Dortmund side that would lift the Cup Winners' Cup two years later, opponents who were competing in the very first season of the Bundesliga after its launch in August 1963.

In the first leg at the Stadion Rote Erde, Inter got off to the dream start when Mazzola powered home a stunning diving header with only four minutes having elapsed. A dazed Dortmund eventually hit back twice within a five-minute span midway through the first half.

Fritz Brungs was the Dortmund hero, flashing in a shot low to Sarti's right for the equaliser before directing a header into the Inter goalkeeper's top corner. It was the perfect response by the West German champions and gave Herrera much to think about as the half-time interval loomed, only for Mario Corso to intelligently level the scores once again four minutes from the break, when he stole in on the edge of the penalty area before taking the ball around the Dortmund goalkeeper Hans Tilkowski and rolling it into the net from an acute angle.

A goal each from Mazzola and Jair in the return game a fortnight later cemented Inter's place in the 1964 European Cup Final. With having to wait another week for the inevitable confirmation that their opponents would be Madrid, Herrera and his side had just under three weeks in which to prepare for facing up to Miguel Muñoz's five-time champions of Europe at the Praterstadion in Vienna.

In the Austrian capital, it was Madrid who possessed most of the experience in what was their 60th game in the European Cup, compared to an Inter side taking to the pitch for just their ninth appearance in the tournament. It was Di Stéfano's last game in a Madrid shirt but it was not to be a winning finale to his time with Los Blancos.

There was a marvellous symbiosis at play in the final. Not only was it the last appearance of Di Stéfano for Madrid, but it was also a game that marked the validation of Mazzola, a player blessed, cursed, and damned to be the son of the eternal figure that was Valentino Mazzola.

Valentino had been part of the legendary Grande Torino side, the Turin giants who had dominated the Italian game throughout the 1940s, but he was one of the victims who tragically perished at the Basilica of Superga in May 1949 when the entire team, their coaching staff, and all on board the flight home from a friendly against Benfica were killed as the FIAT G.212 they were travelling in crashed into a retaining wall at the back of the Basilica when badly off course and disorientated by a low-lying mist, strong winds, and a potentially defective altimeter.

Forever compared to his gifted father, the young Sandro was often dismissed as being a pale shadow of the player Valentino had been. It was unfair to put such pressure on a player of increasing potent, but more than that, it must have been devastating at times to have the spectre of the parent he lost, when aged only six, used as a tool to beat his own talents with.

A more than compelling answer to Milan's Rivera, for Mazzola and his rival it had to have felt like looking in a mirror when it came to their roles for their respective clubs, and their competition for international recognition.

By nine months, Rivera was the younger of the two, but without carrying the weight of the football career of a talented and tragic father, he was the faster out of the blocks, making his Serie A debut for Alessandria when aged just 15, in June 1959, fittingly against Inter.

Aged 16, Rivera clocked up 25 league appearances as Alessandria battled unsuccessfully to retain their Serie A status, the last season the club ever graced the top flight of Italian football. Yet his performances, which were way beyond his years, earned him just under a quarter of his club's goals, and had he played the entire campaign there must have been a chance he might have saved them from the drop into Serie B.

Rivera's explosion on to the Serie A scene also won him his summer 1960 transfer to Milan, for whom he would serve until 1979, eventually ending his professional career 20 years after it began. A career of perfection, his last act would be to help his team over the finish line for their tenth Serie A title, winning them not only the trophy but also the star which proudly sits above the badge on their shirts.

In comparison, Mazzola's Internazionale debut came two years after Rivera's for Alessandria, and it wasn't until the 1962/63 season that he claimed a regular place in Herrera's plans. By then, the Serie A-winning Rivera already had the first of four World Cups under his belt, having been part of Italy's bruised and battered squad at the 1962 finals in Chile, where not yet 19 he had played against West Germany before being spared the exposure of a game of violent intent against the hosts that was christened the 'Battle of Santiago'.

Mazzola would soon make up ground on his rival, however. His introduction to the Inter team was the point of ignition, and while Rivera was helping Milan to glory in the 1963 European Cup Final, Mazzola's ten goals in 23 games went a long way in I Nerazzurri wresting the Serie A title from their great rivals. Before the 1962/63 season had come to an end, Mazzola had also broken into the national team.

At the 1964 European Cup Final, Mazzola blew away any remaining doubts over his right to be playing his football on such an elevated stage. The scorer of two goals, the first and the last of the contest, Mazzola's strikes were scene-setters. His first broke a tense deadlock and his second ended Madrid's hopes of clawing their way back into the game.

Catching Madrid off guard with his opening goal, it came during what seemed to be a gentleman's agreement between the two teams to meander to the half-time interval. With only two minutes remaining, Aristide Guarneri played a beautiful diagonal ball out of the Inter defence, which was collected by the overlapping Giacinto Facchetti on the left-hand side of the pitch. Wonderfully controlled, the ball was rolled the short distance to Mazzola, who was positioned just to the left of the D on the edge of the Madrid penalty area, from where he took two touches to adjust his trajectory, and one glance goalward for directional purposes, before dispatching it beyond a stunned José Vicente, possibly benefiting from a subtle deflection along the way.

Just beyond the hour, Vicente was tormented once again, this time when he allowed an Aurelio Milani effort low and to his left to brush past his fingers and sneak into his net just inside the post. With Mazzola involved in the build-up, while Inter's first goal had been a swift and brutal punch to the stomach when Madrid had marginally let their guard down, the second goal was a more self-inflicted wound. Mazzola and Milani were given too much space to operate and it was ultimately a goal that Vicente should have kept out, potentially deceived as the ball bounced a yard or two in front of him.

With 20 minutes left to play, Madrid reduced the arrears when Felo planted the ball into Sarti's top-right corner with a spectacular scissor kick, benefiting from one of Puskás's many probing corners. It was here that Herrera and his team's nerve was tested, and they passed with an assured excellence.

Within five minutes, Inter had re-established their two-goal lead. First slowing the game down, drawing the sting of Madrid's momentum and the ire of many in the stadium, they then took advantage of the unlikely charity and unexpectedly poor defending of José Santamaría, the man who would go on to coach Spain in their ill-fated hosting of the 1982 World Cup.

Milani was this time the provider for Mazzola with what had been no more than a hopefully looped ball forward, and there was nothing that Vicente could have done on this occasion as he was left badly exposed to the ruthless Internazionale number eight. Mazzola accepted the gift presented to him, converting intelligently for a goal taken with the outside of his right foot and in off the post as he advanced on the Madrid goalkeeper.

Deflated, Madrid didn't have the strength to rise again and Herrera and Inter were crowned champions of Europe for the first time, in turn making Milan the first, and to date the only city to boast more than one team to have won either the European Cup or the Champions League.

With the potential for a double celebration, 11 days later Inter were involved in a historical Serie A championship play-off match against Bologna at the Stadio Olimpico in Rome after the two teams finished level on points. The first, and so far only game like it in Italian football, it was Bologna who took the domestic prize, thus both clubs were among the competitors for the 1964/65 European Cup.

While Bologna fell at the preliminary round, lacking in any fortune whatsoever after being drawn against a fast-improving Anderlecht, it was after a tie that took three games and a deciding toss of a coin to split the Italian and Belgian champions.

Bologna had been seconds away from obtaining a place in the first round, until Jacques Stockman snatched the goal that set up a play-off match in Barcelona at a sparsely populated Camp Nou. There were no goals in regulation play, and with penalty shoot-outs still over half a decade away, it all came down to that toss of the coin, which went the way of Anderlecht. Little did Bologna know, but their only shot at European Cup success had been and gone.

Conversely, Inter went all the way to the final for a second successive season. Awarded a bye at the preliminary round stage, thus not beginning the defence of their title until the first round, the holders ruthlessly dispensed with future European Cup semi-finalists Dinamo Bucharest, 7-0 on aggregate, before being paired with British opposition in the quarter-final and the last-four.

Against Bucharest, while all the usual suspects were on the scoresheet, in the second leg at the Stadionul August 23, recent recruit Angelo Domenghini made his presence felt with the only goal of the game.

Barely breaking into a sweat prior to facing Rangers, Inter's powers of endurance were stretched to the limit at Ibrox Park in the return game after a bludgeoning flurry of early second-half goals in the first leg had left the Scottish champions with a seemingly impossible task to turn the tie around.

Rangers had largely frustrated Herrera's team in the first half at the San Siro, only to see their arduous work undone within six minutes of the restart. Whether or not Scot Symon's side had been grossly underestimated, the visitors had rendered Inter a pale shadow of their true self for 45 minutes, only to walk straight on to a succession of devastating blows within a bewildering three-minute blizzard of goals from the 48th minute.

With Herrera's half-time words likely ringing in their ears, Suárez was the first out of the blocks, emphatically breaking the deadlock before Mazzola was the creator of two goals in a minute for the Spanish international Joaquín Peiró.

Peiró had come the closest to scoring in the first half, when he struck the Rangers crossbar from distance. As an Inter player he would spend most of his time on the periphery of the side, but in the 1964/65 quarter-final he proved to be the pivot upon which his club's European Cup defence tilted towards success.

Midway through the second half, Jim Forrest pulled a goal back for Rangers when converting a beautifully weighted cross from Willie Henderson, and with self-preservation at the forefront of Herrera's approach, Inter opted for containment throughout the remainder of the game.

A fortnight later in Glasgow, Ibrox afforded Inter a red-hot reception on what was a bitterly frozen night. With four inches of snow having been cleared from the pitch on the morning of the game, the other pre-match concerns surrounded the fitness of Suárez, who was carrying a cold that Herrera played on, declaring his star man a doubt for the encounter only for him to miraculously recover sufficiently to take part. In the opposite corner, Rangers were again without the gifts of the legendary Jim Baxter, who had suffered a fractured leg in the previous round against Rapid Wien.

Needing to win by a two-goal margin just in order to take the game to a Stuttgart play-off, Rangers got off to the dream start when Forrest struck once more with only seven minutes on the clock.

Roger Hynd had been brought into the team as an extra defender to subdue the threat of Mazzola and Peiró, but it was in the Inter half that he posed greater problems when a low drive of his bounced back off Sarti for Forrest to pounce and guide the loose ball home.

Rather than panic and go for blanket defensive tactics, Herrera's players calmly found space and kept the ball for long periods, even hitting on the break, where from one such attack they almost scored when the Rangers captain Eric Caldow had been forced to hook the ball off the goal line.

Prompted by the far from incapacitated Suárez, his subtle movement and economy on the ball dictated the dangers posed by Jair and Mazzola. With the snow piled high at pitchside, Inter were not playing as if skating on thin ice.

Amid an atmosphere that regularly veered from passion to apprehension, Rangers struggled against the greater technique of the Inter players but also lacked a crucial element of luck. After the hosts had been denied a first-half penalty when Jimmy Millar went to ground, in the second half George McLean had Sarti comfortably beaten only to see the ball crash against the underside of the crossbar.

Yet, across the breadth of the game, it was the visitors who looked to be in control of proceedings. Despite this, Giacinto Facchetti was forced to limp through the latter stages after sustaining a knee injury, which meant he was pushed into the Inter forward line where he was able to float around as a pedestrian with intent. With Peiró covering for him at left-back, Herrera's side were never as vulnerable as they should have been, while without Baxter, Rangers lacked the creativity to take advantage.

Two months later, Inter were back in the United Kingdom and 219 miles south of Ibrox at Anfield, the home of Bill Shankly's Liverpool, who three days earlier had won the FA Cup for the first time in their history.

Herrera had been at Wembley to witness Liverpool overcoming Don Revie's Leeds United on an energy-sapping and sodden pitch, on a day when the pre-match rain had been torrential. He had also watched the progression of Shankly's side throughout, and confessed he had hoped to avoid them, at least until the final.

Liverpool's path to the semi-final, on what was their maiden European campaign, had taken them past the challenges of Knattspyrnufélag Reykjavíkur, Anderlecht, and 1. FC Köln. While the Icelandic team had offered only a token resistance, and the Belgians had been impressively dismissed, it had taken Shankly's side three games and a winning toss of a disc to separate them from the West German champions.

A trilogy of games that attracted over 155,000 spectators, where almost as many were in attendance for the play-off encounter at De Kuip in Rotterdam as there had been at Anfield, it had been such a stalemate that even when the disc was tossed into the air to decide the outcome, it landed side-on in the mud. Liverpool prevailed on the second attempt.

So, it was with a sizeable amount of momentum that Liverpool went into the semi-final, albeit shorn of two vital players. Influential midfielder Gordon Milne had missed the FA Cup Final through a knee injury, while at Wembley, left-back Gerry Byrne had played through the pain barrier with a fractured collarbone. Geoff Strong had been the beneficiary of Milne's misfortune, while against Inter the veteran Ronnie Moran returned to cover the absence of Byrne.

With the gates open four and a half hours before kick-off, Anfield was packed to the rafters for the first leg on what, for many, remains the famous old stadium's most atmospheric night. Prior to the players taking to the pitch, Shankly produced a masterclass in gamesmanship when ordering the injured pair, Byrne and Milne, to walk the perimeter of the pitch with the newly acquired FA Cup. The electricity levels of a crowd already in a high state of anticipation escalated further.

Despite fielding a 5-3-2 formation that would ask a lot of questions of any team in need of goals, within three minutes Liverpool had the lead when Roger Hunt, positioned on the penalty spot and allowed all the space he could possibly want, swept the ball into the Kop end net after receiving a fine cross from the right by Ian Callaghan.

Encouraged by their dream start, Liverpool attempted to press home their early dominance and advantage but were caught on the break just seven minutes later, with Peiró stealing in on the hesitancy of Ron Yeats. Set free on goal, he unselfishly rolled the ball to Mazzola to equalise.

Inter then retreated into their shell, handing the remainder of the game to Liverpool, within which they scored twice, had another effort contentiously disallowed, and squandered other excellent opportunities to increase their winning margin.

Liverpool reclaimed the lead just after the half-hour, Callaghan finding the bottom-left corner of Sarti's net when converting a beautifully worked free kick routine involving Willie Stevenson and Hunt.

Before the interval, Liverpool should have had their third goal when Chris Lawler linked brilliantly with Callaghan and Tommy Smith when cutting in from the right to drive the ball past Sarti. Yet, the goal was disallowed, with Hunt erroneously adjudged to have unsighted the Inter goalkeeper when in an offside position.

To add to the frustration, Hunt was then sent through on goal for a one-on-one with Sarti after excellent work by Ian St John and Peter Thompson had again breached the usually watertight Inter defence. However, the ball ricocheted off Sarti's knee and to safety. A hat-trick of gilt-edged chances came and went as Yeats struck the crossbar with a powerful header with virtually the last move of the half.

Rather than dwell on the blow of being denied a perfectly good third goal, Liverpool continued to dictate the pace and the flow throughout the second half, fending off Inter's early attempts to counter-attack and eventually gaining their deserved reward with just under 15 minutes left to play.

The move was instigated by Callaghan and Smith, then the ball was advanced to Hunt, who effortlessly turned inside his marker to force Sarti into a smart save, only to see the rebound fall directly to the feet of St John. The Scottish international made no mistake.

With no further goals added, it leant an air of delighted uncertainty to the outcome. Liverpool had performed heroically and quite rightly celebrated their victory, but denied a bigger lead with which to travel to the San Siro eight days later there was also a sense of foreboding about what might lie ahead. A goal cruelly disallowed, a commanding performance by Sarti and a carelessly conceded goal left a high quantity of ambiguity over whether Liverpool could finish the job in Milan. Not long after the final whistle had been blown, Shankly was being told his team would not prevail at the San Siro.

And so the prophecy came to pass. The San Siro proved to be a bearpit too far for Liverpool, and with suspicions over the even-handedness of the referee, José María Ortiz de Mendíbil, it is a game that has gone down in the annals of footballing shade. It was a game that haunted Shankly, a man who remained militant in his belief that corruption was at play.

Within ten minutes, Inter had wiped out their two-goal deficit, while arguments raged in the Liverpool camp over the validity of the strikes. Mario Corso struck the first with a wonderfully taken free kick, which has long been debated as having been awarded as an indirect free kick but one which was scored directly. Looking at the footage, however, the free kick seems entirely legitimate, and at no point does Mendíbil signal an indirect free kick.

Not much more than 60 seconds later, Peiró had the ball in the net for Inter's second. Again the protests were long and loud. Tommy Lawrence, having claimed the ball and collided with Peiró in the process, was bouncing it and looking up to see where to send it when the Spanish international picked himself up from the turf and closed swiftly on the Liverpool goalkeeper, dispossessing him of the ball, and then turning it into the unguarded net.

This goal harbours more ambiguity as while the ball is certainly in play, and fair game while being bounced, Peiró does at least make partial contact with Lawrence to retrieve it.

This in a game played in a country and refereed by an official from a nation where physical contact with goalkeepers was readily penalised. Also, in the build-up came a throw-in that was wrongly awarded to Inter, and there was a hint of offside to Peiró's initial run.

For Inter, none of this mattered, as not only where they now level on aggregate with 80 minutes still to play, they had also argued that St John's goal in the first leg should have been ruled out. Herrera's men would have felt karma was in operation.

Having drawn themselves level, Inter were willing to play the patient game rather than be drawn into any potential errors at the back or committing too many numbers going forward. Liverpool composed themselves very well, finding a degree of rhythm and keeping possession of the ball for longer periods than they might have expected. The problem came in the final third, however, as they failed to break down the stubborn home defence.

With 28 minutes remaining the final blow came as Facchetti strode forward to join the attack, scoring from outside the penalty area at the end of a hypnotic passing move. This goal was Herrera's Inter at their very best; confident, precise, skilled, composed, and ruthless.

From then on there was no way back for Liverpool. With Inter happy to sit deep, frustrating the visitors, and hitting on the break whenever the urge surfaced, the holders cruised into the 1965 European Cup Final.

In time Liverpool would go on to great success in the European Cup, using the lessons learned in the San Siro to stunning effect and winning the tournament four times between 1977 and 1984. In May 1965, however, it was a bitter pill to swallow, and Mendíbil's name would go down in the chapters of Anfield infamy, a referee who certainly emitted intermittent clouds of smoke throughout his career.

Back at the San Siro for the final, Inter's opponents were the two-times winners Benfica, who had been in imperious form during their run, including a 5-1 destruction of Real Madrid in the quarter-final at the Estádio da Luz.

In what should have been one of the all-time classic European Cup Finals, the game was largely blunted by a waterlogged pitch and the loss of Benfica's goalkeeper, Costa Pereira, early in the second half. With substitutes yet to be permitted, it meant that Germano took on the goalkeeping duties, doing well enough to stop Herrera's side adding to Jair's first-half strike. It was to be the only goal of the game, and it had relied upon a touch of good fortune with the ball squirming beneath Pereira and only just creeping over the goal line.

Retaining the European Cup made Inter the new contemporary benchmark, with Madrid's last success in the competition now five years in the past, and having been beaten by Herrera's side in the 1964 final, I Nerazzurri had now defeated the team who had broken Madrid's run of success, by winning the 1961 final, themselves retaining it the following year. They had also swiftly eclipsed Milan's solitary European Cup success.

When Inter and Madrid went head-to-head in the 1965/66 semi-finals, it was the European Cup's version of George Foreman going up against Muhammad Ali in Kinshasa boxing's 'Rumble in the Jungle' bout with the world heavyweight championship at stake. This was shaping up to be yesterday's legends being led to the slaughter against today's big-hitting alpha male.

Just as was the case eight years later, however, the old dog proved that it could still learn some new tricks and Miguel Muñoz's Madrid outfoxed Herrera's Inter when taking a narrow first-leg lead to the San Siro, from which Amancio scored the opening goal. Turning the tables on European football's masters of frustration, it could be suggested that Madrid beat Inter at a variant of the game Herrera had invented.

Surely it would have been incredulous to consider it at the time, but beyond winning the 1965 European Cup Final, it would be 45 years before Inter were crowed the champions of Europe once again when defeating Bayern Munich, in the 2010 Champions League Final at the Santiago Bernabéu.

Yet, aside from a first-round exit in their previous campaign, in 1989/90, within the era of the European Cup, Inter remained a significant threat whenever they gained entry to the tournament. They would go on to reach the final again in their next two attempts, in 1966/67 and 1971/72, while they made it to the semi-final in 1980/81.

It was a tournament that Inter felt very much at home in, and alongside Rocco's Milan they did as much as Béla Guttmann's iconic Benfica side in that first decade to help the pacesetting Madrid provide the European Cup with its increasingly vibrant existence.

After a Mediterranean monopoly of the first 11 seasons of the European Cup, however, the outliers of a once suspicious British Isles were poised, very much ready to break this cosy southern European hegemony.

5

Immortals

WHEN CELTIC won their 20th Scottish league title, in 1953/54, the birth of the European Cup was just one year away. Their first league success since the Second World War came as part of a league and cup double, captained by the driven and often abrasive Jock Stein.

Rather than act as the doorway to a new era of glory, it would be 12 years before Celtic laid their hands upon the domestic championship once again. When they did so, they were managed by the driven and often abrasive Jock Stein.

Over the course of the first 11 years of the European Cup, Celtic's supporters had had to watch from the cheap seats as not only Rangers, but Hibernian, Heart of Midlothian, Dundee, and Kilmarnock set sail on voyages of varying length in the continent's most prestigious club competition.

Hibs, by default of Aberdeen not taking up their place in the inaugural playing of the European Cup, had reached the 1955/56 semi-final, a run that Rangers and Dundee emulated in 1959/60 and 1962/63, respectively.

English clubs, too, had gone no further than the last four. Manchester United had fallen at this seemingly insurmountable hurdle in 1956/57 and 1957/58, while Tottenham Hotspur and Liverpool had come unstuck at the same stage in 1961/62, and 1964/65, respectively, before the team from Old Trafford were left distraught once again in 1965/66. It was as if Béla Guttmann, in his spare time, had elected to curse British teams as well as Benfica.

Stein, having initially seen his way to the manager's office barred at Celtic Park when he was the club's reserve team coach, had polished his burgeoning managerial abilities at Dunfermline Athletic and Hibs before being belatedly offered the top job at a struggling Celtic in March 1965.

In an arid period of Celtic's history between the league title successes of 1953/54 and arrival of Stein as manager, they had won just two Scottish League Cups, yet when gaining entry to the European Cup Winners' Cup in 1963/64, having lost the 1963 Scottish Cup Final to double winners and bitter cross-city rivals Rangers, the club had taken to the competition with great enthusiasm.

A run to the semi-final of that 1963/64 Cup Winners' Cup unfolded for Celtic, and a place in the final would have been theirs had they shown more defensive discipline in the second leg against MTK Budapest. Having won the first leg 3-0, they shudderingly lost the return game 4-0.

After a painful lesson learned, under Stein's watchful eye in 1965/66 they again reached the semi-final of the Cup Winners' Cup, where they were narrowly defeated by Bill Shankly's Liverpool.

Given what was to come for Celtic over the course of the next decade, where they would win nine successive league titles and a glut of domestic cups, inclusive of claiming the first domestic treble, and four further doubles, it was nothing short of astonishing that they went from almost nothing to virtually everything in what seemed the blink of an eye.

This success came without wholesale change. Of the 11 players to take to the pitch for the 1967 European Cup Final, Stein had inherited ten of them. Celtic's revolution was a self-perpetuating one, a giant lay largely dormant, awaiting the right man to stir the pot.

Stein was most certainly the right man. From an eighth-place finish in 1964/65, the new manager having arrived two months before the end of the campaign, Celtic were champions the following season, with only Rangers able to keep up with the relentless pace. With the 1965/66 league title came entry to the 1966/67 European Cup and Celtic's debut in the competition.

Short work was made of FC Zürich, and Nantes before winter, and the most impressive thing about Celtic's progression to the quarter-final was just how belligerent they were on their travels, scoring three times in both Switzerland and France. While against Zürich these had been second-leg goals, scored against increasingly demoralised opponents, against Nantes they were first-leg goals, scored after the French champions had struck first.

Confidence and stubbornness were allied by style and substance. Stein's Celtic were the steel fist contained within the velvet glove, and with it their 1966/67 campaign was to be the perfect storm. They won every trophy available to them, defeating Rangers in October's League Cup Final, then overwhelming Aberdeen in the final of the Scottish Cup, a week before clinching the title at Ibrox Park. They had even claimed the Glasgow Cup too.

So utterly dominant, so quickly, under the tutelage of Stein, there was a footballing magnetism at play. In the last eight of the European Cup they were drawn to face FK Vojvodina of Yugoslavia, opponents masterminded by their young and visionary technical director Vujadin Boškov.

A talented side, with the quirk that their Yugoslav internat-ional goalkeeper Ilija Pantelić was also their penalty taker, in winning the 1965/66 Yugoslav First League Vojvodina had not only broken the existing monopoly of the Belgrade giants but they had usurped the powerbases of Zagreb and Split, in being the most likely threat to do so.

Going into the first leg, Vojvodina were without the services of the suspended pair Dobrivoje Trivić and Vasa Pusibrk after both were sent off in a volatile second-round play-off encounter, against Atlético Madrid, in which they clawed their way back from having conceded twice in the first five minutes to win it in extra time, despite ending the game with nine men. Added to this, during the winter break, Vojvodina's top scorer Silvester Takač had been sold to Stade Rennais.

Offsetting this, Celtic's prolific Joe McBride had succumbed to a serious knee injury which would effectively end his time with the club. With his team-mates going on to win the ultimate prize without him, McBride would seek pastures new when unable to break his way back into the first-team picture.

With both sides unremittingly committed to their causes, Celtic defended resolutely and hit on the break occasionally, while Vojvodina came forward in wave upon wave of attacks, only to be blunted by the combination of Stein's deep-lying two banks of four. Milan Stanić prodded home the only goal of the game with 20 minutes remaining after a mistake from Tommy Gemmell.

A week later, and treading the fine line between patience and frustration, it took Celtic almost an hour of the second leg to level the aggregate scoreline. When the breakthrough came, it was Stevie Chalmers who took advantage of an over-stretching Pantelić. Just as the game looked set to be drifting towards a Rotterdam play-off, Billy McNeill arose the highest to meet a last-gasp Jimmy Johnstone corner. A devastated Vojvodina had no more than the time to kick off for the restart before the referee brought the game to an end.

Faced with the perennial Half Man Half Biscuit favourites, Dukla Prague, in the semi-final, Celtic were now the seventh British club to try clearing the last hurdle and reaching the European Cup Final. It wasn't an easy task as to reach the last four, Dukla had ejected the fast-improving Anderlecht and the swiftly evolving Ajax, who themselves had scored five on a misty night in Amsterdam against Liverpool.

In the first leg at Celtic Park, the power and physical superiority of Stein's men, backed by 75,000 passionate home supporters, was enough to overcome the technical brilliance of Dukla. They ran out 3-1 winners but it was an oddity of a game that could have just as easily ended with a narrower scoreline as it could a larger winning margin.

Dukla started the brighter, prompted by the legendary Josef Masopust, while Celtic were perhaps weighted by the sense of expectation. The home side were lucky not to be breached during the opening quarter of an hour, yet from there they began to take control of proceedings. The Czech champions were left to count the cost of the loss of the services of Ivan Mráz, the talented Sparta Prague striker, who Dukla, as the football branch of the army, were able to field while he was partaking in his national service.

Despite the fine play of Dukla not bearing the fruits that it potentially deserved, conversely, Celtic were denied extra goals of their own by the woodwork and a harshly disallowed effort from Chalmers. Level at the break thanks to Stanislav Štrunc snatching an equaliser shortly before the interval to cancel out Johnstone's opener, Celtic dominated the second half, during which William Wallace struck twice within a six-minute span either side of the hour.

Defiant defending two weeks later saw Celtic through to the final. At times up against an insurmountable eight-man wall, even Masopust could not find a way through. Amid this, Dukla were left to worry about the threat of the breakaway, especially from Johnstone. While it was not pretty, it was certainly effective, and Britain had its first European Cup finalist.

Standing in their way was a fearsome sight: Internazionale, twice winners, and not shy in using sleight of hand if required. Helenio Herrera was the master tactician, yet the foe Stein had wanted to pit his wits against. It was the Celtic manager's dream scenario, and it was to be played out against the backdrop of Lisbon's Estádio Nacional.

Inter had impressively downed the holders, Real Madrid, in the quarter-final, but then struggled to sneak past Bulgaria's CSKA Red Flag in the semi-final, having earlier laboured with other eastern European opponents in the first round, Torpedo Moscow.

Although all but Wallace had already been at the club when Stein arrived, this was very much a team within the image of its creator. Hard-working and durable, several elements had appeared to be upon the cusp of the exit door at Celtic Park under previous management.

Chalmers, Bobby Lennox, and John Clark had all laboured for a while before Stein gave them fresh impetus, the returning Berti Auld had been converted from an ailing winger into a central midfielder of composure and solidity, Jim Craig had gone from amateur university student to front-line overlapping full-back of potency, while the veteran goalkeeper Ronnie Simpson was playing some of the best football of his long and illustrious career. Even Billy McNeill, Celtic's iconic captain, was a man reborn. Incredulously, all 11 players on duty for Celtic against Inter were born within 35 miles of Celtic Park.

Stein had taken what he inherited and by sheer force of will, he insisted that it evolved at breakneck speed. Within two months of his arrival, the Scottish Cup had been won by defeating the first club to take a chance on appointing him manager, Dunfermline. Twelve months on, Celtic had swept the entire board.

In Lisbon, there were no nerves on an evening when Celtic played as if they were the team who had already won the European Cup twice before. Even the blow of conceding the first goal, an early Sandro Mazzola penalty, was brushed off and Simpson was forced into only one save of substance.

Relentless Celtic unsettled Inter magnificently. Herrera's side were simply unable to cope with the numbers that Stein's men committed to attack. Johnstone and Lennox were impossible to contain, both supported consistently by Gemmell and Craig. It made for a disorientating 90 minutes for Inter, which made a Celtic win seem inevitable, despite the equaliser not arriving until the 63rd minute and the winner being delayed until six minutes from the end. Inter, without the services of Luis Suárez and Jair, had a lack of inspiration just when they needed it the most.

Gemmell's driven effort from outside the area equalised, and then Chalmers deflected in the winner. The pressure was too much for Inter. Had it not been for the wonderful goalkeeping of Giuliano Sarti, and the positioning of the crossbar, Celtic would have had the lead long before they did.

Iconic images of McNeill lifting the new trophy high into the Lisbon sky remain as evocative now as they were impassioned then. Bursting into the Celtic dressing room after the game, Bill Shankly implored to Stein that he was immortal now.

It was a shift in power in the European Cup and Celtic had broken the spell the south of the continent had seemingly had on the tournament. Spain, Portugal, and Italy had now made way for Scotland, and soon England, the Netherlands, and West Germany would prosper too. It was time for the north to rise, and Stein's Celtic were the instigators.

For Inter, their season would totally unravel. Having led the Serie A table from the start, they needed only one point from their delayed last league game to retain their title, only to lose away to mid-table Mantova, draw specialists who had won only five times in Serie A prior to that day. At one stage, looking at an almost probable treble, Inter would also lose in the semi-final of the Coppa Italia. It was a stunning capitulation.

Having climbed their mountain in winning the 1967 European Cup, Celtic's defence of their prize was a short one and they were eliminated in the first round by Dynamo Kyiv. As the semi-finals rolled into view it was with a sense of familiarity that Real Madrid and Benfica loomed on opposite sides of the draw. The north had been loaned the European Cup, but now the south wanted it back. To strengthen this concept, Juventus were there too.

Representing the north were Matt Busby's Manchester United. A decade on from the Munich air disaster, the club had regenerated to stunning effect. A new team had emerged, built around Bobby Charlton, where he formed a holy trinity of attacking talent in tandem with the magnificent Denis Law and the imperious George Best.

This rebirth was not an easy one. As late as 1962/63 a relegation battle had been beckoning Busby's side as consistency proved difficult to locate, despite the talent they possessed. This was offset by winning the FA Cup, defeating Leicester City in the final, a success that acted as the springboard for the rest of the decade.

First Division titles followed in 1964/65 and 1966/67, along with a series of stumbles when deep in contention in cup competitions both domestically and in Europe. FA Cup semi-finals were lost in 1962, 1964, 1965, and 1966, while they had reached the last four in the Inter-Cities Fairs Cup and the European Cup in 1965 and 1966, respectively.

After an inconsistent start to 1966/67, United had been consistency personified beyond Christmas; remaining unbeaten in the First Division after a Boxing Day defeat away to Sheffield United, Busby's side comfortably held off the challenges of Nottingham Forest, Tottenham, and Leeds United to reclaim the league title, and gain with it a shot at the 1967/68 European Cup.

Too strong for Hibernians of Malta in the first round, the sterner tests came from the second round onwards. United were cautious away and made to sweat at home against FK Sarajevo and then Górnik Zabrze in the second round and quarter-final, respectively. The introduction of the away goals rule left the former fixture a little too close for comfort in the final minutes of the second leg at Old Trafford.

Against the Polish champions in the last eight, the team Manchester City would overcome in the 1970 European Cup Winners' Cup Final, United threw everything they could into attack, if sometimes a little too reliant upon high balls into the penalty area. It was the type of approach that had failed against the same opponents in the previous round for Kyiv.

Visiting goalkeeper Hubert Kostka was in incredible form, and had it not been for him then Busby's side would surely have won the first leg with a greater degree of comfort. As it was, they were to rely upon a Stefan Florenski own goal to break the stalemate on the hour and a Brian Kidd effort with almost the last kick of the game. In a display of wonderful sportsmanship, the United supporters arose to acclaim Kostka at the end of the game for the quality of his performance, while Busby's players also felt compelled to applaud him from the pitch.

A fortnight later, United faced the figurative and literal storm in Chorzów. At a snow-shrouded Silesian Stadium, Górnik eked out a 1-0 victory that was not enough to halt the march of Busby's men into the semi-final.

On a blanket-white pitch, adorned with red line markings, there had been much conjecture over whether the tie should take place or not. Of the travelling Manchester United contingent, Best was the only person to speak up in favour of the game going ahead, and indeed, especially during the first half it was played out amid blizzard conditions, in temperatures so cold that the local supporters took to lighting bonfires on the terraces for some much-needed warmth.

When the gifted Włodzimierz Lubański scored, United were left with 20 minutes to hold out, which they did with a steely determination. Tellingly, this had been the first goal they had conceded upon their 1967/68 European Cup travels.

Given the stellar line-up of teams left in the competition for the semi-final, there was no easy option available in the draw. Despite this, being handed the assignment of taking on the might of Miguel Muñoz's Real Madrid would have provoked a sharp intake of breath at Old Trafford.

Having looked well equipped to retain their league title for much of the season, in mid-February the domestic wheels began to wobble and United went on to lose seven of their last 15 First Division fixtures, opening the door for their cross-city rivals from Maine Road to glide in and dethrone them.

With their eggs entirely in their European Cup basket, Busby and his players were left with just four days with which to deal with the disappointment of throwing away the league and to prepare for their trip to the Santiago Bernabéu for the second leg of the semi-final.

Three weeks earlier at Old Trafford, Best had scored the only goal of the first leg against a Madrid side that could no longer call upon the genius of Ferenc Puskás and Alfredo Di Stéfano. Regardless, they still had the electric talents of Paco Gento, a man who had borne witness to all those early glorious European Cup days, plus a phalanx of newer dangers.

A strong spine of Ignacio Zoco, Pirri, Amancio Amaro, and Roberto Grosso were now prompted by their ageing captain, Gento. This was largely the thrust of the team that had won the European Cup two years earlier. Crucially, however, Amancio was suspended for the first leg after picking up a needless red card in Prague in the second leg of their quarter-final against Sparta. In his absence, his team would depart Salford without a goal to call their own, something that would lend the second leg its open and attacking nature.

An evening of frustration unfolded for United at Old Trafford, however, as Madrid's well-organised, and disciplined defence set out to absorb the expected pressure that was applied by the home side.

Madrid, dependent upon the agility of their reserve goalkeeper Antonio Betancort to keep out an early effort from John Aston, were for much of the evening stretched to the very limits of their physical capacity and mental durability. Within this initial onslaught, Pat Crerand also struck the woodwork.

Best, at the hub of his team's most dangerous moments when linking beautifully with Charlton and Crerand, broke the Madrid resistance nine minutes before the interval, forcefully finishing a move which was wonderfully crafted by the teenage Brian Kidd, and Aston. Yet, it was to be Best's only true sight of goal, expertly shadowed for the evening by Manuel Sanchís.

Rather than open the floodgates, Best's goal simply strengthened Madrid's defensive resolve, so unwilling was Muñoz to be drawn into a slugfest. Cleverly exploiting the pockets of space in the centre ground vacated by the marauding

United players when stepping forward, Pirri proved to be Madrid's pressure release component. Taking possession as often as possible, his was a performance of great intelligence, vital in redirecting the forward momentum of the red-shirted players.

Busby, perhaps unsettled on his team selection for the return game, or maybe looking to undermine Madrid's preparations, took a squad of 18 players to the Spanish capital, this at a time when only one substitute was allowed to be selected, and that to be a goalkeeper.

With Law suffering a recurrence of a lingering knee problem, much of the build-up surrounded the perceived likelihood of the Scottish international being asked to play through the pain barrier. It was all shadow puppetry as he had little to no chance of playing, but this was something that Busby did not need Muñoz to be aware of.

Erring upon caution in the first half, Busby deployed David Sadler in a deep-lying role in the hope that his team could be as stubborn in defence as Madrid's had been at Old Trafford.

This simply handed the keys to the game to the six-times European Cup winners, and with Amancio available once again, it soon became a very one-sided event, although United did exceptionally well to keep Madrid at bay for over half an hour before four goals flew in during the last 14 minutes of the first half.

It was within these 14 minutes that the dream seemed to end for Busby's side; a fourth European Cup semi-final set to culminate in defeat. Madrid were magnificent during this period and everything they attempted appeared to come off. At the interval, nobody could have expected anything other than more of the same in the second half.

Pirri had headed the opener, getting on the end of an Amancio free kick, before Gento burst through on goal for the second ten minutes later. In the last two minutes before half-time, Madrid conceded carelessly as Zoco flustered to slice the ball into his own net after a long and hopeful lob forward from Tony Dunne. Within seconds, Amancio had turned and converted through a crowded penalty area to restore Los Blancos' two-goal advantage on the night.

Still, this only translated into a slender one-goal aggregate lead, and despite United being a clear second best to Madrid in the first half, there was much to play for. In the second half Busby tweaked his tactics, and Sadler was pushed forward with a switch in formation to 4-3-3.

Madrid, arguably guilty of believing the job had been completed already, went into cruise control, and they would have had little cause for concern as the game crept towards the last 15 minutes. A club who had seen and done it all before were more than equipped to close the game out and claim a place in their ninth European Cup Final.

Then came the unexpected punchline as first Sadler and then Bill Foulkes bludgeoned the goals that rewrote the presumed script. Best was involved in both, flicking a header on for the first then using his special brand of magic to set up the clincher.

There was something incredibly apt about Foulkes being the unexpected hero of the hour. Having survived the Munich air disaster by the most fortuitous way imaginable, then to be handed the captaincy of the club in succession to the tragic Roger Byrne, he along with Charlton had spanned the full stretch of the club's odyssey to reach a European Cup Final.

There were only two weeks between the semi-final second leg and the final itself, where Benfica lay in wait after they had comfortably dispensed with Juventus. Basing themselves at the Saxon Inn Hotel in Harlow, they set about a marvellous charm offensive, handing out flags, pennants, and any other Benfica-embossed items to the gaggle of children who converged upon their selected pre-match location.

With Benfica heading into their fifth European Cup Final, and even taking into account the outcome of the game, it seems a peculiarity that Manchester United were so emphatically billed as the favourites. Yes, Wembley was the venue, and Busby's side had overcome Madrid in the semi-final, yet it was Benfica who had all the experience and knowhow. From a British perspective, however, much was made of the English team's 5-1 victory in Lisbon from two years earlier.

Without the services of Law, who had succumbed to knee surgery a week before the final, but boosted by the return to fitness of Nobby Stiles, it meant that Aston and Kidd were to join Best in a three-man forward line for Manchester United, while Otto Glória's side largely picked itself. Both managers were bold enough to name their teams 48 hours before the game, as if they too had been caught up in the pre-match mutual respect, and general buoyancy of mood.

Given the expectation of a festival of football, the first half leaned toward the physical aspects instead with both teams guilty of leaving their mark on one another. With an estimated global audience of 250 million television viewers, they were served up a much better spectacle during the second half, and beyond.

After the two sides had swapped early near-misses, Sadler passing up a golden opportunity and Eusébio rattling Alex Stepney's crossbar, it was Charlton who made the breakthrough by glancing in a header after fine work from Dunne and Sadler just eight minutes into the second half.

Backed by nine of every ten spectators at Wembley, it would have been understandable had United eased away from this point, yet Benfica were stubbornly resistant. Sadler should have made it 2-0 when picking up on a loose ball, after a hypnotic run and shot from Best brought out a parried save from José Henrique, but the Benfica goalkeeper cleared the danger with his feet.

Another mazy Best run could have led to a goal, but profligacy was the only potential threat to United's hopes. Sure enough, then, Jaime Graça netted the equaliser with just over ten minutes remaining when capitalising on a towering header from José Torres.

Emboldened by this turn of events, and perhaps mindful that they would not have the energy for extra time, Benfica swept forward in their droves and Stepney was to prove the match-winner as much as any of United's goalscorers as he pulled off a remarkable late save from the suddenly effervescent Eusébio.

United might have spent most of the evening with the look of the team most likely to win but all could so easily have been lost in those last ten minutes of normal time. By the finest of lines, the fate of the game was handed back to Busby's players as soon as the full-time whistle was blown on the initial 90 minutes.

Within nine minutes of the extra period beginning United had claimed three goals as Best, Kidd, and then Charlton once more struck the fatal blows to Benfica's dreams. It was as brutal as it was swift.

First it was Best, with a magical piece of skill in slaloming his way past Henrique following what was initially a long kick downfield from Stepney which was flicked on by Kidd, who made it 3-1 five minutes later when heading into the roof of the Benfica net. It was then left for Charlton to clip in the fourth after excellent play down the right by Kidd.

With the wind removed from Benfica sails, the second half of extra time was a more prosaic event with one more fine save from Stepney denying Eusébio the goal his endeavours deserved.

Having reached the peak of the mountain Busby had set out to conquer over a decade earlier, Manchester United's shoulders relaxed a little too much and a year later they were narrowly denied a place in another European Cup Final as Milan defeated them in the semi-final, while domestically a slow puncture emerged that would eventually lead to their 1973/74 relegation, the club never suitably adapting to life beyond the retirement of their metronomic manager.

Given the nature of qualification, United never again returned to the European Cup beyond 1968/69, eventually rising to success again in the Champions League era under Alex Ferguson.

As for Celtic, they were to remain part of the European Cup furniture, reaching a further final and two more semi-finals before drifting as a continental threat as the second half of the 1970s progressed.

On the back of 1967 and 1968, however, nobody could have speculated that this new Stein- and Busby-generated powerbase would be a fleetingly successful one. Surely more successes were to come for them in the European Cup, yet instead, after a compelling riposte from the San Siro in 1969 it was to be a new movement from the Netherlands that would soon absorb all available matter and light.

6

1968/69 – The Shifting Tectonic Plates of the European Cup

AN UPRISING was coming, but not before a salutary lesson was learned in Madrid at the hands of Nereo Rocco and his ageing yet supremely talented AC Milan team. So many elements about the 1969 European Cup Final would be repeated 25 years later for Johan Cruyff in Athens.

In the build-up to the 1969 encounter, at the Santiago Bernabéu, much was made of Ajax's youthful and aggressive nature. In domestic league terms, Rinus Michels' side had fallen narrowly short of an average of three goals a game in finishing as Eredivisie runners-up, to their sworn rivals from Rotterdam, Feyenoord.

Rocco's men had been much more frugal over in Serie A, both in attack and defence. Admittedly plying their trade in a league of a more defensive air, Milan had eked out 31 goals from their 30 league games, barely breaking even, while they had conceded two-thirds fewer than Ajax had.

In continental endeavours, upon a leveller playing field, during their respective runs to the final, the team from Amsterdam had scored twice as many goals as the outfit from the San Siro, albeit with two extra games at their disposal after Milan were awarded a bye in the second round due to a large-scale withdrawal of teams from the Eastern Bloc.

This was a situation that arose when UEFA had insisted that eastern Europe's teams be drawn against one another in the first round in a bid to partly traverse the political minefield that was created by the Soviet-led invasion of Czechoslovakia.

So when Ukrainians Dynamo Kyiv were ushered together with Poland's Ruch Chorzów, and Bulgaria's Levski Sofia were paired up with the Hungarians of Ferencváros they all downed tools, with Carl Zeiss Jena following suit when refusing to face Red Star Belgrade.

In riposte, Czechoslovakia's representatives Spartak Trnava brazenly took to the 1968/69 European Cup field, going all the way to the semi-final where they almost overturned Ajax in a stirring second-leg fightback after losing 3-0 in Amsterdam. It was a season where Slovak footballing inspiration was in plentiful supply as over in the European Cup Winners' Cup, their compatriots Slovan Bratislava went on to lift the trophy by defeating Barcelona in Bern.

An iconic season in the history of the European Cup, this would be Milan's last success in the tournament for 20 years, while it also marked the last time that Manchester United took part, under the tournament's original name and format. Added to this, Real Madrid limped out meekly in the second round to Rapid Wien and would be three decades away from becoming champions of Europe once more, with Internazionale's wait for a third coronation stretching to four decades.

Unbeknown to anybody, it would be almost two decades before Benfica graced another European Cup Final, whereas Celtic were a year away from their second and last appearance in European football's biggest occasion. Essentially, 1968/69 represented the shifting of football's tectonic plates; the winds of change were most definitely blowing.

Milan began their run to glory inauspiciously.

In Sweden against Malmö FF for the first leg of the first round, Rocco's team fell behind to two sucker-punch strikes either side of the half-time interval, the first off the inside of the post by Kurt Olsberg and the second a 25-yard piledriver from Rolf Elmstedt that flew into Villiam Vecchi's top-left corner. It was a shock to the Milan system and they were left to be content with obtaining just the one away goal, procured by a beautiful run and dink by the magnificent Gianni Rivera.

There must have been a part of the Milan psyche that hadn't been shocked at all by Malmö's performance, however, as I Rossoneri had long been admirers of Sweden's finest players. The famous Gre-No-Li combination of Gunnar Gren, Gunnar Nordahl, and Nils Liedholm had brought both fine football and a glut of trophies to the club throughout the 1950s, while the 1968/69 vintage boasted the services of winger Kurt Hamrin, who alongside Gren and Liedholm had played against Brazil in the 1958 World Cup Final. In years to come, Liedholm would twice lead Milan as coach, while in more contemporary times Zlatan Ibrahimović has twice served them with a never understated distinction.

Even the 4-1 victory with which Milan navigated the second leg wasn't without its issues, as Anders Ljungberg opened the scoring at the San Siro for Malmö with an intelligently guided finish after a smart one-two in the approach.

While the magical Pierino Prati had the scores on the night level just beyond the half hour, sweeping home from a Rivera cross, it wasn't until the last 30 minutes that Milan took charge of the tie thanks to an Ángelo Sormani diving header, another Prati effort that the Malmö goalkeeper Nils Hult should have kept out, and a late Rivera penalty that Hult almost redeemed himself with by when getting close to.

After returning to European Cup action following the turn of the year, it was nothing but the most monumental of opponents for Milan as they had to face the previous two winners of the tournament, before taking on Ajax in the final.

In the last eight it was Jock Stein's Celtic, the 1967 champions, who arrived at the San Siro for the first leg, where they displayed a defensive aptitude that Rocco would have been proud to call his own on what was a snow-covered pitch. Absorbing everything that Milan could throw at them then hitting on the break, Celtic also dealt adeptly with the hostility of the locals, who sent a barrage of fireworks towards the pitch throughout. With the game petering out to a goalless draw, the closest Milan had come to breaking the deadlock was when Sormani had hit the post early in the second half.

Rightly applauded for the job they had done in Milan, Celtic were viewed by many as the favourites to progress in the second leg. Had it not been for a carelessly gifted goal with only 12 minutes on the clock then it might well have been Stein's side reaching the semi-final.

When Billy McNeill collected a throw-in from Jim Craig just inside the Celtic half, there appeared little danger, until he miscontrolled it, then Prati dispossessed him, advanced on John Fallon and confidently dispatched his shot low into the Celtic net.

It was not only an open invitation to score, but it was also the cue for Milan to make themselves stubbornly impregnable. Rivera, at his most majestic, was everywhere, clearing danger in the six-yard box, battling for possession in midfield, and instigating his team's occasional breakaways. It was a masterclass of a performance, amid which the only genuine scare for the visitors came right at the beginning of the second half when Luigi Maldera was lucky not to have a penalty awarded against him after handling a Jimmy Johnstone cross.

When Celtic did manage to catch a sight of goal, they found themselves thwarted by the excellent goalkeeping of Fabio Cudicini, the father of future Chelsea custodian Carlo. In response, Hamrin and Prati would strike forth for Milan. It was the perfect performance from Rocco's players. Having dispensed with Stein and his Celtic side, the semi-final threw Milan together with Matt Busby and the holders, Manchester United.

Labouring domestically in the middle of the First Division, all of United's eggs were in their European Cup basket. Having picked apart Waterford in the first round, they had been stretched by Anderlecht, then breezed past Rapid Wien.

By the time they rolled into the San Siro for the first leg, Busby was spinning several plates in his team selection, with injuries keeping Alex Stepney, Tony Dunne, and David Sadler out of contention. Given that no British team had ever won at the San Siro, the task for United was one of containment, to the point that Denis Law was handed the role of shadowing Rivera, a job that led to the Milan captain exiting the game early after a mistimed tackle by his marker.

Assured and simply too strong, Milan picked off a 2-0 lead to take to Old Trafford, Sormani plundering the first with a sharp effort that Stepney's understudy Jimmy Rimmer should possibly have kept out, while after the interval he had absolutely no chance when Hamrin got on the end of a beautifully carved move to finish from close range. Fortunate that it was not even worse, Busby's side played out the last 15 minutes with ten men when John Fitzpatrick's frustrations in trying to subdue Hamrin got the better of him.

On an electric and action-packed night in Salford, United, in their away colours, came desperately close to overturning their first-leg deficit, denied only by a Milan side with a steely determination to hold on, and arguably a first-half propensity for hesitation in the final third of the pitch.

With Rocco happy to allow Busby's players all the possession they could possibly want, while flooding his defence and midfield to present United with a forest of opponents to pick their way through, it made for an opening 45 minutes that was akin to footballing arm wrestling, where the hosts came closest to blinking first.

Within 15 minutes, Hamrin had the ball in the net for Milan only to see it disallowed for offside. It was a marginal call, but by the footballing laws of the day it was probably the correct one. It is an incident, however, which has been used as currency ever since, in response to an even closer call that came during the frenetic finale.

If the first half had been something of a chess match, the second half was incendiary. Within seconds of the restart Cudicini was prone on the turf in front of the Stretford End, struck as coins rained down around him. With warnings of a potential abandonment made over the tannoy system, focus swiftly returned to events on the pitch – and they didn't disappoint.

Over the course of the second half United turned the screw, with Law, Bobby Charlton, and George Best spinning in perpetual motion in their efforts to create pockets of space in and around the Milan penalty area. The visitors' retaliation to this was to get Rivera on the ball as often as possible, from where he would release Prati, Hamrin, and Sormani, off and away on intermittent counter-attacks, two of which forced Rimmer into crucial point-blank stops.

Footballing rope-a-dope was at play, and the approach of both teams represented differing works of art. Law and Roberto Rosato were locked within a raging battle that saw both players literally spitting blood, Rosato eventually being forced out of the game and replaced by Nello Santin, while Giovanni Lodetti was given the mission to shackle Charlton, who in turn would draw his shadow deep in a bid to leave gaps for Brian Kidd, Willie Morgan, and Pat Crerand to exploit. At the centre of this maelstrom, Best often found himself trailing two, or even three opponents around the pitch.

After a series of fine saves from Cudicini, Charlton eventually made the breakthrough with 20 minutes still to play, powering the ball high into the Milan net from an angle after a wonderful and weaving run by Best. Old Trafford was alive with noise and expectation of a miracle.

With United applying pressure, and Milan protecting their goal line resolutely, the game lifted itself to a stunning crescendo, no better encapsulated than with ten minutes left to play when Law was convinced he had smuggled the ball over the line.

The contentious moment came after Charlton had just forced Cudicini into a smart save after sweetly catching a half-volley on the edge of the penalty area. As the parried ball became a hot property it eventually fell to Best, in turn laying it to Kidd, who instinctively sent it to Crerand on the right, where the Scottish international drove it powerfully across the six-yard box, his compatriot Law managing to flick it past Cudicini only to see it desperately halted on the line by Santin, the man who had replaced Law's nemesis, Rosato.

Despite the passionate and ultimately embittered protests of Law and his team-mates, no goal was awarded. Conjecture and argument have reigned ever since, but just as with Hamrin's disallowed goal, the footage available is completely open to interpretation, yet it narrowly points to the correct decision having been made by the officials. The final images of the incident are of Law remonstrating his frustration with Santin, who is still laying across the goal line.

Some 36 years prior to Luis García's much debated goal for Liverpool against Chelsea in the 2005 Champions League semi-final, Law's effort against Milan could feasibly be cast as the original European Cup 'ghost goal', or at least a ghost goal that never was.

From there, Milan staunchly ensured that that would be as close as United would come to an equaliser, stubbornly fighting their way to the full-time whistle and their place in the 1969 European Cup Final.

For United and their supporters, they could never have guessed it then but it was to be their last appearance in the tournament under the banner of the European Cup. Incredulously, not only would they not be champions of England for almost a quarter of a century, but they would slip to relegation from the First Division just five years later, having struggled to find a way forward beyond the retirement of Busby.

Winners in 1968 and five times a semi-finalist, the first English club to take part in the tournament when Busby defied the wishes of English football's insular bureaucrats, Manchester United had been one of the European Cup's most influential participants during its formative first decade and a half. Their exit from the landscape beyond 1969 was totally in keeping with the new direction that would be taken during the 1970s, however, and those flickering images of that second leg against Milan have an almost lunar appeal to them, a bit like the footage of Eugene Cernan three years later, when he gained the notoriety of becoming to date the last man to walk on the moon.

For that Milan era there was a similar theme at play, but one which would be gloriously completed in Madrid where they faced Ajax. You then have the book-ending of their relationship with the European Cup, created by Arrigo Saachi, as the 1980s met the 1990s. Whereas Manchester United were left with an experience of an unrequited love from the European Cup after 1969, Milan were able to renew their vows before the Champions League era dawned. There was a defined reconciliation.

Going back to moon terminology, if 1970/71 were to represent Apollo 11 for Ajax, and one small step for a football team, then 1968/69 would have to be Apollo 8, or 10, and a first circuit around the dark side of the moon, or a flirtation to within eight and a half nautical miles of the surface.

It had been less than a decade since Ajax had effectively been playing on an amateur footing, while as recently as 1964/65 the club had vaguely threatened relegation from the Eredivisie when the return to De Meer of Vic Buckingham had not gone as smoothly as hoped.

Buckingham had been the Ajax coach between 1959 and 1961, leading the club to Eredivisie and KNVB Cup success, but when he returned for a second spell in charge in the summer of 1964, after a three-season interlude at Sheffield Wednesday, the club had regressed.

By January 1965, after five months of inconsistent toil, Buckingham had departed when offered the manager's job at Fulham, and his replacement was Rinus Michels. Positioned in mid-table when the dapper Englishman left for west London, Ajax's results for the remainder of 1964/65 were worse after the loss of the former Bradford Park Avenue and West Bromwich Albion manager. Despite a bright start under the new man, their top-flight status became ever more precarious yet they avoided the unthinkable, albeit by just three points and having failed to pick up a win in their last seven league fixtures.

Despite the travails of 1964/65, Buckingham, in his short second spell at the club, had given Johann Cruyff his Ajax debut and left a sizeable impression on a young man who had first met him when a waif-like but prodigiously talented 12-year-old, a child who would so very nearly go on to conquer the world that lay beyond the continent he had the undoubted measure of.

From the start of the following season, improvements under Michels were swift and the Eredivisie was won for the first time since Buckingham had led Ajax to it six years earlier.

With that success came Michels' first tilt at the European Cup, in 1966/67, a run that was narrowly ended in the quarter-final by the more worldly wise Dukla Prague with a late winner via a Frits Soetekouw own goal. It was an unfortunate exit that came not before disposing of Bill Shankly's Liverpool in two iconic and fog-shrouded games, the first of which in Amsterdam saw Anfield's legendary manager laying claims to have walked on to the pitch during play, completely undetected by the officials.

Although knocked out of the following season's tournament at the first hurdle, another valuable lesson was absorbed by Michels and Ajax against Real Madrid, in which it took extra time for the Spanish giants to progress. Notes were taken by Cruyff and business between the two clubs would be resumed five seasons later, with an alternative ending.

In 1968/69, although denied glory, Ajax truly set a marker for what was to follow. Ruthless against Max Merkel's self-destructive Bundesliga winners 1. FC Nürnberg, a team who would end their reign as West German champions by being relegated, Michels' side also breezed past Fenerbahçe, setting up a stunning quarter-final with the incredible Benfica.

In a set of games that amounted to ambush and counter-ambush, Ajax had seemingly blown their chance when they were beaten 3-1 in the first leg at Amsterdam's snow-dusted Olympic Stadium by Otto Glória's Portuguese champions.

With experienced opponents again looking likely to be their undoing, Ajax had fallen behind to a Jacinto Santos penalty just beyond the half-hour, and five minutes later they were 2-0 in arrears when an error gifted José Torres the opportunity to ram the ball past a cruelly exposed Gerrit Bals.

Following the introduction of Inge Danielsson at the beginning of the second half, the Swedish international was soon on the end of a beautifully worked goal for Ajax to offer his team the glimmer of a potential salvation.

This was a reprieve that lasted for only 13 minutes, however, as Benfica earned themselves a third goal with a towering back-post José Augusto header as a corner went completely unchallenged. Formulaic a goal as it arguably was, his celebration was a work of art as he dived headlong into the snow piled up at the pitchside, then climbed to his feet and stooped to lift a huge lump of snow high into the air, as if the European Cup itself, before throwing it into the night sky.

A week later, at the Estádio da Luz, Ajax should have been the artistic lambs to the slaughter but with 32 minutes on the clock they had swept to a 3-0 lead on the night, taking with it the aggregate advantage.

Danielsson was again the man with his team's first goal, but not before having had one disallowed, taking out everyone who stood between him and the loose ball, whether they be friend or foe, in his attempt to give Ajax the dream start.

It was a disappointment that would only be short-lived as Danielsson had his team up and running with a wonderful glancing header which was then followed by a Cruyff brace, the first a work of brutal determination, the second with heavy shades of a goal he would score six years later, at the 1974 World Cup against Argentina.

Ajax then managed to keep an increasingly desperate and at times physical Benfica at bay until Torres' looped in a header with 20 minutes left to play. Levelling the aggregate score, Glória's side were now in the ascendency with Michels' players holding on. Three hours of football tilted one way then the other before balancing perfectly in the pre-penalty shoot-out era meant that a play-off was required a fortnight later at the Stade Olympique Yves-du-Manoir in Paris.

The venue of both the 1924 Summer Olympics and the 1938 World Cup Final, the Stade Olympique Yves-du-Manoir was packed to its capacity rafters as more spectators flooded through its turnstiles than had been the case in either Amsterdam or Lisbon.

Almost 180,000 supporters and football lovers had been in attendance across the breadth of this incredible trilogy of games, and in Paris the interest was so intense that many of those who were locked out of the stadium resorted to climbing adjacent trees in their attempts to gain a vantage point.

After a tense game in front of a rapturous crowd, despite some golden opportunities for Benfica to snatch victory during the 90 minutes, the two teams could not be split and extra time came into play.

Within this extra 30 minutes, Ajax's greater fitness told and in a hypnotic duel between Cruyff and Eusébio, it was the pretender who won the day as he broke the deadlock just two minutes into the extended period. Leaning on a stroke of luck, Cruyff's effort looped up and over José Henrique and just beneath the crossbar.

Still a threat at 1-0 down, Benfica's hopes were extinguished when Danielsson was on hand to take advantage of a loose ball in the penalty area just before the interval. It was then the same man who powered through a heavy-legged defence four minutes after the restart to complete a 3-0 scoreline that provided a certain sleight-of-hand given how close a contest it had been across 300 minutes of football.

It was a fork in the road as victory paved the way for Ajax to go on to their first European Cup semi-final, Benfica were subtlety deflected away from their position of prominence, and despite one last great run in 1971/72, for this majestic Portuguese generation it was the beginning of the end. It would be 1988 before they contested another European Cup Final.

Avoiding Manchester United and Milan in the semi-final draw, Ajax went up against the determined Slovaks of Spartak Trnava, with the first leg at the Olympic Stadium in Amsterdam.

Quick out of the blocks, Cruyff led wave upon wave of Ajax attacks with two very good early chances being squandered, one a free header central to goal and the other when the ball bounced back off the post.

Rather than frustration being allowed to build, Ajax simply turned the screw tighter still with the lead coming their way in the 28th minute, shortly after another opportunity went awry when a fine passing move resulted in an untaken cross flashing across the edge of the six-yard box.

Surreally, the catalyst to gaining the advantage seemed to be the pitch invasion of a giant rabbit, hastily removed by a pitchside photographer. Within minutes, Cruyff had the ball in the visitors' net. A corner was swung over from the right and a towering header from Danielsson was blocked on the line by Trnava goalkeeper Josef Geryk, only for Ajax's most valuable commodity to be on hand to slam the loose ball home.

It was a lead that Michels' side fully deserved, and incredulously the half-time score remained at 1-0 despite Danielsson having a shot stopped on the line by a Trnava defender who was sat on the turf. It was a narrow advantage but Ajax really would have been good value had they gone in for the break with a 5-0 lead.

For all their first-half profligacy, in the first 20 minutes of the second half Ajax were steely eyed in front of goal. Sjaak Swart swept home their second seven minutes after the restart and not long after the hour the magnificent Piet Keizer stretched every neck muscle in directing a header beyond the desperate reach of Geryk for 3-0.

The second leg was conducted 11 days later in Trnava, just 24 hours after Milan had won the first leg of their semi-final against Manchester United.

Presumed notions of an inevitable Ajax vs Milan final were almost blown out of the water by Trnava, however, as they mounted an impressive fightback on home territory. As if losing the services of Cruyff after just 24 minutes wasn't bad enough for Ajax, to concede in such needless circumstances only three minutes later made it a devastating double blow.

On a terrible pitch, Ajax had been forced into a desperate rearguard action and when Bals comfortably collected a through ball that he opted to send down field far too eagerly, scuffing it and sending his clearance no more than 30 yards, it fell straight into the possession of Ladislav Kuna who beautifully dealt with the awkward bounce before volleying the ball with his left foot as it dropped perfectly for him. As the desperate Bals tried to recover ground, Kuna's venomously struck shot was agonisingly out of reach for the Ajax goalkeeper and dipped into the net.

While definitively outplayed in Amsterdam a week and a half earlier, Trnava had at least shown they were confident when on the ball, and this was spectacularly proved in the second leg as for large swathes of the game they outplayed Michels' carriers of the flag for technically impeccable football.

With the obligatory firecrackers disrupting the game here and there, given how well Trnava were performing, it is hard to say which team was the more unsettled by the stoppages. Half-time arrived, however, with the scoreline at 1-0.

Trnava emerged for the second half like lightning, as if they knew any chance of overturning Ajax's lead was highly dependent upon scoring before more pyrotechnics materialised. Within seconds of the resumption a shot flashed past the foot of Bal's right-hand post, and inside ten minutes Kuna had scored again, this time with a flicked header that the Ajax goalkeeper had no chance of stopping.

Armed with 35 minutes in which to level the aggregate score, Trnava threw everything at Ajax. Another chance rolled past the wrong side of Bal's left-hand post and he then made a wonderful save, tipping the ball away for a corner when a goal looked a certainty. It was one of a string of important stops, and when added to a growing sense of anxiety in Trnava's attackers, the home side's frustrations escalated as the clock ticked down.

Riding out the storm, despite defending deep not being a natural situation for his side, Michels and Ajax crept over the finish line and into their first European Cup Final, embracing this with both delight and relief.

Despite the final being a clash that was billed as all the Ajax young dudes against the Milan elders, the average age of the two teams was split by a gap that stood at less than a year and a half, while Ajax had almost as many players as Milan who were in their 30s.

Perceptions were somewhat distorted, and this belief that there was a wider age gap between the two teams can only have been a product of their respective styles of play, and deeds so far done during the first decade and a half of organised European club competitions. Whereas this was the first time that Ajax had explored beyond the quarter-final of a major continental tournament, Milan had not only won the European Cup six years earlier but had also contested the 1958 final, and reached the semi-final in the tournament's inaugural season. Added to this, only 12 months had passed since they had won the European Cup Winners' Cup.

When you factor in the Italian national team twice being World Cup winners and the reigning European champions, and the Netherlands having not taken part in a major international tournament since 1938, it all helped to propagate a not untrue concept of the new currency taking on the old currency. There was a clear historical disparity between Serie A and the Eredivisie, and this meant that being older of footballing consciousness was erroneously translated to the actual age of the players.

So while it was expected to be the stubbornness of the experienced and defensive Italians, up against the ebullient young bucks of the broad-minded attacking Amsterdam artisans, more accurately it was the footballing textbook vs the blank sheet of paper. The 1969 European Cup Final would represent a bridge too far for Ajax, but they would then use that blank sheet of paper to brush the most beautiful of abstracts rather than write the type of quill-inscribed scriptures that catenaccio had been spun from. It all, arguably, set the stage for the European Cup's most fascinating final of the lot.

Pre-match stereotypes were ditched by the Serie A team and Milan made a fast start, with Prati at the centre of it. Within 45 seconds he had hit the post, and then evaded Wim Suurbier with the sort of turn that Cruyff would later make famous. In the seventh minute he opened the scoring, and Ajax never fully recovered from it. Prati would end the game with a hat-trick yet somehow remain a subplot to the duel between Rivera and Cruyff.

Milan's opening goal was created by Sormani when he managed to turn and lose the man who would be his shadow for much of the game, Barry Hulshoff. Creating space on the left, Sormani sent in the perfect cross for Prati to flick his header out of the reach of Bals and into the net, high towards the right-hand post.

Socks around his ankles from the start, Prati benefited throughout the game from the promptings of Rivera, and with Sormani acting as a magnet for Hulshoff it gifted the Milan number 11 acres of space to exploit. Suurbier, struggling to keep tabs on him, was replaced at half-time, but not before Prati had struck again five minutes before the interval.

Suurbier had been dispossessed of the ball deep in the Milan half, picking up an injury in the process, from a challenge his team-mates had felt to be an unfair one. From there, Rocco's men broke swiftly and when Rivera worked his way across the edge of the Ajax penalty area, he sent a back-heel into the path of Prati, who struck from distance.

It was a punishing moment for an Ajax side who had enjoyed most of the possession of the ball between the two Milan goals. They had, however, been largely kept at bay by a resolute Milan defence and the huge frame of Cudicini, who had saved impressively from a Cruyff shot when he wonderfully twisted and turned his way past Angelo Anquilletti. It was to be Ajax's best chance of the first half.

Despite Ajax enjoying greater possession, the clearer chances continued to fall to Milan and Hamrin rolled the ball just wide, while a Sormani header caused concern. Rocco's side had been minimalists when it came to time on the ball, yet they had been very effective when they had it. Conversely, Ajax had not done much wrong but had been made to pay whenever they momentarily let their guard down.

Along with Suurbier failing to return after half-time, Henk Groot was also replaced. Klaas Nuninga and Bennie Muller were thrown into the fray.

In a tempestuous start to the second half, Cruyff had claims for a penalty ignored but also a blind eye turned by the referee when he went over the top of the ball on Giovanni Lodetti. In between these two incidents, Sormani again came close with a header.

Just before the hour, Ajax worked their way back into the reckoning when Lodetti upended Keizer, to gift Velibor Vasović a penalty that he confidently converted at the second attempt, having pulled up halfway through his initial run-up due to Cudicini having an outside chance of making it to the ball first.

Rather than panic, Milan immediately tested Ajax's powers of concentration, when Rivera came painfully close to restoring his team's two-goal advantage, this being quickly followed by Hamrin forcing Bals into a smart save.

Put off balance by Milan's positive response to conceding, it seemed to be Ajax who froze at this point and Sormani was the man to punish them. Shackled for most of the game, he had been dangerous on the handful of occasions he managed to slip the close attention of Hulshoff, setting up Prati for the opening goal and flashing two headers close.

In the 67th minute it was Sormani who dealt the killer blow at the business end of a classic Milan counter-attack. With the Ajax defence backing off, it was a basic invitation for the Brazilian-born striker to try his luck, and when he did the perfect left-footed effort was narrowly out of reach for Bals and tantalisingly just inside his right-hand post.

Incensed at how his team had wasted their opportunity of a route back into the game, Cruyff was soon clipping the outside of Cudicini's left-hand post, but it was to be Ajax's last chance of true substance. With Lodetti having just threatened, a fourth Milan goal was delivered by Rivera for Prati with 15 minutes remaining.

Breaking through an Ajax defence that was now encamped on the halfway line, Rivera was soon into a one-on-one with Bals, from which he was forced wide when being knocked off stride by the Ajax goalkeeper and captain.

Keeping his feet when the easy thing would have been to go to ground and accept the penalty that surely would have been awarded, Rivera took his time to await the arrival of Prati in the penalty area, picking him out with an inch-perfect cross from which he completed his hat-trick by heading the ball back across the scrambling Bals.

Game all but over, Ajax made two last unsuccessful efforts to narrow their losing deficit in what was almost an exhibition of football for the last 15 minutes. Swart skewed a shot wide while Saul Malatrasi produced a stunning block on Cruyff. Milan, meanwhile, ploughed forward to relieve the pressure, and even Giovanni Trapattoni tried a speculative effort to join the goalscorers.

At full time, Milan had gained their second European Cup success, while Ajax had absorbed a priceless tutorial that would be the springboard for the glorious nights of the early 1970s to come in London, Rotterdam, and Zagreb.

Unwittingly, the tectonic plates of European club football had shifted beneath the pitch at the Santiago Bernabéu. It might have felt like business as usual in Madrid, but change was coming.

7

Lowlands Uprising

AJAX MIGHT not have taken the trophy at the 1969 European Cup Final, but they walked away from it as the unsuspecting future of the tournament. It was to be Feyenoord who brought the Netherlands its first success, however.

Eredivisie champions in 1968/69 as part of a domestic double while Ajax were falling short against Milan, Feyenoord had grabbed the golden ticket for 1969/70. No stranger to European football's biggest competition, they had reached the semi-final of the European Cup in 1962/63, the best run by any Dutch club until Rinus Michels took his team to Madrid.

Feyenoord's enduring rivalry with Ajax was already set in stone and by the end of the 1960s they represented the two most successful clubs in Dutch football. Rotterdam, and Amsterdam, two markedly different cities, with alternative outlooks on life, and their own interpretations of football. Ying and Yang in operation.

Ajax would soon eclipse the European Cup deeds of Feyenoord, but the team from De Kuip were the first of the two to reach the promised land.

Ernst Happel took the reins at De Kuip in the summer of 1969, recruited from ADO Den Haag after Feyenoord's double-winning coach Ben Peeters bowed out. The Austrian had won the KNVB Cup in 1968, and in seven years with his previous employers he had turned them from a struggling top-flight entity into one of the most consistent teams in the country. For his next trick, Happel would ambush Celtic in the 1970 European Cup Final.

Still viewed by some as at best an emerging nation when it came to football, and at worst a backwater by others, without the tangible success of continental club success or a visible national team to have made an impact in the finals of a major international tournament then, it was all too easy for the rising threat some countries posed to not make it on to everybody's radar.

This was certainly the case for a presumptuous Celtic in 1970. Having overwhelmed Don Revie's Leeds United in two titanic 'Battle of Britain' encounters in the semi-final, on the back of dispatching both Benfica and Fiorentina – the former on the toss of a coin – it must have been with a degree of entitlement that Jock Stein's side approached their second European Cup Final. The hard work had seemingly been done and Feyenoord were just meant to be part of Celtic's second coronation.

For Happel's team, the 1969/70 European Cup became the primary focus of their campaign. Although only defeated once in the defence of their Eredivisie title, they drew too many games, which allowed Ajax to reclaim the prize. Combined with an early exit in the KNVB Cup, it meant that Feyenoord were to befall an arid domestic season.

In the first leg of the first round, Feyenoord made the trip to the Icelandic capital to take on Knattspyrnufélag Reykjavíkur, where they indecently scored 12 times, three times as many goals as they would score in the return game in Rotterdam.

This was followed by an infinitely far sterner test, and one that was expected to end their involvement in the 1969/70 European Cup. A trip to the San Siro, to face the holders, Milan, ended in a 1-0 defeat, which could easily have been by a much wider margin. Happel's side stubbornly held on and made their illustrious opponents pay a costly price in the second leg at a packed De Kuip.

Within six minutes of start of the return game, the future Celtic manager Wim Jansen had looped in one of those goals where it was difficult to decipher if it was intended or not. Regardless of whether it was precision optimism or a miscued cross, the ball dropped in and the net rippled.

Feyenoord's faithful brought themselves into play from this point. A vibrant atmosphere inspired their heroes onward to victory in a stark contrast to the low attendance at the San Siro a fortnight earlier for a game that was played out on a weekday afternoon.

Conversely, under the De Kuip floodlights, the second leg felt like an event rather than an idle afterthought. Willem van Hanegem headed home the winning goal with only eight minutes remaining to cause a seismic shock.

The result put Feyenoord squarely on the map and it was nothing short of careless of Celtic not to take note. Feyenoord would emerge from the winter break to face two eastern European opponents, firstly Vorwärts Berlin in the quarter-final where the Dutch champions again turned around a 1-0 first leg reversal with a 2-0 victory on home soil, and then Legia Warsaw in the semi-final.

On each occasion, beyond the first-round demolition of the Icelandic champions, Happel had preached discipline on the road, and a fast incisive passing game back at De Kuip, having been blessed to be drawn away in the first leg in every round on their way to the final.

Happel lined up his team with essentially a 4-1-2-3 system, which was largely the formation he used to take the Netherlands to the 1978 World Cup Final. A forward thinker, he would go on to become the first coach to win the European Cup with two different teams and even took a third to another final.

None of these teams were the perceived great and the good at the point of impact, either. Beyond Feyenoord, Happel took Club Brugge to the 1978 final and then won the European Cup with Hamburger SV five years later.

This Feyenoord team was one of subtle purpose. Beyond van Hanegem and Jansen, both of whom would go on to play in a World Cup Final, Feyenoord were packed with fine players. Rinus Israël was another member of the team who would be present at the 1974 World Cup Final, in his case as an unused substitute, while they were also blessed by the attacking talent of the prolific Swedish international Ove Kindvall and the iconic Coen Moulijn, a skilled free spirit who Johan Cruyff had idolised as a youngster.

Israël, captain and lynchpin of central defence, was partnered by Theo Laseroms and flanked by the full-backs Theo van Duivenbode and Piet Romeijn in a unit that was ably overseen by the former Ajax goalkeeper Eddy Pieters Graafland, who himself had been in keen competition for the number one shirt with Eddy Treijtel. The entirety of this defensive unit were full internationals while Van Duivenbode had also been in the Ajax team for the 1969 European Cup Final prior to his transfer to Feyenoord. Treijtel was to be another member of the Netherlands 1974 World Cup squad.

In midfield, Jansen and Van Hanegem were joined by the Austrian international Franz Hasil; Kindvall and Moulijn were supplemented in attack by the Netherlands international Henk Wery. Still, Celtic sleepwalked into the 1970 European Cup Final.

On the eve of the game at the San Siro, Stein questioned the levels of fitness and fight in the Feyenoord side, brushing them off to a degree, at least in comparison to the Leeds team who had fought tooth and nail against Celtic in the semi-final. It was dangerous territory into which the Scottish champions were clumsily treading.

There is more than one way to win a game, however, and Celtic could not match Feyenoord's levels of technical ability and speed of thought. Tommy Gemmell opened the scoring for Stein's side, but that was against the run of play, and Israël equalised within a couple of minutes, restoring both parity and the persistent running current of the game, which was flooding towards the Celtic penalty area.

Amazingly, Celtic took the game into extra time, and to within three minutes of a replay. Hasil twice hit the frame of goal while Evan Williams pulled off fine saves from Kindvall and Wery. Eventually the dam broke, however, and Kindvall struck the decisive goal.

For Celtic, this was like 1967, except in reverse. This time they had been overwhelmed by opponents who were billed as being inferior. Van Duivenbode successfully blotted out the threat of Jimmy Johnstone, and with that Stein's side seemed to be bereft of ideas.

This was a defined shift in footballing culture. Ajax took the foundations that Feyenoord had laid and on top of them created the most esoteric brand of football imaginable. Yet it was a concept grounded in simplicity and freedom. Evolution was at play.

From football in the Netherlands still being on an at least tenuous amateur footing as the 1950s ended, to one of its clubs reaching a European Cup Final before the 1960s drew to a close, improvements were rapid. Long having embraced a short passing game, something that stems all the way back to the days of Jack Reynolds' involvement with the club, via the influence of Vic Buckingham, Ajax's future fell into the hands of Michels at the beginning of 1965.

After an initial period of volatility, by 1965/66 Michels had transformed them into champions. Blessed by the emergence of some of the finest talents in global football, let alone the domestic game, they soon took a stranglehold. The next two league titles also fell their way and inroads were beginning to be made in Europe.

Tentative steps forward soon became giant strides, and despite there surely being a temptation to stick rather than twist on the composition of his team, in the wake of having reached the 1969 European Cup Final, within a year almost half of that line-up had been moved on.

Surviving the cull was, of course, Cruyff, but Michels also kept faith with Velibor Vasović, Barry Hulshoff, Wim Suurbier, Sjaak Swart, and Piet Keizer. Across the following European Cup-winning seasons, this wonderfully gifted group was enhanced by the additions of Heinz Stuy, Johan Neeskens, Horst Blankenburg, Ruud Krol, Arie Haan, Gerrie Mühren, and Johnny Rep. Michels would see Ajax to their first European Cup success, in 1971, before accepting an offer of employment from Barcelona. His successor was Ștefan Kovács and over the next two years Cruyff and his team-mates went supernova.

Under Michels, it was undoubtedly mind-expanding football, yet he also kept tighter hold of the reins than Kovács would. Control was everything, and without either Michels' insistence upon it, or his successor's relaxing of it, Ajax would not have attained the highs that they did.

Wembley in 1971 marked the realisation of Michels' vision. Panathinaikos were Ajax's surprise opponents, a team led from the touchline by a man who was no stranger to European Cup finals, Ferenc Puskás.

Impressively knocking out Slovan Bratislava, Everton, and Red Star Belgrade on their way to the final, Panathinaikos were not there by accident. Having brushed Jeunesse Esch aside in the first round, Slovan were only 18 months beyond defeating Barcelona in the 1969 European Cup Winners' Cup Final, a night when Puskás' dismantled the Catalans at the Leoforos Stadium.

To prove that it was no fluke, when Panathinaikos headed to Goodison Park for the first leg of the quarter-final, they came away with a hugely valuable 1-1 draw that had been seconds away from being a 1-0 victory, against opponents who had high designs of winning the tournament. Everton had been stylish and dominant First Division champions in 1969/70 and were highly motivated by the final being at Wembley, feeling that they could emulate what Manchester United had achieved three seasons earlier.

Harry Catterick's side had eliminated the blossoming Borussia Mönchengladbach in the previous round, prevailing in what was the European Cup's very first penalty shoot-out, and Panathinaikos will have been viewed as a free pass into the semi-final. Frustratingly for Everton, they were bundled out by the Greek champions on away goals.

In the last four Panathinaikos were to all intents and purposes dead and buried when beaten 4-1 in Belgrade by Red Star. Yet they stormed to a 3-0 second-leg win, which instead sent them on to the final. The first two goals were claimed by the prolific Antonis Antoniadis, a rangy striker who was difficult to mark. Dangerous in the air yet useful with the ball at his feet, he possessed no shortage of pace and carried a powerful shot. He was to be the 1970/71 European Cup's leading goalscorer.

In turn, although perhaps not in such bewitching extremes, Ajax's run to the final was similarly one of peaks and troughs. Vaguely unsettled by the Albanians of 17 Nëntori Tirana in the first round, and brushing aside Basel with ease in the second round, the real tests were encountered in the quarter-final against Celtic and then in the semi-final against Atlético Madrid.

Jock Stein's men, perhaps with their experiences against Feyenoord too fresh in mind, were eventually comfortably beaten in Amsterdam in the first leg of their last-eight clash. Ajax ran to an impressive 3-0 first-leg win at the Olympisch Stadium, yet were kept at bay for over an hour before taking control in the final third of the game.

Their opening goal was shockingly direct, yet not without skill. After a three-man move from goalkeeper to goalscorer, Cruyff was the man to pick Celtic's defensive lock. A Hulshoff free kick and a late magical piece of Keizer skill put the tie beyond Celtic, and despite the Scottish champions winning the return game, the deficit was to be too insurmountable a mountain for the 1967 European Cup winners to climb.

In the second leg of the semi-final, it took Ajax just eight minutes to level the aggregate scoreline, having narrowly lost in the Spanish capital to Atlético. An unstoppable Keizer free kick ripped into the visitors' net, and they must have feared the potential onslaught, yet it was not until the last 15 minutes that Michels' side secured their place in the 1971 final.

Prospering firstly from a speculative effort from distance by Suurbier, which Atlético goalkeeper Rodri should have kept out, Ajax's nerves were then settled in the last few minutes when Neeskens guided in his team's third.

With lessons learned from their defeat in the final two years earlier, Ajax overwhelmed Panathinaikos at Wembley thanks to a tactical masterclass. Michels' side scored early through a glancing header by Dick van Dijk and then threw a defensive blanket over Antoniadis.

With Panathinaikos's Plan A having failed, there simply was no Plan B on offer. With just three minutes remaining, and after playing an impressive game of keep-ball, Haan was at the end of a magnificent team move to make it 2-0. Ajax were deserving champions of Europe but with such success came the suitors. Barcelona could not yet have Cruyff, but they did take Michels.

Fears for Ajax's future without Michels were entirely understandable, and these were not initially eased by the appointment of Ştefan Kovács, a man who himself seemed quite surprised that he had been handed the job. In response to this development, he promptly purchased a short-term return ticket to Amsterdam, feeling that he would not keep the position for too long.

There was a mixed reaction to Kovács's appointment from the Ajax squad, and he was immediately tested at his first training session as a waist-high ball was hit in his direction at speed, which he impressively controlled and dispatched in one fluid movement. Challenge accepted, and overcome, the bohemian culture that would escalate over the course of the next two years at Ajax was engendered in the blink of an eye.

Kovács had quickly earned the respect of his players, and the majority would back him to the hilt, although one or two would confess frustrations that the discipline of Michels was allowed to slip dramatically. From the point of view of the new man in charge, he was handing his players responsibility and degrees of autonomy that they had never possessed.

No soft touch, Kovács was not afraid to stand up to the egotistical power plays that were beginning to creep into the modern game. When Cruyff suggested he was not fit enough to play in one match due to an ankle injury, the Romanian took out a bank note and rubbed it on the reputedly painful area.

Cruyff, fully understanding the message, took to the pitch and was the star of the show.

What Kovács showed to his players was that he was willing to loosen the reins and treat them like adults, with the caveat that in return they must act like adults. It was an approach that reaped the most wondrous of dividends but also placed an unwitting best-before date on the concept. Ajax under Kovács would burn brightly, but to do so there would be a fade to come.

Tomorrow was not something to concern Ajax as they began the defence of their European Cup in 1971/72. They swept to their third final without losing a single game. Dynamo Dresden, Olympique de Marseille, Arsenal, and Benfica were the lambs to the slaughter, each of whom were able to bask in the glow of association with escalating greatness.

This new air of freedom was soon on display. Against Dresden, a 2-0 first-leg victory should have been 3-0 as a piece of Cruyff magic was rendered redundant when his team-mates were erroneously penalised for a foul on the East German goalkeeper.

Confidence rising, Ajax then headed to the south of France to silence a volatile and intimidating Stade Vélodrome. From 1-0 down, Kovács and his players walked away with a 2-1 win before again coming from behind in the return for an even more emphatic winning margin on an Amsterdam evening that by its conclusion had taken on the aura of exhibition match.

In the quarter-final, Arsenal must have been happy with their away goal during a 2-1 defeat in Amsterdam in the first leg. Ray Kennedy had opened the scoring before Gerrie Mühren struck twice. All this hard work was undone within 15 minutes of the start of the second leg at Highbury, however, when George Graham glanced in a well-placed own goal. It was to be the only goal of the game.

Up against Benfica in the semi-final, signs of nerves, or at least respect to the two-times winners, meant that there was significantly less freestyling from Ajax. Swart headed home the only goal over the course of both games, midway through the second half of the first leg. It was an impressive display of discipline that Michels would have been proud to call his own.

With Rotterdam playing host to the 1972 European Cup Final, for Ajax to retain their title in the home of their great domestic rivals, thus overtaking them in number of tournament victories, was the dream scenario come true.

Internazionale should have exited at the second round, having conceded seven goals away to Borussia Mönchengladbach only to have the result overturned due to Roberto Boninsegna being struck by a can. Running with the reprieve, Giovanni Invernizzi's side had picked their way through to their first European Cup Final since losing in 1967 to Celtic, the team they had beaten on penalties in the 1972 semi-final.

A footballing cat with nine lives in 1971/72, despite being able to call upon the talents of Sandro Mazzola and Jair, Inter were never likely to be anything other than the fall guys to Ajax in this one. Cruyff was at the peak of his Amsterdam powers, scoring both goals in his team's 2-0 victory, and giving the watching world his iconic celebration. Expansion consumed pragmatism and it was joyously embraced.

In Belgrade a year later, Ajax arguably seemed as bored with themselves as the those watching them were enraptured. Rep scored the only goal of the game against Juventus, but with the frame of Dino Zoff's goalposts being struck a couple of times and near-misses galore, their bewildered opponents could just as easily have absorbed a wide losing margin.

On their way to the 1973 European Cup Final, Ajax had been stylish of movement and dismissive of threats. CSKA Sofia and Bayern Munich had been ruthlessly dispatched, before in the semi-final their supreme self-confidence reached its zenith in the shape of a wonderfully assured and vaguely arrogant piece of skill from Mühren at the Santiago Bernabéu against Real Madrid, in which he punctuated the game with the most hypnotic display of ball juggling. It was a piece of magic that could only ever come from those teams and players who are completely at one with themselves.

Juventus were a far stronger opponent than Inter had been the year previously. They had taken two trips behind the Iron Curtain and beaten Brian Clough's Derby County in the semi-final. Yet, they were no contest for Kovács's team.

However, with control relinquished by Kovács in the summer of 1973 and Cruyff set to be reunited with Michels at Barcelona, change was coming. The Netherlands' rise was ending and a new Germanic movement would emerge. A fresh hat-trick of European Cups would unfold, except without the charm of what Ajax managed to conjure up. It was to be an overlap of thinking, methods, and principals that would also spill over on to the international stage at the 1974 World Cup finals.

8

Bavarian Bravado

ELEVEN YEARS prior to Bayern Munich walking out at the Heysel Stadium for their first European Cup Final, the Bundesliga was born. The Bavarian giants to be were not invited to the christening.

A belated introduction to West German club football of a top-flight professional league, up to the summer of 1963 the system in operation was the Oberliga, in which a series of regional leagues took place from which the top two teams would progress to the championship play-off round. This would eventually simmer down to a final, where the winners would be crowned the champions. It was something akin to the structure of the NFL except on a nominally amateur footing.

When the Bundesliga was formed, the teams to be initially involved were decided upon by a combination of recent on-pitch achievement and geographical location. While some clubs' involvement was an obvious decision, others were vehemently argued over as the clubs cut adrift angrily stated their own cases for inclusion.

One of the rules drawn up for the inclusion of teams for the inaugural Bundesliga was that no one city would be permitted multiple clubs. This was to be a problem for Munich, and despite Bayern's gradual growth, in 1963 it was 1860 Munich who had the greater track record.

Swept aside to the Regionalliga system, it would be two years before Bayern won promotion to the Bundesliga under their own steam, but they would soon make up for lost time and by 1967 they had already won their first major European honour when defeating Rangers in the 1967 Cup Winners' Cup Final.

From Zlatko Čajkovski's promotion, DFB Pokal, and Cup Winners' Cup-winning teams to Branko Zebec winning Bayern their first Bundesliga title, Udo Lattek was the man to be handed the task of taking the club to its next objective within the wake of their quarter-final exit from the 1969/70 European Cup.

Also charged with the task of fending off the growing rise of Borussia Mönchengladbach, Lattek was a fascinating character who would eventually represent both sides of a divide that heavily defined not only West German football but the wider spectrum of the game in the 1970s.

Mönchengladbach, under Hannes Weisweiler, took the Bundesliga title in 1969/70 and 1970/71, before Bayern and Lattek wrested it back in 1971/72 for the first part of a hat-trick of domestic league successes.

Bayern, a team blessed to possess the spine of West Germany's 1972 European Championship and 1974 World Cup-winning teams, could boast the services of Sepp Maier, Franz Beckenbauer, Paul Breitner, Hans-Georg Schwarzenbeck, Uli Hoeneß, and Gerd Müller.

In the cases of Maier, Beckenbauer, and Müller, they were survivors of Bayern's Regionalliga days, and they would traverse the distance between being excluded from the Bundesliga to champions of Europe.

Even Bayern's backing dancers were players of substance. Jupp Kapellmann would be another to pick up a World Cup winners' medal, albeit without making an on-pitch appearance, while the Swedish international Conny Torstensson would appear in all but one of his nation's games at the same tournament. Another Scandinavian influence was the wonderful Danish full-back Johnny Hansen.

Franz Roth was a massively important component of the Bayern side, whose international recognition was criminally low, while Rainer Zobel and Bernd Dürnberger were hugely unfortunate never to receive a call-up from Helmut Schön.

Much of this strength that Bayern possessed was either taken for granted by the rest of the continent, unacknowledged as routine or shrouded in what some saw as them being the European Cup's pantomime villain.

With last-minute equalisers in extra time, persuading referees to disallow goals that seemed set to stand, and square goalposts helping deflect success their way, Bayern enjoyed more than their fair share of luck in completing their own hat-trick of European Cup wins in succession to the aesthetically compelling version that Ajax had spun.

Scratch below the surface, though, and you'll find a wonderful sense of cohesion offset by a ruthlessness that cost Lattek his job. Like a heat-seeking missile, Bayern's focus and attention to detail was scientific compared to the art of Ajax, yet it was not without a bespoke beauty of its own.

In an era of Total Football, only West Germany and Bayern could come up with an answer that was truly worthy of the question that was posed by the Netherlands and Ajax. Pragmatism combined with speed of body and mind, in which Beckenbauer was the puppeteer, Hoeneß was the go-between, and Müller was the assassin, made for a relentless entity where winning was the only statutory demand.

Make no mistake, Bayern could play, but they were not against doing the ugly things to gain a victory; leaning toward the dark arts was embraced when deemed necessary, but fine, flowing football was allowed too. First and foremost, the win was the primary target, and if it could be obtained stylishly too then that was seen as a bonus. Fun was permitted only if the risk assessment said it was okay. Bayern's path to glory was arguably more inclusive than the more niche version peddled by Johan Cruyff.

Bayern's hat-trick of European Cups could have been sunk at the very outset, however. In the 1973/74 first round they were taken to a penalty shoot-out against Åtvidabergs FF. Playing for the Swedes was Conny Torstensson, scorer of two goals in the second leg and one of the players to succeed from 12 yards in the shoot-out. Lattek's side were momentarily behind on aggregate and it took a strike from Hoeneß take the tie to extra time.

So impressed were Bayern by the performances of Torstensson that they swiftly swooped to sign him, and were able to include him in their European Cup squads from the quarter-final onward.

Three further steps took Bayern to their first European Cup Final, all of which involved trips behind the Iron Curtain, to East Germany, Bulgaria, and Hungary. Comfortably dealing with CSKA Sofia in the last eight and Újpesti Dózsa in the semi-final, during which Torstensson immediately showed his worth, the hardest task had been posed by Dynamo Dresden in the second round.

While the European Cup possessed many iconic games, it was quite rare for the two legs of one tie to offer as much as Bayern and Dresden did in this one. In the first leg at the Olympiastadion, Lattek's side trailed 1-0, led 2-1, trailed 3-2, then came back to win 4-3 thanks to a late goal from Müller in a game embossed with an admirable lack of trademark Germanic discipline.

It was not that it was a dirty match, more that defensive shapes were easily dissolved. It was a goalscorer's paradise and akin to that controlled and studious colleague who let loose at the staff party, drunk after one pint, on an evening in which they all too briefly display that they have a marvellous alter-ego to go alongside the on-point workaholic you usually see.

At the Rudolf-Harbig-Stadion in the return game, the theme of the first leg was faithfully re-enacted. From 2-0 up to 3-2 in arrears, Bayern edged through with a 3-3 draw, for a magnificent 7-6 aggregate win after a night of counter-punching football that swept from one end to the other.

In the 1974 European Cup Final, Bayern went up against a talented yet uncompromising Atlético Madrid at the Heysel Stadium in Brussels. The Spanish side were fined £14,000 by UEFA for violent and anti-sporting conduct during the first leg of their semi-final, against Celtic, in which they had three players sent off. It was the highest penalty that UEFA had ever imposed up to that point.

Three-match bans were conferred upon Ruben Ayala, Ruben Diaz, and Quique. The rancour did not stop there either as seven other Atlético players picked up yellow cards, three of them causing further second-leg suspensions. But in a turnaround, the La Liga champions took the second leg 2-0 without a single yellow card being brandished at them.

The 1974 European Cup Final was expected to be tilted heavily towards Bayern, with Atlético defending deep from where they would launch the occasional breakaway. Conversely, it was the West Germans who were pinned back, and the Spanish who were dominant, at least until extra time when Bayern's greater fitness began to tell.

Despite Lattek's team sensing that should there be a victory in the late stages then it would fall their way, it was Atlético who broke the deadlock when Luis Aragonés curled in a wonderful 114th-minute free kick. They were just seconds away from glory when Schwarzenbeck popped up as the unlikely Bayern saviour, driving the ball home low and powerfully, beating Miguel Reina to his right. With no penalty shoot-out scheduled, in meant that the European Cup would have its first, and ultimately only, final replay just two days later.

So close to success in the first encounter, Atlético were simply overwhelmed in the replay, both by the ferocity of Bayern's attack and their own psychological scars. Lattek named an unchanged line-up whereas Juan Carlos Lorenzo opted to field the 11 players who had ended the original game rather than those who had started it.

After shadow-boxing their way through the first half-hour, Bayern proceeded to toy with Atlético for the remaining 60 minutes, Hoeneß hitting the first and last goals of the evening and Müller clinical with his team's second and third, his second strike being a magical lob over a desperately back-peddling Reina.

Having set his players the task of stopping Atlético playing in the first game, when Lattek instead deployed his team to embrace their attacking potential in the replay, the plan reaped the ultimate reward. This performance was bewitchingly Bayern at their very best, a display that could easily be held up to scrutiny as one of the European Cup's greatest team performances in a final.

Suffering something of a hangover the following season, sluggish domestic form cost Lattek his job just after the turn of the year. Having approached the Bayern hierarchy stating that change was needed, while agreement was forthcoming, their interpretation was that rather than an influx of new signings the coach should go instead.

It was a seismic event, and by the beginning the 1975/76 campaign Lattek had resurfaced at Mönchengladbach as the successor to Weisweiler, who himself had accepted a lucrative offer to take over from Rinus Michels at Barcelona.

Within a year, Lattek had taken his new employers to the Bundesliga title, and a season later to the 1977 European Cup Final. Back in January 1975, however, at Bayern he had relinquished the reigning champions of Europe to the much-desired Dettmar Cramer.

Cramer, a footballing nomad who was seen as something of a technical genius, had rebuffed the advances of many Bundesliga clubs before but found Bayern impossible to turn down. Domestically he would be frustrated in his bid for trophies, despite the talent at his disposal, but in the European Cup it was a very different matter.

Lattek had still been at the helm when 1. FC Magdeburg were faced in the second round of the 1974/75 European Cup campaign. Recipients of a bye in the first round, when Bayern's defence belatedly began, it was with a titanic clash with the East German champions and in a similar theme to the Dresden encounters of the previous season, the gloves were off.

Magdeburg, holders of the Cup Winners' Cup, were something of a renegade club in East Germany. Reportedly their coach Heinz Krügel was offered the chance to listen in on the bugged Bayern dressing room prior to the second leg, but he said no.

Krügel would soon be run out of both Magdeburg, and football itself, by the East German powers that be. It was brave response to an unethical offer made by dangerous figures. Bayern had won the first leg but with the score having been 3-2 after the holders had fought back from 2-0 down at half-time, Krügel's team were still well positioned to turn the tie around.

An assured Bayern performance won the second leg 2-1. It would be a fork in the road for both Lattek and Krügel. By the time Bayern took to the pitch against Ararat Yerevan in the quarter-final, Cramer was at the helm.

Throwing off their domestic demons, Bayern nervously cleared the last eight before going up against the blossoming Saint-Étienne in the semi-final. With percentages played in the first leg at the Stade Geoffroy-Guichard, back at the Olympiastadion Bayern's experience told as they eased to the 2-0 victory that sent them through to a second successive European Cup Final.

Facing them at the Parc des Princes were Leeds United. Another team to have hastily dispensed with the manager they began the season with and to have offset domestic difficulties with excellent form in the European Cup, Jimmy Armfield's side had defeated FC Zürich, Újpesti Dózsa, Anderlecht, and Barcelona, to reach Paris.

Particularly impressive had been the way Leeds had overcome Anderlecht and Barcelona. This had been an Anderlecht that was powered by the inimitable Rob Rensenbrink, the star turn for opponents who would go on to reach three successive finals of the Cup Winners' Cup from the following season onwards.

Meanwhile, Barcelona were fuelled by the visionary Michels and the dazzling Cruyff. The script had deemed that the 1975 European Cup Final was going to be another head-to-head between Beckenbauer and Cruyff, only for Leeds to tear it up.

What followed was one of the most contentious finals there has ever been. Leeds, dictating the flow of the game for the majority, were denied a clear penalty for a challenge by Beckenbauer on Allan Clarke, while even under the offside rule of the time Peter Lorimer was desperately unlucky to see an effort disallowed.

To be on the rough end of one of those two instances would have been a blow, but to absorb both was the undoing of Leeds. Within a short few minutes of Lorimer's disallowed goal, Bayern had the lead thanks to a well-crafted strike from Roth. Ten minutes later, Müller netted a second. With some Leeds supporters contending that a conspiracy was in operation, violence erupted on the terraces.

Conversely, Leeds had been fortunate to complete the game with 11 men. Terry Yorath had ended Björn Andersson's game after only four minutes with a horrific tackle after the whistle had already been blown for a free kick, while Frank Gray was another who sailed close to the wind with a terrible challenge on Hoeneß. Rather than any conspiracy, the game just needed officials who were that little more observant.

A year later, Bayern completed their hat-trick of European Cups in Glasgow when up against Saint-Étienne. Again they rode their luck in the final, but on their way to Hampden Park they had largely been in commanding form apart from being made to sweat in the second round until the last half-hour of the second leg by future finalists Malmö FF.

Now reinforced by the emergences of Udo Horsmann and Karl-Heinz Rummenigge, Bayern were being regularly eclipsed domestically by Lattek's Mönchengladbach but remained dominant in Europe.

Prior to their problems in dealing with Malmö, Cramer's side had dispatched Jeunesse Esch with ease, and it was into the spring that Bayern's campaign really picked up pace. Thrown together with Benfica in the quarter-final, a goalless draw ensued in the first leg at the Estádio da Luz, a stasis that remained intact for the first half of the return game. From there the stabilisers were removed and a blizzard of goals emerged.

Bayern ran out 5-1 winners, constantly cutting through the Benfica defence with an inordinate simplicity. Rummenigge, an unused substitute in the 1975 final, had now made himself indispensable, initially as a winger before being converted into an out-and-out striker.

Müller was still the master at this point, however. After two goals against Benfica, he scored the all-important away goal in the first leg of the semi-final against Real Madrid, after a rare Beckenbauer misunderstanding with Horsmann had handed the hosts the lead with Roberto Martínez the beneficiary on an evening when Maier was attacked on the pitch by a frustrated Madrid supporter.

Bayern had weathered the early storm as wave upon wave of Madrid attacks was impressively repelled, apart from that one slip-up. This was a mature performance and one of Cramer's finest nights against a team that was conducted on the pitch by the magical Günter Netzer, yet surprisingly missing the former Bayern star Paul Breitner, who had made the move to the Santiago Bernabéu the previous summer.

Three minutes before the interval, Bayern were level when Müller pounced with such ruthlessness that he beat not only the Madrid goalkeeper and defence but also the Spanish television director and cameramen too. Catching only the ball hitting the back of the net and the goalscorer's trademark celebration, they had instead been lingering on a replay of a missed Martínez effort, which could easily have just made it 2-0 to Madrid. Gaining increasing control throughout the second half, Bayern dampened Madrid's enthusiasm and by the end had another goal occurred then it was more likely to be one scored by Cramer's players.

A fortnight later, Breitner was available to Madrid, but it made no difference. Bayern cruised to a comfortable 2-0 victory, with Müller magnificently scoring both goals. These were his 49th and 50th in the European Cup. These semi-final encounters between Bayern and Madrid could easily have been an all-West German affair. Mönchengladbach had been hugely unlucky to bow out in the quarter-final to Madrid on away goals, on an evening when they had two perfectly good goals disallowed. The Spanish champions had lived a spirited but charmed life in the 1975/76 European Cup, even overturning a 4-1 first-leg deficit in the second round against Derby County.

Bayern had proved to be an entirely different proposition, however, and Cramer and his players moved on to face Robert Herbin's stylistically pleasing Saint-Étienne, who had battled their way to the final past Kjøbenhavns Boldklub, Rangers, Dynamo Kyiv, and PSV Eindhoven.

Too strong for the Danish, and Scottish champions, Saint-Étienne had shown their hidden streak of steel in the quarter-final when turning around a 2-0 first-leg loss against a Kyiv side that many considered to be the favourites to dethrone Bayern. Beyond this fine comeback, Herbin's side held their nerve in the semi-final when going to Eindhoven to face a talented PSV with only a one-goal advantage.

While future Saint-Étienne vintages would be propelled by Michel Platini and Johnny Rep, they would never possess the verve and panache that the mid-to-late 1970s version did. Inspired by Dominique Rocheteau, Christian Sarramagna, Dominique Bathenay, Christian Lopez, Jean-Michel Larqué, Jacques Santini, and the brothers Hervé and Patrick Revelli, among a cast of many others, green was very much in vogue as the 1976 final approached.

Marking the 21st birthday of the European Cup Final, Hampden seemed the perfect choice of venue to celebrate the occasion given the famous old stadium had hosted the greatest final of all 16 years earlier.

The 1976 version could never live up to the standards set by Ferenc Puskás and Alfredo Di Stéfano against Eintracht Frankfurt, but in its own contemporary setting it did offer style and pathos aplenty.

With Rocheteau restricted by a muscle strain to a place among the substitutes, Saint-Étienne started at the disadvantage of being without their most potent player. Surprisingly, it was to be a game that lacked the hoped-for romance, yet it did make up for that with technical brilliance and one of the European Cup's most compelling hard luck stories.

One goal settled the game, Roth striking for Bayern shortly before the hour with a powerfully driven free kick that went low and to Ivan Ćurković's right. If a goal must break the heart of a nation, it was a fitting one. Many outside the Auvergne-Rhône-Alpes, and even beyond the borders of France will have felt the pain of it all. Twice, Saint-Étienne struck the Bayern crossbar in the first half, cursed as they were by Hampden's infamous square goalposts. First it was Bathenay with a 20-yard effort, the rebound from which was headed straight into the arms of Maier by Hervé Ravelli, and five minutes later a Santini header found almost the very same spot. It was an incredibly tormenting passage of play.

Bayern had threatened too, however, and between Saint-Étienne's two flirtations with Maier's crossbar, Rummenigge had almost broken the deadlock. When Roth did score, the French champions began to steadily deflate, although they would return home to a hero's welcome.

For Bayern, just like Ajax, a hat-trick of European Cups would be too much of a weight to bear; just like Ajax, Bayern would not become champions of Europe once again until the Champions League had come into existence.

Cramer, having struggled on the domestic scene, went on to suffer a similar fate to Lattek in being unseated from his job within a year of him having led Bayern to European Cup glory. For a generation, only frustration would lay ahead for the Bavarians, but between 1974 and 1976 they had deservedly etched their name deep within the trophy three times.

Completely the opposite to Ajax in many respects, when Lattek was replaced by Cramer, Bayern seemed to lose some of their freedom. They became a more mechanical version of themselves to an extent. It was the reverse journey that was made in Amsterdam, when the switch was made from Rinus Michels to Ştefan Kovács, yet it proved to be just as fruitful a change. Added to this, at Ajax, Kovács never had to go up against Michels domestically in the way Cramer did with Lattek at Bayern.

A fascinating era, and a wonderful entity, shrouded behind their persona of being football's great pantomime villain, of all those clubs to be deemed European royalty it is Bayern who everyone should learn to love that little bit more.

9

With Such Simplicity, the European Cup Surely is Won

WITH HIS shock of red hair and turn of pace, it was with stereotypical jet-heeled behaviour that David Fairclough closed in on goal before rolling the ball under the condemned and helpless goalkeeper.

This was not AS Saint-Étienne and the second leg of the 1977 European Cup quarter-final, however; this wasn't even a goal scored at Anfield's famous Kop end. It was instead a goal plundered down at the Anfield Road end, coming almost a year prior to that legendary night against Robert Herbin's stylistically pleasing French champions.

It was an unreasonable 11am kick-off, on the first Saturday of April 1976, that arguably proved to be the launchpad for Liverpool to take the baton of European Cup domination from Bayern Munich.

A game against Everton that took place on the morning of Grand National day; a short few hours before Rag Trade held off the challenge of Red Rum at Aintree, the 126th Merseyside derby seemed to be petering out to an unhelpful goalless draw.

By the 88th minute, Fairclough, with the number 12 on his back, had been on the pitch for 24 minutes of fruitless toil before he nipped in to pluck the ball from Everton's possession after a tired exchange between Martin Dobson and Roger Kenyon just inside the visitors' half. From there, Fairclough fended off the desperate Dobson before a run that saw him accelerate away from John Connolly and cut inside Kenyon, carrying the ball without being accosted until Dave Jones dared the teenager to cut wide again 25 yards from goal.

This Fairclough did, again striding away from the despairing lunge of Connolly, who had attempted to keep pace after his initial attempt to win the ball towards the halfway line. Into the penalty area he swept, but with the angle on goal narrowing exponentially, Fairclough could do one of two things – either aim a cross through a sea of blue shirts to find the advancing Kevin Keegan or use his momentum to shoot for goal.

Fairclough took a shot. The ball fizzed past the converging Mick Lyons and Bryan Hamilton, blindsiding Everton goalkeeper Dai Davies and arrowing low at his left-hand near post. Bedlam ensued around Anfield as the ball flew into the net. Not only had local bragging rights been secured but a toehold was maintained in a closely fought title race with Queens Park Rangers.

The win put Liverpool level on points with Dave Sexton's side, at least until Stan Bowles earned QPR their own last-gasp winning goal against Newcastle United at St James' Park a few hours later.

A fortnight later, the battle for the title turned Liverpool's way while as Bob Paisley's side won an eight-goal thriller at home to Stoke City, QPR were beaten at Carrow Road by Norwich City. Had Liverpool dropped a point against Everton two weeks earlier then it is not beyond reasonable speculation to suggest the 1975/76 First Division title might have been redirected to Loftus Road rather than Anfield.

Had that been the case then Liverpool would not have been at Rome's Stadio Olimpico in May 1977 to lift their first European Cup. By such fine margins do empires unfold. In this respect, Fairclough's goal against Everton, in April 1976, carries as much weight, if not more, than his goal against Saint-Étienne the following March.

In Rome, at the 1977 European Cup Final, Fairclough was among the substitutes, seemingly the most likely to be called upon given how much time he spent warming up on the touchline during the second half. Yet the way that Liverpool were disarming Udo Lattek's very gifted Borussia Mönchengladbach side meant that Paisley became reluctant to make the alteration he had promised.

Four days earlier at Wembley, Liverpool had lost to Manchester United in the FA Cup Final. It was a game that Paisley had been unwilling to allow roll into a second game as given the positioning of the midweek European Cup Final, the looming onset of the British Home Championship and the impending tours of South America for the England and Scotland national teams, the projected replay wouldn't have taken place until Monday, 27 June 1977.

Had circumstances been different then Paisley would have approached the FA Cup Final differently. He would have played the percentages and not been afraid to have taken the long game to glory. Instead, his hand forced to a large degree, the Liverpool manager opted for a 4-3-3 formation rather than the extra man in midfield, or the concept of a split-striker, a role that Steve Heighway would sometimes be deployed in.

With Ian Callaghan the sole substitute, it left a straight choice between Fairclough and David Johnson for the number ten shirt at Wembley. The more experienced Johnson got the nod, and within Paisley's attempts to console Fairclough, the dejected youngster was told he would be playing a part in Rome.

While Fairclough picked up a winners' medal in Rome, it was to be as an unused substitute. Against Saint-Étienne two months earlier he had been the man to salvage Liverpool's dream of the ultimate continental success, which had looked perilously close to slipping away.

On the back of his marginalisation by Paisley at the business end of the 1976/77 season, a year later Fairclough travelled to the 1978 European Cup Final with a written transfer request in his pocket, to be handed over in the eventuality of finding himself on the sidelines once again come kick-off time.

This time a place in the starting line-up was his but given the way the next five seasons would pan out for Fairclough, the remainder of his professional career might have taken on a vastly different complexion compared to the frustration he encountered had he missed out against Club Brugge at Wembley.

Back in Rome in 1977, while Fairclough cut a pent-up figure on the touchline, it was another striker around whom the story revolved. The 1977 European Cup Final was Kevin Keegan's last game in a Liverpool shirt and, while he ended it without a goal, he spent it running the majestic Berti Vogts to a standstill, eventually obtaining from him the penalty with which Phil Neal scored his team's third goal of the evening, thus ending any remaining doubt over the outcome.

For Liverpool, success at the Stadio Olimpico was the crowning glory of a journey that was started from a position of Second Division decay by Bill Shankly in December 1959 and completed by Paisley.

Paisley had reluctantly inherited a beautifully balanced team in the summer of 1974 from Shankly. Liverpool had just won the FA Cup with a dominant performance against Newcastle United and were a year on from having claimed a First Division and UEFA Cup double in 1972/73. Just as in Rome, Liverpool defeated Borussia Mönchengladbach in the 1973 UEFA Cup Final.

Refusing to rest on the laurels he was handed by Shankly, despite fielding seven survivors from the 1974 FA Cup Final, by the time of the 1977 European Cup Final Paisley's team had evolved markedly.

One of those to line up at Wembley in 1974 had been in a Newcastle shirt that day. Terry McDermott had been one of the few plus points for the team from Tyneside on an afternoon when his team-mates had badly underperformed. By November of the same year he was a Liverpool player.

The burden of expectation and the responsibility of wearing a Liverpool shirt initially weighed heavily on McDermott and it took him over two years to pin down a regular place in the team, aided by some of his midfield rivals falling by the wayside due to advancing age and injury.

McDermott's delayed blossoming was part of a restructuring of the Liverpool midfield, in which Jimmy Case took over on the right and Ray Kennedy was transformed from a misfiring striker into a left-sided midfielder of silk, steel, and innate vision, who still retained an eye for goal.

Within this, wingers were largely dispensed with as the wide midfielders tucked in, allowing the full-backs the freedom to overlap. As part of these changes, Steve Heighway's role became a much more varied one as opposed to that of an out-and-out winger. He was still asked to add width occasionally, but more often played in the hole, operating as the link between midfield and attack.

At the centre of it all, Callaghan was able to enjoy such a compelling Indian summer to his career that he eventually won a recall to the England team at the age of 35, over 11 years after his previous appearance, at the 1966 World Cup finals.

Added to the world-class goalkeeping of Ray Clemence, plus the switch of central defensive ethos from traditional British stoppers to ball-playing alternatives in the shapes of Emlyn Hughes and Phil Thompson, both of whom had been moved back from midfield, it all meant that Paisley's Liverpool were unlike any English side of the past. Their system was bespoke yet European in nature, insisting upon short passing and perpetual movement, building from the back and pressing high up the pitch. It went against the contemporary First Division vogue for two wingers and space aplenty through the middle, something that Case and Ray Kennedy exploited on a week-to-week basis.

It made Paisley's Liverpool the natural European Cup heir to Ajax and Bayern Munich. Each side had their own variant of footballing intelligence and it made for a marriage of skill and pragmatism, belligerence and confidence, all of which was grounded in simplicity. The easy ball was king and whichever player was in possession was never in short supply of passing options.

Liverpool's way was christened pass and move, a simple moniker that played down its impact. It was understated yet brilliant. Detractors and rivals, who could neither combat the system nor replicate it, would brand it predictable, without being able to overcome it. It was a system that would provoke paranoia in other teams, and the perceived magical secrets of the Boot Room and Melwood would be obsessed over. New signings would arrive, expecting to be bestowed with the groundbreaking wisdom of Paisley and his cabal of coaching soothsayers, only to find no magic spells in operation. Everything was shockingly simple.

UEFA Cup success in 1975/76 was the springboard to Liverpool winning their first European Cup a year later. It had been a second success in UEFA's third-ranked tournament in four seasons, and there would be a neat sense of symbiosis as the teams that they defeated in those two finals would also be the same opponents vanquished in Liverpool's first two European Cup Finals: Mönchengladbach and Club Brugge.

While the threat posed by Brugge in the 1976 UEFA Cup Final had been a severe one, it was the grown-up way Liverpool defeated the Barcelona of Rinus Michels and Johan Cruyff in the semi-final that spoke of their potential to finally win the biggest prize. Following a 1-0 victory at the Camp Nou in the first leg, Paisley's side eased through to the final after negating the Catalan offensive in a 1-1 draw back at Anfield in the return game.

When Liverpool set off on their bid to win the 1976/77 European Cup, it was their fourth attempt. They had been deprived of a place in the 1965 European Cup Final by reputed unfair means against Internazionale, while footballing lessons had been absorbed in 1966/67 and 1973/74 against an emerging Ajax and a clinical Red Star Belgrade, respectively.

Their loss to Red Star has since taken on a mythical place in Liverpool's history, viewed as the defining moment of eureka in which Shankly and Paisley were convinced that to succeed in the European Cup then being able to play the ball out of central defence would be key.

Liverpool's style against Red Star was vastly different to the one they had developed by 1977. Heighway and Callaghan operated the wings, while the high pass into the area for John Toshack was a much-utilised tool, with Keegan working to pick up the loose ball.

Liverpool's full-backs had that familiar freedom, but apart from set pieces, the centre-backs would be required to sit back and be stereotypical stoppers. The central midfield was a place where vision was allied with high energy. As effective and busy a system as it was, when it came to the high ball for the classic Toshack-Keegan one-two, it was a tactic that was far more percentage playing than the style that would evolve under Paisley. It was not that it was an outmoded style of play, it was just a clash of ideologies, and Liverpool would eventually make what was the brave choice to move towards a continental European approach in their quest to lift the European Cup.

This was a Liverpool with the uncompromising Tommy Smith and Larry Lloyd marshalling the centre of defence, a pairing that had provided the solid foundation stone to what was known as Shankly's second great team. When Smith was unavailable for the second leg against Red Star, Hughes dropped back from midfield to cover the absence with Thompson stepping in to deputise for Hughes in the engine room.

Thompson started out as a burgeoning midfielder yet by the time the 1974 FA Cup Final was being won, he had formed a new, lasting, and ball-playing central defensive partnership with Hughes. This, however, was not something that was born from the immediacy of Liverpool's loss to Red Star.

When Smith returned to fitness, he did so just as the right-back Chris Lawler picked up a lengthy injury lay-off of his own, meaning that he was asked to pick up the number two shirt rather than return at centre-back. Lloyd, meanwhile, remained in the side until he too suffered fitness problems in early February, and this was the turn of events that brought Hughes and Thompson together in central defence. It was a union that was born three months beyond Liverpool being knocked out of the European Cup by Red Star.

Thus, rather than an epiphany, the games against Red Star arguably acted more like a significant stepping stone to change. Liverpool had already faced the Total Football of Ajax and the

Bayern Munich of Beckenbauer, yet had not walked away from those encounters with notions of altering their style of play.

A year beyond their experiences against Red Star, another fluid passing side put Liverpool out of Europe. This time it was Ferencváros in the European Cup Winners' Cup, a team who Shankly and Paisley had crossed paths with twice before, in the 1967/68 and 1970/71 Inter-Cities Fairs Cup. Both sets of games were keenly contested, the first meeting going the way of the majestic Hungarians and the second being edged by Liverpool.

Within this, the way that Liverpool's new-look defence came together was arguably as much due to circumstances as it was through that much believed moment of eureka against Red Star. While it was an evolution which was still likely to have occurred, it was one that was given a nudge of encouragement by fate. Many lessons had been learned along the way.

What can be said for certain, however, is that once Liverpool had opted for this new ideal of defending, they never turned back. Lloyd would not play another first-team game for the club, while Smith's switch to right-back allowed him to get in touch with the spirit of his earlier years in football, when he operated further up the pitch. As much of a hard man image he quite rightly garnered, there was an underlying subtle deftness to his abilities, which were no better showcased than in his contributions to Liverpool's third goal in the 1974 FA Cup Final.

With central midfielders converted to central defenders, a goalkeeper who began his career as an outfield player, a left-sided midfielder crafted from a striker, and the central midfield dictated by a former winger, Paisley created a team that consisted entirely of thinking footballers. It made for a collective of intelligent fighters.

Once Lloyd was dispensed with, and once Paisley had eased out Toshack as a traditional target man, it was quite telling that none of the players he recruited or called up from the reserves could have been classed as an Anglo-Saxon footballer. Even beneath the combative exteriors of Case and Graeme Souness lay artistry.

Added to this evolution, Phil Neal was brought in from Fourth Division Northampton Town, and then in the summer of 1977 came Kenny Dalglish and Alan Hansen. Before Paisley vacated the manager's office at Anfield he had also signed Alan Kennedy, Mark Lawrenson, Ian Rush, Ronnie Whelan, and Steve Nicol.

In collecting their first European Cup in 1977, Liverpool got off to a stuttering start at home to the Belfast side Crusaders. Restricting the Reds to a 2-0 victory at Anfield in the first leg, the underdogs went for blanket defending, venturing forward only rarely and failing to win either a corner, or fashion a shot on target.

Yet in their heroic rearguard action, Crusaders magnificently frustrated Liverpool's team of experienced internationals, with their goalkeeper Roy McDonald in inspired form, and the ten players in front of him putting their bodies on the line time and time again with Walter McFarland, Bob Gillespie, and Drew Cooke proving particularly stubborn.

Crusaders had been stirred the evening before the game by the advice and confidence given to them by the Everton manager Billy Bingham, and his midfielder Bryan Hamilton, both sons of Belfast themselves.

Although Liverpool ran out 5-0 winners at Seaview a fortnight later, the final score masked how arduous their task had been. Crusaders launched themselves at their more illustrious opponents in the opening exchanges, where Ronnie McAteer hit both the crossbar and the post, before Keegan broke the home side's resistance, from whence Paisley's team ruthlessly picked off four more goals in the last ten minutes.

From a tie in which Liverpool where fully expected to progress, it was the impressive 27-minute cameo by McDermott that had the most value. It proved to be the turning point in his Anfield career, winning him a recall to the starting line-up four days later for the First Division visit of Middlesbrough.

Prior to the trip to Belfast, Paisley had admitted that McDermott's form in training and for the reserves had been so good that he felt his unhappy midfielder was unlucky not to be finding a way into the first-team reckoning. Doing so meant that another crucial component in Liverpool's European Cup successes to come had belatedly fallen into place.

In the second round, Liverpool were drawn to face the Turkish champions Trabzonspor, a club whose talents and successes were largely shrouded in the mists of time until their 2019/20 return to greater prominence. Six times Süper Lig champions in a nine-season span between 1975/76 and 1983/84, their rise coincided with the eye of Liverpool's storm and temporarily ended the hegemony that had long been enjoyed by Fenerbahçe, Galatasaray, and Beşiktaş.

Just as against Crusaders, Liverpool experienced an uncomfortable first leg against Trabzonspor. Although Paisley's team seemed to control much of the proceedings, they did so without threatening enough in the final third and shortly after the hour they conceded the only goal of the game, from a heavily disputed penalty, which was tucked away off the inside of the post by Cemil Usta, sending Clemence the wrong way.

Within 18 minutes of the start of the second leg at Anfield, Liverpool had scored the three goals that took them into the quarter-final. It was a brutal riposte and prompted an antagonistic air to the remainder of the game, culminating in a red card for Cemil towards the end.

England international Keegan had approached Paisley in the summer of 1976 to inform him of his desire for a new challenge away from Anfield, although he was persuaded to stay for one more season and aid Liverpool's bid for a first European Cup. The response of the club's supporters to the transfer request was a mixed one. While some were philosophical about this turn of events, others made their displeasure known.

At the Stade Geoffroy-Guichard, against Saint-Étienne in the first leg of the quarter-final, Liverpool coped admirably with the threat of the team who had become the widely admired darlings of the continent.

Expected to face a difficult night in the Auvergne-Rhône-Alpes, the visitors were assured and largely in control of the game. Frustrating their hosts, Liverpool took the sting out of the intent of the French champions, provoking the ire of the local support. In a textbook away European performance, Thompson had a goal disallowed, while Heighway curled an effort that unluckily struck the post. It was almost an insult to Paisley's team when they conceded the only goal of the game, to Dominique Bathenay from a corner, with 12 minutes remaining.

The result might have been a different one had Keegan not failed a fitness test on the morning of the first leg. It simply meant that the Liverpool number seven was eager to make up for lost time in the return.

In the meantime, Paisley had lost the services of Thompson, who had been forced to undergo a cartilage operation that would rule him out for the rest of the season, bringing Smith back into the team to play alongside Hughes in central defence. Two dominant personalities in the Anfield dressing room, while they did not see eye to eye as people they showed the highest professionalism on the pitch, leaving their issues with one another at the touchline.

Linking Keegan and Toshack together for what would unwittingly be the last time, Paisley stood McDermott down to the bench with Heighway adding width to the Liverpool midfield. On the most electric of Anfield nights, Keegan levelled the aggregate scoreline in under two minutes with an audacious effort from way out on the left-hand side, after collecting a short corner from Heighway, as he and his team-mates attacked an Anfield Road end that was as much awash with green as it was with red.

Whether Keegan meant what he did is wide open to debate, as he drifted his effort over the desperately back-peddling Saint-Étienne goalkeeper Ivan Ćurković and beneath the crossbar. To the naked eye, it could just as easily have been intended as a cross.

Shaken, Saint-Étienne eventually composed themselves and began to venture forward, Liverpool perhaps dwelling a little too long on their dream start. The magnificent Dominique Rocheteau soon forced a smart save from Clemence and would have a goal disallowed, while Bathenay increasingly imposed himself on proceedings and Jean-Michel Larqué hit a speculative effort from distance. In response, Callaghan came close, Toshack should have done better with a free header, and Case joined Rocheteau in seeing a strike chalked off.

After a first half played at breakneck speed, the unremitting nature of the game did not ease up during the second half. In the opening few minutes Rocheteau tested Clemence yet again, and Kennedy hit back with a show of intent.

Only six minutes had passed after the break when Liverpool took the viciously beautiful body blow of Bathenay's equaliser, as he shrugged off the attentions of Case to stride into the Liverpool half and unleash a tremendous swerving and dipping shot from an almost indecent distance. Clemence, in a largely imperious frame of mind, was beaten all ends up. It would be the French champions' only goal of the evening, and a testament to just how special an effort it took to put the ball past the Liverpool goalkeeper.

Saint-Étienne held the direction of the game in the palm of their hand, with Liverpool now needing two goals without further reply to progress to the semi-final.

With a huge choice to be made on whether to opt for containment or to go for more goals, Saint-Étienne did neither. Their response to the situation was like that of Liverpool's after Keegan had scored.

Just before the hour, Liverpool were in the lead on the night once more. A short throw-in by Heighway on the right was received by Callaghan, who quickly squared the ball to Neal, from which he clipped it forward with a beautifully weighted first-time pass towards the penalty spot. Toshack was there to receive it, timing his left-to-right run to perfection, spinning his marker and wonderfully laying off the ball to the loitering Kennedy, just inside the area, who drove it beneath the dive of Ćurković, where it nestled among the tossed toilet rolls that had congregated in the back of the Kop end net.

A goal that was greeted with a deafening roar of approval, it put Liverpool level on aggregate yet still at the disadvantage of an away goal, although armed with half an hour in which to find the winner.

Nerves were fraying and with Saint-Étienne pushing forward for a goal of their own, one which would have left Liverpool with the need to score twice to progress, Paisley had rolled the dice with just over 15 minutes to play in replacing Toshack with Fairclough.

It was a preordained tactical tweak with Toshack carrying an injury into the game, so Paisley had planned to switch him for Fairclough after an hour only to persevere with the Welsh international for an extra 15 minutes after the part he played in Kennedy's goal. Toshack's 74-minute exertions against Saint-Étienne would come at a cost, however, with the night proving to be his last appearance of the 1976/77 season.

For Fairclough, a date with destiny and the defining moment of his career lay ahead, although not before Rocheteau almost took advantage of hesitancy between Neal and Clemence on the edge of the Liverpool penalty area.

Calamity averted, two and a half minutes later the ball was in the back of the Saint-Étienne net once again with only six minutes to spare. It was a piece of eternal magic from Fairclough to earn Liverpool their semi-final berth as he got on the end of a looping ball forward by Kennedy, outstripping the visitors' defence and rolling it underneath the advancing Ćurković, igniting a heightened sense of bedlam both on and off the pitch. Often cited as Anfield's greatest night, it had been a coming together of two of Europe's finest teams; it had been a game of football that would not have been out of place as the final itself.

In comparison, Liverpool's semi-final against an overconfident FC Zürich was something of a successful anti-climax, Paisley's team cruising through 6-1 on aggregate.

With the First Division title retained but the FA Cup Final lost, a focused and reflective Liverpool headed for their date with destiny in Rome. Speculative notions of Toshack being fit enough to be involved were ended on the morning of the game, and even the temptation to have him sat on the bench to unnerve a Mönchengladbach side who struggled against his aerial presence in the first leg of the 1973 UEFA Cup Final was resisted.

Selecting the 11 players who had been on the Wembley turf as the final whistle was blown on the FA Cup Final, Paisley's approach to taking on Lattek's Mönchengladbach was markedly different to Shankly's approach when faced by Hennes Weisweiler's version four years earlier.

It would have been an understandable thing to do, to try and replicate the tactics of 1973, but this was not only a different Liverpool; Mönchengladbach had also evolved in the years since their UEFA Cup encounter.

Paisley, perhaps with the memory of Liverpool's successful disarming and dismantling of Lattek's Bayern Munich in the 1970/71 Fairs Cup in mind, opted for a formation in Rome that offered greater midfield protection than his team had enjoyed in the FA Cup Final.

While Shankly's Liverpool had overcome Lattek's Bayern in 1970/71, the roles were reversed the following year, in the Cup Winners' Cup. These face-offs had left a huge impression on Lattek and by the time of the 1977 European Cup Final he was a vocal advocate on the style of play that Paisley had cultivated, the West German recognising that Liverpool were continental in their approach to the game and even considering his opponents to be the best team in Europe. It was rich praise indeed from a man who was a tactical and technical genius in his own right.

As the game loomed, both teams were counting the cost of their injuries. Toshack's failure to prove his fitness left him on the sidelines with Thompson. Added to this, while Callaghan won a starting role, it was only his second start since picking up an injury of his own in the second leg of the quarter-final against Saint-Étienne.

For Lattek, the biggest question mark was embossed upon the legendary Jupp Heynckes, who had been nursed back to fitness almost specifically for the European Cup Final, while the loss of Horst Köppel had been a sizeable blow.

Both teams adapted magnificently, and what played out was an open and entertaining European Cup final that was wholly unrepresentative of the cluster of 1-0 outcomes to follow in the finals that bridged the 1970s to the 1980s.

Perhaps feeling that it was too much of a gamble to go toe to toe with Liverpool, despite boasting the talents of not only

Heynckes, but also luminaries such as Berti Vogts, Rainer Bonhof, Allan Simonsen, Herbert Wimmer, and Uli Stielike, Mönchengladbach went into the game with a caution-first approach.

Shadow-boxing to an extent, it was not that Mönchengladbach weren't coiled and waiting to strike, they were just content to wait and pick off their chances. Half an inch here and a greater degree of composure there and they might have just pulled it off.

Fulfilling Lattek's prophecy, however, it was Liverpool's greater sense of expansion that won the night. When in possession of the ball, Paisley's side slowed the game down, dictating the flow and pattern of play, and when they lost possession they pressed relentlessly to win the ball back.

Tellingly, when Lattek had made personal scouting missions to watch Liverpool in big First Division encounters with Ipswich Town and Manchester United prior the final, Paisley's side were without the services of Callaghan, and playing a formation that translated into 4-3-3 when on the front foot and 4-5-1 when falling back.

In Rome, the reintroduction of Callaghan meant that Liverpool were essentially playing a 4-4-1-1 formation that would morph into 4-2-3-1 when in full flow. As part of this, McDermott had the central midfield remit to provide late runs from deep, one of which was responsible for the opening goal.

Either fearful of the threat of Keegan or buying into the urban myth that the Liverpool number seven did not adapt well to close attention, Lattek deployed Vogts to man-mark a player who was about to become a Bundesliga rival at Hamburger SV.

Keegan was unremitting in his work, dragging Vogts, the West German captain, consistently out of position throughout the game, and out of shape by the time it ended. Always available to receive the ball, Keegan created space aplenty for his team-mates to exploit. When McDermott scored the first goal of the evening, after 28 minutes, it was the fruition of a 50-yard run to get on the end of a perfectly weighted pass from Heighway before tucking the ball into Wolfgang Kneib's bottom-right corner.

While Liverpool had enjoyed the best of the game up to this point and would continue to dominate the remainder of the first half, it was Mönchengladbach who had come closest to scoring prior to McDermott breaking the deadlock, when Bonhof struck Clemence's right-hand post from distance.

The Germans were then gifted an equaliser during the early exchanges of the second half when Case miscontrolled the ball into the path of Simonsen, who dispatched it into the top corner of Clemence's net, and for the next 12 minutes the game was delicately balanced.

Simonsen markedly grew in confidence after his goal, and he was soon glancing a free header wide of the post, while he also sent Stielike through on Clemence, who pulled off a magnificent save upon which the game turned back to Liverpool.

In what was meant to be his last game in a Liverpool shirt, in the 64th minute Smith met a Heighway corner with a thunderous header to make it 2-1 and the goal deflated Mönchengladbach. Paisley's team retained complete control of the game for the remainder, and when a besieged Vogts brought down Keegan in the penalty area with eight minutes to go, Neal was calmness personified in converting the penalty.

It had taken nine years for English football to claim a second European Cup, Liverpool being the first English club to win it away from their homeland, but this new success was to mark the beginning of a new domination in which First Division teams would win six of the next seven.

Liverpool would go on to conquer Brugge at Wembley and Real Madrid in Paris in 1978 and 1981, respectively, but in terms of glory the European Cup would always be about Rome for the club. It was to be the location where they would be crowned champions of Europe for the first time, and where they would be coronated for the fourth time when defeating Roma in their own stadium.

While the 1978 European Cup Final does not deserve the negative press it tends to get, the 1981 final was an undeniably poor game, played out by two teams of which so much more was expected, on a pitch where the grass was ridiculously long.

Alan Kennedy decided the outcome in 1981, storming in on the left, and planting the ball past an exposed Agustín after picking up a throw-in from Ray Kennedy with just eight minutes remaining. It was a glorious end to a forgettable game and it was a blessed relief that the final did not drift into extra time.

Three years earlier, by the same single-goal scoreline, a piece of Souness vision and a slice of Dalglish magic settled an evening in which another goal or two would have been entirely deserved by Liverpool. Dalglish and McDermott both passed up excellent opportunities to score against a disappointingly negative Brugge.

Liverpool's best nights during the 1977/78 and 1980/81 European Cups were experienced on their way to the respective finals. Dominant at home to Dynamo Dresden, majestic against Benfica home and away in 1977/78, they also won their semi-final rematch with Mönchengladbach.

Having been beaten 2-1 at the Rheinstadion in Düsseldorf in the first leg, a Ray Kennedy masterclass was the inspiration behind Liverpool's 3-0 victory in the second leg. He scored the first goal then created the second and third for Dalglish and Case, respectively.

Sat amid the collection of Anfield's finest European nights, it tends to be a game that falls under the radar – although maybe as a sign that such outstanding European Cup performances were becoming customary to Liverpool's supporters – the Mönchengladbach semi-final rarely gets a mention in conversations about the Reds' finest European hours. Yet this was the result that confirmed their success of 12 months earlier was no flash in the pan.

Three years later, it was again Ray Kennedy who was the semi-final hero, this time at the Olympiastadion against a very presumptuous Bayern. A goalless draw in the first leg at Anfield had prompted the reigning Bundesliga champions to print leaflets prior to the return game, which were handed out to supporters, containing travel details for Paris.

An understrength Liverpool were undeniably up against it in Munich, with injury ruling out Thompson and Alan Kennedy. Matters worsened further when Dalglish was forced from the game after only nine minutes with an ankle injury sustained in an uncompromising challenge by Kalle Del'Haye.

On an evening when Souness, and David Johnson played but were not fully fit, Dalglish's exit brought into play the little-known Howard Gayle, whose fearless performance put the Bundesliga champions on the back foot until his own departure from the game 61 minutes later.

Tormenting Wolfgang Dremmler, Gayle was asked to work the left flank while Ray Kennedy was pushed back into his old striker's role. The Liverpool substitute was repetitively hacked down by the West German international, with one such incident being a blatant foul in the Bayern penalty area which went unpunished.

Eventually, Paisley withdrew Gayle, who had picked up a yellow card for retaliation, the manager being concerned that his player would be shown a red card if he responded a second time. It made for a sweet and sour evening for Gayle, the first black player to represent the club. On one hand he had unbalanced Bayern, while on the other, Paisley had not placed his trust in him to remain disciplined for the last 20 minutes.

Combined with Sammy Lee's wonderful man-marking job on Paul Breitner, and the fine defending of reserve regulars Colin Irwin and Richard Money alongside the more experienced Neal and Alan Hansen, Bayern were comprehensively stifled.

With seven minutes remaining, Ray Kennedy grabbed the crucial away goal, and despite Karl-Heinz Rummenigge levelling the aggregate scoreline four minutes later, Liverpool eased through to the final thanks to that Kennedy strike.

It was the culmination of a run which had seen Liverpool put ten goals past Oulun Palloseura, before overcoming Alex Ferguson's fast-improving Aberdeen, and the dangerous CSKA Sofia, against whom Souness gave one of the finest performances of his entire career. The 1980/81 season was an outstanding success for Paisley and his players during what had been an inconsistent domestic campaign, one which was blighted by injury problems.

Added to by his 1978 success, the European Cup became Paisley's domain. Three times a winner, he handed over a healthy and revamped squad to Joe Fagan, in the summer of 1983. Clemence, Case, Ray Kennedy, McDermott, and Johnson had all been moved on, while Thompson would swiftly drop from contention under the new manager. In their places had come Bruce Grobbelaar, Mark Lawrenson, Ronnie Whelan, Craig Johnston, Steve Nicol, and Ian Rush.

After back-to-back quarter-final exits in 1981/82 and 1982/83, Fagan's ascension to the top job at Anfield brought a defined focus to a squad of players who were determined to succeed for him.

And succeed they did as Fagan's players delivered him the First Division title and the League Cup in 1983/84. Within a season unremittingly dominated by Merseyside, Everton also got in on the act by lifting the FA Cup, having lost the final of the League Cup. Even the FA Youth Cup went to the Goodison Park outfit.

Considering so much of the season fell perfectly into place for them, in the European Cup Liverpool were intent on doing it all the hard way. Having been stubborn opponents in the first round on their own turf, Richard Møller Nielsen's Odense Boldklub were comfortably beaten in the return game at Anfield, but from there Fagan's side were drawn to play the home leg first all the way to the final.

It was not detrimental but that Athletic Club, Benfica, and Dinamo Bucharest all travelled to Anfield with the intent to contain and frustrate. They largely succeeded too, as while Grobbelaar kept three clean sheets, his outfield team-mates were restricted to scoring just two goals across the span of those three games.

A goalless draw in the second round against an at times ferocious Athletic side was thought to be a fatal slip, yet Liverpool scored the only goal of the second leg midway through the second half, via a rare Rush header from a right-footed Alan Kennedy cross. As goals go, it was quite the collector's item, and it eerily silenced the San Mamés.

Benfica in the quarter-final, led by a youthful Sven-Göran Eriksson, followed the Bilbao blueprint in the hope that they could escape Anfield with a result that would make the second leg competitive. Suffering only a 1-0 defeat, Rush again the marksman, on a rainswept night, the Portuguese champions were well-positioned to strike for the semi-final, only to capitulate to a 4-1 reversal at the Estádio da Luz, overpowered by a devastating Liverpool display.

With the hard work seemingly done, Liverpool avoided Roma and the impressive Dundee United in the semi-final, instead drawing Dinamo Bucharest, the Romanian champions. It was a step into the unknown and a first leg of violent intent unfolded, in which Souness broke the jaw of Lică Movilă after a series of stern challenges from the Dinamo number six went unsanctioned.

On a fast-paced, but frustrating night, Lee scored the only goal of the game, later having a second effort disallowed, just as Rush had during the early exchanges. A late shout for a penalty was also turned down in the final seconds.

Souness's altercation with Movilă, and the narrow first-leg scoreline, meant that the return game was to be played out within a magically volatile atmosphere. Liverpool's captain, drawing as much of the local ire as possible, helped facilitate the space for his team-mates to prosper despite the high levels of on- and off-pitch intimidation. Two goals from Rush saw them through to the final on an evening when many Liverpool players departed the field at the end nursing the wounds of a stunningly physical encounter.

Out of the frying pan and into the fire; to win the European Cup again, Liverpool would have to achieve something that no other team had before managed in the tournament and beat opponents who were blessed to be playing the final in their very own stadium.

When arriving in Rome in their droves seven years earlier Liverpool's supporters had been welcomed with open arms, but in 1984 there was an entirely different reception awaiting them as they came to play one of the eternal city's very own teams.

Rather than the kind and friendly nature of 1977, which engendered such a party atmosphere, this time danger lurked around many corners and a gauntlet was run to the

Stadio Olimpico by many as the pre-match mood turned increasingly dark.

Roma, fully expecting their anointing as the new champions of Europe, were defeated on penalties after a 120-minute chess game of a football match in which Liverpool struck first through Neal, and Roma levelled shortly before half-time thanks to a Roberto Pruzzo header.

Bedlam ensued after the game as Liverpool supporters eventually exited the stadium, many to find their scheduled transport had deserted them, throwing them to the lack of mercy on the increasingly mean streets of the Italian capital. Paying guests were not permitted access to their hotels by angry and anxious owners, while the British Embassy became something of a refuge for a sizeable diaspora.

On the pitch, however, the 1984 European Cup Final became Liverpool's finest moment.

This was not an era in which the tickets for the final were split evenly, with small percentages going to each team, and residents, while the rest went to the friends and commercial partners of UEFA; this was an era in which each club asked for a defined allocation, and the rest were picked off on general sale.

While an admirable amount of Liverpool supporters made the pilgrimage to Rome in 1984, especially given the hardships endured by the city in the 1980s, the final truly was a home game for a Roma side who had not conceded a single goal on home soil on their way to their date with destiny.

Led by the legendary Nils Liedholm, their team was packed with talent. Beyond the predatory instincts of Pruzzo, the attacking intent of the side was also boosted by the presence of Francesco Graziani and Bruno Conti, who had both been part of Italy's 1982 World Cup-winning team.

In midfield they were inspired by the magnificent Falcão, whose freedom to roam was handed to him by the discipline of both his Brazilian international team-mate Toninho Cerezo and the focused son of Rome, club captain Agostino Di Bartolomei, all of whom more than made up for the absence of the injured Carlo Ancelotti.

It was difficult to find any weaknesses in a wonderfully balanced side that was built upon the sound foundations of the fine goalkeeper Franco Tancredi and a defensive unit that was commanded by Sebastiano Nela. Despite never having reached the European Cup Final before, the bookmakers had Roma as the clear favourites going into the game.

Liverpool's experiences in Bilbao, Lisbon, and Bucharest had been the perfect preparation for what appeared to be a final that was impossible to win. Outside the stadium, T-shirts had already been doing a roaring trade, emblazoned with slogans proclaiming Roma as the champions of Europe.

To diffuse the potential pre-match tensions, Fagan took his squad away for a week of relaxation prior to the final, where the players were allowed to let loose. While it was not necessarily the most focused of preparations, the team spirit garnered was priceless.

In the tunnel, as the two teams lined up and awaited the nod to walk out on to the pitch, it was a pensive-looking set of Roma players while Liverpool seemed supremely relaxed. From towards the back of the Liverpool line, David Hodgson, one of the substitutes, broke out into a chorus of the Chris Rea song 'I Don't Know What It Is but I Love It' and was soon accompanied by the rest of his team-mates, much to the bemusement of Roma's superstars. Psychologically, Liverpool had already won.

When it came to the penalty shoot-out some two and a half hours later, the weight of expectation was too much for Roma's players, despite Liverpool's spot-kick preparations having consisted of losing an impromptu shoot-out against a cluster of their own youth-team players.

As with the rest of the final, Liverpool were able to embrace the situation in an air of having nothing to lose. All the pressure belonged to Roma, and it should have eased when Nicol sent the first effort high over the crossbar with the advantage seized by the Italians when Di Bartolomei converted his penalty.

Next up for Liverpool, however, was their expert taker, Neal, who made no mistake, and when Conti surprisingly failed to find the target the scales had evened out once again. Souness and Ulbaldo Righetti then held their nerves. Three spot-kicks each and the score was 2-2.

After Rush tucked his penalty away, he visually confessed to having been nervous. Then, just as shockingly as Conti having missed, Graziani did likewise, unsettled by Grobbelaar's antics on the goal line. The two players to have missed for Roma had been their World Cup winners, players to have experienced football's most unique triumph.

Alan Kennedy was now in possession of the ball. Score and the European Cup would be Liverpool's yet again; miss and Roma would have a kick to take it to sudden death. Several of Liverpool's players could not bring themselves to watch, so sure were they that he would fail.

In Kennedy's penalty went, though, and the trophy was theirs. The Liverpool number three, the most unlikely of heroes, had now scored a European Cup Final-clinching goal for the second time.

European champions for the fourth time in eight seasons, just as with other footballing empires it seemed like the success was set to roll on and on for Liverpool in the European Cup. A violent fork in the road was up ahead, however, which would change both the club and football forever.

10

Midland Bank

IF YOU love football, somewhere in your subconscious mind there will be a point of genesis, where you were unwittingly hooked.

Personally, I cannot remember a time without football being an omnipresent figure in my existence. Yet I'd suggest that for a while it was just something that was part of the furniture in the same way our cat was, or that Wednesday meant egg, chips, and beans for tea, or that Thursday night was always the big shop, and that Sunday night meant bath night.

Football never truly dropped off the weekly radar, but Saturday was the holiest day of the week at our house as it was the day where football was at its most resplendent. *Grandstand*, *Football Focus*, and *World of Sport* all broadcast, at separate times if you were lucky, the results service, followed by *The Dukes of Hazzard*, or *The Pink Panther Show*, then *Match of the Day* as the perfect excuse to stay up late, with usually a few hours of Subbuteo in between.

If you had the bonus of clicking through a turnstile to watch a game in person then it was a borderline idyllic existence, just if you ignored the occasional outbreak of terrace violence here and there.

Growing up in the Granada region, this spectacular feast of football on a Saturday was bookended by our ITV franchise's Friday night half-hour preview show, *Kick Off*, and a Sunday afternoon helping of *The Kick Off Match*, both fronted by Gerald Sinstadt and then Elton Welsby, with the occasional opt-in to LWT's *The Big Match* if it were a game of wider national interest. In the event of television letting you down and the Subbuteo being packed away, we would be off out to kick a ball around.

Among my very earliest memories I can summon up the incredibly hot summer of 1976, and being in awe of Lee Dalgleish's Scotland shirt, which will have been sourced via his Scottish mother's side of the family. I'd often end up with bag of hand-me-down clothes once Lee had outgrown them, but that Scotland shirt never did come my way.

It will have been the late 1970s when I inherited a cluster of football shirts including the red Liverpool V-neck Umbro shirt, in which the European Cups of 1977, 1978, and 1981 were won, later to be torn at the armpit; the white Admiral England shirt of the Don Revie era; plus a blue Everton effort, the one with the Umbro diamonds down the sleeves and EFC emblazoned where a badge was meant to be, circa 1976–78.

A dark secret considering I am a Liverpool supporter, but even the Everton shirt was worn a few times before it was outgrown and upcycled into rags.

Other stand-out memories of that period when football was there without having truly taken a vice-like grip include Scotland supporters bringing down the goalposts at Wembley after defeating England in 1977, a silk 1977 European Cup winners scarf knocking around the house that I wish was in my possession today, and my dad celebrating the 1978 success over Club Brugge by handing out four-finger Kit Kats to us kids. I kid you not. Four. Fingers.

Then came February 1980 and Liverpool on *Match of the Day*, away at Carrow Road, against John Bond's Norwich City. A mad eight-goal thriller in which a red-headed fella by the name of David Fairclough scored a hat-trick. Hair a copper sort of colour, just like mine, it struck a chord. Suddenly football was relatable. I was sure he had prevailed at the sport despite being called Duracell at school.

Liverpool won the game 5-3, but that wasn't the end of it by any means. I was also taken with a goal that Ray Clemence had conceded – Justin Fashanu's marvellous strike which won that year's Goal of the Season award.

The movement of the ball from left to right, from Greg Downs to Kevin Bond and on to John Ryan. Ryan's first-time pass to Fashanu, and Fashanu teeing the ball up for himself with the instep of his right foot, shifting his body weight and causing Alan Kennedy to almost sink into the soft turf before catching his shot perfectly on his left to send it with unerring precision just out of Clemence's despairing reach and marginally inside the left-hand post. Everything about the goal connected with me.

There is a wonderful juxtaposition between Fashanu's nonchalant one-finger salute and the ebullience of Barry Davies's commentary. The commentator framing the moment by letting loose his feelings while the goalscorer is stomping away, almost unmoved by what he has just done.

In one neatly packed set of highlights I had fallen completely in love with both the team I had long been told is the one our family supports, and the wider aspects of the game.

Even now, over four decades on, I still harbour a soft spot for Carrow Road, and I wish Norwich City the best of health. That isn't meant to be possible when you also hold a warm glow for Bobby Robson's Ipswich Town of John Wark, Frans Thijssen, and Arnold Mühren.

Three months later I had every intention of watching the 1980 FA Cup Final, which I tried to do before being lured outside by the beautiful sunshine and the request of Austin Buckley to go out to play.

By 1980/81 I had all the finer points of football assimilated. The league pyramid was studied in the Sunday papers when we'd go to visit my nan, I had a healthy-looking Panini album, and a full understanding of both the club and international game. If there was football to imbibe, be it in person, on television or in print, then I was there.

As part of this, suddenly football had introduced the aspect of peril. Rivals were there to try and take away the trophies your team had made their own, and the biggest threat wasn't posed by local foes but by interestingly named teams from the Midlands.

Who needed to be a City, Town or United when you could be a Forest or a Villa instead? These bespoke football clubs didn't choose to follow the crowd in being an Athletic, or even a Wanderer. I supported a team that didn't even opt for a suffix. Was this a good or bad thing thing? I couldn't be sure.

I take a little bit of tongue-in-cheek enjoyment as I say it, but when I reached my point of footballing genesis, Everton might have resided in the same city as my team but as a force they were not all that relevant in February 1980.

They didn't pick off too many victories against us, and they certainly didn't seem to win trophies. Everton's time would eventually come, but not yet. Added to this, I was informed that Manchester United were also an enemy, who had a knack of beating us but not the ability to win league titles. Also, despite knowing they had beaten us in the 1977 FA Cup Final, I had no recollection of it. They were essentially the footballing bogeyman. A figment of the young imagination, the monster hiding under the bed but you'd never actually cast eyes upon it.

Instead, the real threat came from the City Ground and Villa Park.

Nottingham Forest had been a clear and present danger, one that had come from nowhere, and in Brian Clough they had a leader to be feared no matter how publicly reverential he was towards Bob Paisley and Liverpool, and Bill Shankly before him too.

Relegated from the First Division at the end of 1971/72, Forest's supporters had had the double dismay in seeing their East Midlands rivals Derby County lift that season's league title under the powerful but volatile partnership of Clough and Peter Taylor.

In a complete about-face, by February 1980 Derby were the team sliding towards relegation from the First Division while Forest were the reigning European champions under the stewardship of Clough and Taylor.

Clough had arrived at Forest in January 1975 via an explosive exit from Derby, a parting of the ways with Taylor at Brighton & Hove Albion, and his iconic 44 days in charge of Leeds United.

Together, Clough and Taylor hadn't only transformed Derby from second-tier water-treaders into champions of England, they had also taken them to within touching distance of the 1973 European Cup Final, where they would have gone head-to-head with an Ajax at the apex of their brilliance.

Having convincingly dealt with Željezničar at the first hurdle, this was followed by an encounter with Benfica in which the two-time European Cup winners could still call upon the skills of Eusébio, albeit when faced with a strategically overwatered pitch during the first leg of the second round at the Baseball Ground, with Clough's team sweeping to a 3-0 victory. Next came Spartak Trnava in the quarter-final, after which Derby found themselves in the last four alongside the holders Ajax, the might of Real Madrid, and the ever-dangerous Juventus.

Although European novices, there was a defined lack of fear from Clough and his team as they headed to Turin for the first leg against Juventus. Arriving three days before the game, the most Derby got to see of their surroundings was the torrential rain through their hotel window.

With the memories of being grossly underprepared for a deluge prior to the first leg of the 1971 European Fairs Cup Final against Leeds, Juventus seemed to be fully aware of the weather warnings this time around. Having protected the Stadio Comunale pitch with a covering that enabled a dry surface for kick-off, the game was never in danger of postponement, unlike two years earlier against Don Revie's side.

Juventus promptly outplayed Derby, picking off a 3-1 victory that still left the visitors with a glimmer of hope for the return game. Post-match, Clough readily accepted the balance of play, albeit with a series of caveats which revolved around his suspicions of foul play.

In a game during which the physical parts of Juventus's approach went overlooked, Clough felt the yellow cards that Archie Gemmill and Roy McFarland picked up were too enthusiastically awarded, while in the tunnel at half-time Taylor was involved in an altercation with uniformed security when he went to question why the Juventus substitute, Helmut Haller, had gone into the referee's changing room, both before the game and again at the interval.

Although these were occurrences that could be easily explained by Gerhard Schulenburg being a compatriot of Haller's, Clough and English football were on high alert due to repetitive rumblings of bribery from Italian teams to match officials.

While the bookings of Gemmill and McFarland were hugely damaging to Clough as it meant that both would be suspended for the second leg, Schulenburg did also caution Giuseppe Furino and Francesco Morini to level up the card count, although they were not suspended for the return.

A fortnight later, Derby were their own worst enemy. In an occasionally tempestuous game, three of the visiting players were flashed a yellow card while the Rams' Roger Davies got himself sent off when reacting to the provocation of Morini.

It was goalless over the 90 minutes of the second leg but could have been so vastly different for Clough and Derby had substitute Alan Hinton not missed a penalty, and had John O'Hare's excellent effort found the back of the Juventus net rather than Zoff's left-hand upright with 15 minutes still to play.

Derby's chance hadn't just been in this late flurry as a string of opportunities fell their way within the first 30 minutes, which lesser teams would have succumbed to. Zoff was the hero throughout, however, pulling off magnificent saves from Hinton and O'Hare, while Davies's threat on the ball made his dismissal even more frustrating for Clough, coming as it did shortly after Hinton had put his spot-kick wide.

By mid-October of the same year, Clough and Taylor had parted company with Derby, the result of brinkmanship in their running battles with chairman Sam Longson and many of his fellow directors at the Baseball Ground.

Whereas a similar stand-off and a serious threat to jump ship for Coventry City had been averted 18 months earlier, this time it came as a shock to Clough that his and Taylor's resignations had been accepted, upon which they were swiftly replaced by Dave Mackay.

Dropping two divisions to accept the offer of employment by Mike Bamber at Brighton, by the summer of 1974 Clough and Taylor had parted ways with each other. While Clough was more than willing to take on the impossible job of succeeding Don Revie at Elland Road, Taylor felt that Brighton deserved his loyalty, electing to stay on to become manager in his own right at the Goldstone Ground.

Fixated on another attempt at the European Cup, a campaign that would ultimately take place without his input, by January 1975 Clough was back in the East Midlands and at the City Ground with Forest. Taylor, meanwhile, would remain at Brighton until the summer of 1976, steadily building a team that would be fit to climb from the Third Division to the top tier by 1979. Brighton would do this without Taylor at the helm, however. After narrowly missing out on promotion to the same Second Division that Clough frequented with Forest in 1975/76, he eventually concluded that both their best work was produced together rather than apart.

Taylor probably had a valid point. Flying solo at the City Ground for his first season and a half, Clough's Forest had made little impact. Sat 11th in the Second Division table yet just five points off the promotion places after his first league game in charge, he then managed to win just another three matches before the end of the 1974/75 campaign. Doubts must have permeated that Clough had lost the golden touch he had been blessed with at Derby.

Clough's first full season in charge of Forest, also Taylor's last at Brighton, had been a polarising one. The first anniversary of Clough's arrival was marked by an ongoing run of poor form that amounted to five losses from six league games, instigating a downward spiral that was complemented by an FA Cup exit at the hands of Brighton's Third Division promotion rivals, Peterborough United.

Forest's axis suddenly tilted as February began, however. From a potential relegation battle Clough guided his team to a respectable eighth-place finish, losing only two of their last 16. Over the same period, Taylor's Brighton won just six times, inclusive of winning only once during their last eight games, running out of steam and agonisingly missing out on promotion.

It is incredulous to consider that within two years of Clough and Taylor being reunited they had transformed Forest into First Division champions, and within three they were the kings of Europe. Even within gaining promotion from the Second Division, Forest had not really shown signs of what was to come as they did so by the skin of their teeth, finishing 1976/77 in third place and just one point ahead of Bolton Wanderers and Blackpool.

As turbulent as Clough's first season and a half at Forest had been, some of the building blocks of his European Cup-winning teams were already at his disposal. The mercurial John Robertson and the intelligent Martin O'Neill had been young components of the Forest squad that had succumbed to relegation from the First Division in 1971/72, while Clough's predecessor at the City Ground, Allan Brown, had signed the former Manchester City midfielder Ian Bowyer, a player who had won the European Cup Winners' Cup as a teenager.

Viv Anderson had also been handed his debut by Brown, the first of a rich youth crop that Clough was able to harvest. Tony Woodcock and Garry Birtles would follow Anderson into the first team, although Birtles' introduction was belated in comparison to his contemporaries. All would become England internationals.

With these core elements in place, Clough and Taylor's external approach was to look for high-quality additions who represented great value. They wanted players with undoubted talent but perhaps with a point to prove.

Clough had already begun stamping his mark, moving swiftly upon his arrival at Forest to rescue John McGovern and John O'Hare from Leeds, players he had taken to Elland Road from Derby. By the summer of 1975, left-back Frank Clark was picked up on a free transfer from Newcastle United, while a year later Taylor's appointment as Clough's number two coincided with the purchases of Peter Withe from Birmingham City and Larry Lloyd from Coventry City, the latter after an initial loan deal.

While Withe would move on before the European Cup successes, he was integral to Forest's promotion and league title-winning campaigns. In the case of Lloyd, a former Liverpool central defender, Clough had retrospectively held Coventry up at gunpoint, procuring a player at a quarter of the fee the Highfield Road outfit had paid out for him two years earlier. It was a stunning piece of business for an experienced central defender who had won England caps, had learned his trade from Bill Shankly, and at the age of 28 in all theory should have been reaching his peak years.

Forest announced their return to the First Division with a 3-1 victory away to an Everton side that harboured aspirations of glory themselves for the 1977/78 season. Within weeks Clough had persuaded the Forest board of directors to spend big on Peter Shilton, and they also recruited, for a much more modest fee, the talented Archie Gemmill from Derby. Prior to this, Kenny Burns had been signed in another raid on Birmingham.

Burns had started out as a central defender but was then converted into a striker of reasonable intent at St Andrew's, yet it was as a partner to Lloyd that Clough had envisaged him operating, thus returning the player to the back line. Here he would win not only trophies as part of the collective but also be named FWA Player of the Year for 1977/78.

Unbeaten in the league from mid-November, Clough's Forest swept to the First Division title with four games to spare, picking up the League Cup along the way after defeating Liverpool in an Old Trafford replay, from where an electric rivalry then flooded through the next three years.

Never far away from the next curveball, Clough sold Withe in the first weeks of the 1978/79 season without showing any urgency in finding a replacement. It did not stop the new champions from continuing their unbeaten run into the new campaign, however. By the time Liverpool ended Forest's incredible unbeaten league record in early December, Clough's side had not tasted defeat in the competition for over a year.

One of the loudest atmospheres ever generated at Anfield for a domestic game of football, both on the pitch and in the stands the reaction to Liverpool's victory was utterly euphoric. Yet, it also spoke of just how much Clough and Forest had gotten under the skin of Bob Paisley's side.

Just over two months earlier, the two teams had walked from the Anfield turf to the tune of a different soundtrack. Liverpool's supporters had been in full voice then too, but on that occasion, it was while singing a rendition of 'we'll support you evermore' in response to their European Cup first round exit at the hands of Forest.

The Anfielders' dreams of completing a hat-trick of European Cups vanished and Liverpool promptly went on to reclaim the First Division title from Forest, whereas Clough's side retained the League Cup by beating Southampton in the final before going on to claim the biggest prize of all at Munich's Olympiastadion.

In peril from the very beginning, Liverpool had fallen to a classic European sucker punch at the City Ground in the first leg after embracing the game as if a domestic encounter rather than an away leg in continental combat. On a chastening night for Phil Thompson and Emlyn Hughes, the strike partnership of Woodcock and Birtles had Liverpool's defence in a regular state of disarray.

Making only his third appearance for Forest, Birtles opened the scoring in the 26th minute, laid on by Woodcock after a glaring error from Hughes in his attempts to cut out a through ball. With just three minutes remaining and Liverpool foolishly chasing an equaliser, this unknown entity of a striker then created a second goal as he outwitted Thompson before crossing for Woodcock to nod the ball down for the unlikely hero, Colin Barrett.

Barrett's career would ultimately be curtailed by a knee ligament injury that he picked up before the second leg, yet that second goal in the first leg put him at the epicentre of one of the most pivotal moments in the blossoming of that wonderful Forest era of the late 1970s and early 1980s.

It remains a mystery as to how Barrett ended up being positioned on the edge of the Liverpool six-yard box in the 87th minute, but it meant the visitors were given a mountain to climb at Anfield, and Paisley cut a quite rightly irate figure on the bench as Barrett and his team-mates celebrated.

An explosive game at the City Ground ended with high antagonism as Thompson had unsuccessfully tried to intimidate the inexperienced Birtles throughout, both physically and verbally. As the players were walking from the pitch, Gemmill got involved in heated conversations with several white-shirted Liverpool players.

Paisley, meanwhile, would have willingly taken a narrow 1-0 reversal, content in the knowledge that his team had overturned such deficits many times before. However, a two-goal disadvantage meant that one goal for Forest at Anfield would leave Liverpool needing four; this basic yet foreboding equation coming before you even took Clough's stubborn defence into account.

Two weeks later, at an Anfield that had put up the sold-out signs before a ball had been kicked in anger in the first leg, Forest's resilience saw them to the goalless draw that was more than enough to see them into the second round.

There are times, however, when the scoreline does not tell the story. Forest's journey to a clean sheet was an arduous one and they travelled as a team tasked with repelling opponents who immediately went for the throat and the ankle, backed by an atmosphere that could have generated the floodlighting. This game came three and a half weeks after Liverpool had put seven goals past the Tottenham Hotspur of Glenn Hoddle, Ricardo Villa and Osvaldo Ardiles, leading Clough and Taylor to warn their players of the dangers of complacency.

Forest held their own, though. Burns's treatment of Steve Heighway was what could best be described as Anglo-Saxon, McGovern was the shadow of Graeme Souness, while Gemmill resumed his compelling running battle with Ray Kennedy, a duel that had been one of the most physical aspects of the first game. In response, Birtles was on the receiving end of a couple of stern and targeted challenges that blunted his effectiveness.

Flooding the edge of their penalty area, Forest presented Liverpool with a thin yellow line that was almost impossible to penetrate, safe in the knowledge that it would need something incredibly special, or outlandish, to beat a peak-of-his-powers Shilton from distance.

Despite Liverpool's excellent build-up play, and the pressure that they applied, most of their attacks floundered in and around the penalty area. Forest arguably had the best chance of the first half when Birtles broke free for a one-on-one with Ray Clemence, but the England goalkeeper intercepted.

Desperation crept into Liverpool's play as the second half wore on, especially after Shilton had twice denied Kenny Dalglish. Pot shots from distance by Jimmy Case and Thompson flew high and wide, and even the introduction of David Fairclough did little to alter the course of the evening. Forest's own attacking intent was reliant solely on occasional counters, one of which, led by Anderson, should have earned them a penalty.

Liverpool's players ran and ran to the very last, but it was to no avail. Forest had refused to buckle under a weight that had accounted for so many wonderful teams before them on those iconic Anfield European nights.

Added to Forest's joy at overcoming the back-to-back holders, they then received the news that big potential threats moving forward had also been eliminated. Juventus had fallen to Rangers, while the previous season's beaten finalists, Club Brugge, had been knocked out too.

Drawn against AEK Athens in the second round, Forest cruised through to the quarter-final. They were 2-1 winners in the Greek capital thanks to an untidy effort from McGovern and Birtles benefiting from some slack defending for the second, the only blemish coming courtesy of Burns giving away a penalty just short of the hour, converted by Tasos Konstantinou.

Clough's side then scored five at the City Ground on an evening when it could have been double the amount. David Needham opened the scoring with a diving header, yet either side of that goal Birtles and Woodcock had both been denied.

Gemmill was another to come close, before Woodcock did finally make it 2-0 by heading home a beautifully weighted cross from Robertson. Within five minutes of Forest's second, Anderson had netted their third, intercepting the ball in midfield, striding forward and striking from distance into the top-left corner of Nikos Christidis's net. There was still time before the interval for Woodcock to be denied what should have been a blatant penalty when brought down by the Greek international goalkeeper.

Within five minutes of the restart, AEK had a goal back when the imposing Yugoslav international Dušan Bajević outmuscled the Forest defence to head beyond Shilton. With such a comfortable aggregate lead, a ripple of polite applause broke out around the City Ground for a goal that would be rendered no threat once a double from Birtles took Forest to a 5-1 victory on the night and 7-2 on aggregate.

His first a piece of penalty box opportunism, Birtles' second was a glancing header at the near post, when cutting across Christidis and his defence. This was after the goalkeeper had pulled off a flying save from a magnificent run and shot by Robertson. On an action-packed evening, AEK even found the time to have another goal disallowed.

The European Cup was put into storage for the next four months and when it resumed for the last eight, Forest found themselves up against Grasshopper of Zürich who, just as AEK had, wilted at the City Ground. The only difference this time around was that the home match was the first leg, and Clough's side were much more fortuitous in accumulating their 4-1 victory than the result might suggest.

When Claudio Sulser opened the scoring after only 11 minutes, it was not exactly a goal that you could claim was out of the blue. Grasshopper had made the faster start and Forest had failed to heed the early warnings.

For Sulser's tenth goal of the European Cup campaign, he was swift to latch on to an intelligent through pass from his captain André Meyer, almost barging his way past Lloyd in order to break free on Shilton, benefiting from the bounce of the ball. On a cabbage patch of a pitch, it was a wonderfully incisive move.

Stung into action, Forest swept forward in great numbers, laying siege to the Grasshopper penalty area. McGovern had an effort cleared off the line by Jonny Hey before Woodcock set Birtles up to level the scores by wrong-footing visiting goalkeeper Roger Berbig.

Level at the interval, Forest were gifted the lead two minutes into the second half after being awarded a borderline penalty that was rolled home by Robertson. It should have been a goal that broke Grasshopper's resolve, yet through a combination of Swiss stubbornness and Forest frustration it was not until the final few minutes that Clough's side snared two extra goals.

Robertson, O'Neill, Birtles, and Needham all came close in an increasingly frantic clash, while at the other end Shilton pulled off a fine reaction save from Sulser, who remained a danger on the break. Finally, however, three minutes from time, Gemmill made the pressure pay when driving the ball into the bottom-right corner of Berbig's net, this via a cross from the unlikely source of Lloyd, with Birtles, as an intermediary, creating panic in the Grasshopper penalty area.

Jubilation and relief erupted, and if Forest felt like they had been lucky to break the resistance of Grasshopper so late in the game, it certainly did not persuade them to cease their advances forward. O'Neill was soon seeing a goalbound header tipped on to the crossbar by Berbig, shortly before Lloyd turned from shock provider to surprise goalscorer when flicking in a Robertson corner that the heroic visiting goalkeeper had been ill-advised in coming for. It was a fourth goal that was nothing short of a gift.

In the return game, Forest overcame the first-half blow of conceding a generous penalty to Sulser when O'Neill bundled in the equaliser five minutes later. It was a goal that killed off the appetite of the Swiss champions for another fight to the finish, this time the game meandering through the second period to its inevitable outcome.

Of the four hurdles that Forest had to clear to reach the 1979 European Cup Final, the first and last were definitively the most difficult.

Hennes Weisweiler, the man who had turned Borussia Mönchengladbach from Bundesliga rejects into one of the most dangerous and respected teams of the 1970s, had departed West German football in the summer of 1975 in order to accept the task of succeeding Rinus Michels at Barcelona.

During his 11 years at the Bökelbergstadion, Weisweiler had guided Mönchengladbach to three Bundesliga titles, one DFB-Pokal and UEFA Cup glory, also losing a further final to Bill Shankly's Liverpool. Building his team around the wondrous talents of Günter Netzer and Jupp Heynckes, it was Weisweiler who had overseen Mönchengladbach when they had their seven-goal haul against Internazionale annulled seven seasons earlier.

Weisweiler must have felt that there was a heavy degree of unfinished business between him and the European Cup as he went head-to-head with Clough.

It was not to be a tie that Weisweiler undertook as Barcelona's coach, however. His stay in Catalonia had ended prematurely, and arguably irrationally, when dispensed with after losing the first leg of the 1976 UEFA Cup semi-final to Bob Paisley's Liverpool.

Weisweiler, a strong-minded individual, had encountered a battle for power at the Camp Nou, not only with the hierarchy of the club but also with the all-encompassing presence in the dressing room of Johan Cruyff. Having fought a similar war with an increasingly powerful Netzer at Mönchengladbach, which resulted in the sale of the player to Real Madrid, this time Weisweiler had found himself with few allies among his employers despite leading Barcelona into a promising position towards the season's run-in.

A free agent, and while still holed up in the Catalan capital, Weisweiler was approached by 1. FC Köln, a club he had not only played for but coached twice before, with the view to him taking over for a third time at of the start of the 1976/77 campaign.

Despite other options on the table, including a notable one from the ambitious Fortuna Düsseldorf, Weisweiler's former employers won his signature. It was partly due to his previous associations with them, certainly, but also thanks to the club sending out a delegation to him directly in Barcelona.

Within a year of his return to West Germany, Weisweiler had taken Köln to glory in the Pokal and won another battle of wills with a high-profile and dominant player, this time the ageing Wolfgang Overath. By the end of his second season the Bundesliga title was claimed, edging out his former club Mönchengladbach despite them putting 12 goals past Borussia Dortmund on the final day of the campaign, while the Pokal was also retained, thus completing the domestic double.

Having accounted for the Icelandic outfit Íþróttabandalag Akraness, Lokomotiv Sofia and Rangers on their run to the semi-finals, Köln had not lost a game by the time they went up against Forest for a place in the final.

Falling off the radar for many knowledgeable football observers when it comes to discussions about the best teams not to have won the European Cup, Köln are damned by how their rise to prominence was preceded by Bayern Munich and Mönchengladbach going toe to toe throughout the 1970s. Theirs were exploits of greatness that could not be contained exclusively within the Bundesliga, instead spilling out across the continent, where both obtained European glory to show off alongside a balanced domestic monopoly.

Added to this, in the four years beyond Köln's flirtation with the 1979 European Cup Final, Hamburger SV went on to steal the limelight, contesting two finals that sandwiched a run to the 1982 UEFA Cup Final for good measure.

Weisweiler's Köln, however, were a brief match for their West German contemporaries, and it isn't outlandish to suggest that it should have been they, rather than Forest, who headed to Munich's Olympiastadion to face the surprise finalists Malmö FF.

Spearheaded by the prolific Dieter Müller, Köln had a strong spine that included part-goalkeeper part-Bond villain Harald Schumacher, West German international Herbert Zimmermann, World Cup winner Bernhard Cullmann, plus the criminally underrated Belgian playmaker and occasional winger Roger Van Gool. The cherry on the cake had been the emergence of the outrageously gifted Bernd Schuster.

There were a lot of dependable components in Weisweiler's squad, a lot of players who had grown up with the club and remained loyal to it. Heinz Flohe had been another Köln element of West Germany's 1974 World Cup-winning squad, while Harald Konopka and Herbert Neumann had also represented their nation, as would Gerhard Strack a few years later.

Weisweiler also had at his disposal the Japanese international Yasuhiko Okudera, a talented midfielder who had become the first player from his country to play top-flight European football. It was the talent and dedication of Okudera that eased Weisweiler's mind when cutting loose a prodigious young Danish player by the name of Preben Elkjær, having grown weary of his unwillingness to toe the strict scriptures of his manager.

Within a year, Forest's Tony Woodcock had been added to Weisweiler's team too.

In the first leg at the City Ground, on an atrocious pitch, the two teams spared no quarter in their attacking intent. Weisweiler had set his stall out to secure an away goal and Van Gool obliged within six minutes.

Already there had been opportunities at both ends, as Birtles had sliced wide when well positioned for Forest and Müller skewed one across the face of Shilton's six-yard box after smart interplay with Van Gool.

Finding himself in space on the edge of the Forest penalty area, Van Gool accepted the invitation to shoot, sneaking the ball low past Shilton and in off his near post. While the Forest goalkeeper seemed to get a hand to the effort and would have been disappointed not to have kept the ball out, it had taken a deceptive bounce off the uneven turf. Regardless of culpability, it was a huge blow for Clough and his team.

It was a dream start for Köln and they were firmly in the driving seat after 20 minutes when catching Forest on the break for a second goal. Neumann gained possession after an attack stemming from a Robertson free kick broke down, and the Köln number ten carried the ball from the edge of his own D to the centre circle before releasing it to Van Gool on the left.

The Belgian international must have been shocked with the amount of space he was afforded by Barrett, who was deputising at right-back for the suspended Anderson. Intelligently waiting for Shilton to advance, Van Gool entered the Forest penalty area and instead of attempting to feed the ball beneath this imposing sight, or to opt to chip him, he squared the ball to the unmarked Müller, who was left with the simple task of rolling it into the empty Forest net.

A lesson in the European game, it was fast turning into a sobering evening for Clough and his players, yet they were admirably stung into action. Moments after falling 2-0 behind, Bowyer was clipping the Köln crossbar, and then in the 28th minute Birtles had got one back for Forest when he was allowed too much time and space in the penalty area to direct the ball beyond a helpless Schumacher.

There were no further goals in the first half but Forest still suffered the blow of losing the influential experience of Gemmill shortly before the interval. It was shaping up to be the type of evening that if something could go wrong for Forest, it would. Clough introduced Clark to slot in at left-back, pushing Bowyer into midfield.

It was a huge setback to lose Gemmill, who had just helped create an opportunity for McGovern which, had it not been for an impressive save from Schumacher, would have levelled the scoreline before the break. Woodcock was also denied by the Köln goalkeeper as the home side ended the first half in ascendency.

None of this protected Forest from the dangers of a Köln counter-attack, though. With Forest ploughing forward in search of an equaliser, Van Gool had broken away with only Gemmill for company before clipping the ball just wide of Shilton's left-hand post. Gemmill picked up his injury in this move, and it would have the knock-on effect that he would be restricted to watching the final as one of Clough's unused substitutes.

With obvious concerns that the departure of Gemmill might disrupt their momentum, Clough simply shuffled his pack, which presented Köln with a different set of worries to deal with. Upon the resumption, things could have turned against Forest swiftly, however, as Konopka stung the palms of Shilton with a goalbound effort.

Despite the scare, it was Forest to land the next body blow.

Gifted possession, Robertson teased the Köln defence on the left before eventually looping a cross towards Birtles that he glanced straight into the path of Bowyer, which he met first time, perfectly, just inside the penalty area, to drive right-footed into the bottom-left corner.

With parity restored, it seemed only a matter of time before Forest claimed the lead. A combination of hard work from Woodcock and a miskick by Müller helped create a chance for McGovern that the outstanding Schumacher tipped over the crossbar.

Ten minutes beyond their equaliser, and not far past the hour, Forest did take the lead via a wonderful diving header by Robertson after intricate build-up play from McGovern, Woodcock, and Birtles. Birtles turned Shuster magnificently to flash the cross across the six-yard box for Robertson to score, diving full length to cut across Konopka in beating him to the ball.

It was a stunning fightback from Forest in what was a game that would have made for one of the all-time great finals had it been played out one round further forward, but having gained the lead Clough's side now subconsciously stalled.

Köln were offered a way back into proceedings and again Van Gool was key to most of their best moments, this time as provider, as he teed up Neumann to strike an effort that went narrowly over Shilton's crossbar when he really should have scored.

It was a stark warning of what Weisweiler's team were still capable of and Müller soon came close once more with an attempted lob that dropped on to the top of the netting, after Shilton had charged from his line to meet him.

Weisweiler, perhaps caught up within the spirit of a marvellously open game, threw on Okudera with ten minutes remaining. Within a minute of his arrival on the pitch, he had snatched the equaliser for 3-3.

Forest, yet again on the front foot, were once more caught on the break. With Lloyd one of the players committed to attack and hunt for a fourth goal to take to the Müngersdorfer Stadion for the second leg, Köln switched from defence to attack with a fluid ruthlessness.

As a testament to how desperately Weisweiler's team were defending in a backs-against-the-wall situation, it was Müller who started the move from what was akin to a defensive midfield position, sending Van Gool away down the right-hand channel. Perhaps through his own sense of footballing vision, perhaps through sheer fatigue, or even a combination of both, Van Gool didn't retain possession for long. He adjusted himself to match pace with the ball and centred it first time to the lurking Okudera, who cleverly took it back across the path of the backtracking Forest defence to create as much space as possible for a speculative effort from 20 yards.

Striking it sweetly with his right foot, Okudera beat not only Shilton but also the cameraman. As true a shot as it was, its trajectory was straight at the Forest goalkeeper, who was too slow to go to ground as the ball crept beneath him. If unfortunate to concede the first, Shilton was certainly to blame for Köln's third.

Still Forest continued to push forward; still Clough continued to send defenders forward. There was a goalmouth scramble that Köln survived, and Barrett was almost the unlikely hero all over again.

Clough and Weisweiler were the consummate politicians in their post-match interviews to ITV's Gary Newbon. Clough spoke of how brilliant a result it was, despite shipping three away goals, even prophetically stating that his team only needed to score once to reach the final. He offset the brazen showmanship with the candid confession that given his defence had no discernible pace, they were always going to be vulnerable to Köln's speed. Weisweiler, meanwhile, in faultless

English, gave all the right answers in being pleased with the outcome yet wary of the dangers still posed by Forest.

A fortnight later it was a vastly different game, much more cat and mouse with chances at a premium, and they were subtle ones rather than glaring opportunities. Müller came the closest during a cagey first half, and when he picked up an injury a few minutes before the interval, just as had happened to Forest with Gemmill in the first leg, his night ended prematurely.

Without Müller, Köln cut a much more nervous collective in the second half, and suddenly Clough's one-goal prophecy began to loom as a very real possibility. It came to pass in the 64th minute with Bowyer in the right place at the right time to head past Schumacher when getting on the end of a Robertson corner, which had been flicked on by Birtles.

With Forest defending deep to negate the threat of Köln's pace, Weisweiler's players were left with the desperation of trying to thread their chances through a consistently crowded penalty area. Frustration was met by further frustration as a meaningful sighting of the whites of Shilton's eyes failed to materialise.

After the loss of Müller, Köln could not create the type of chances they had throughout the first 135 minutes of the semi-final. Their best opportunity during this late siege of the Forest penalty area was a Konopka effort from distance, which Shilton was alert to, although he still required a second attempt to smother the danger.

So entrenched in defence were Forest that even in the last few seconds, when able to counter, there was a reticence in vacating space in midfield. It might have been a scrappy way to reach the promised land but for Clough it had been a tactical masterclass, and a classical game of two halves, after Köln had spent so much of the first half moving forward as if in possession of the key to unlock the Forest defence. In the second period, it was as if Weisweiler's players had mislaid the key.

Essentially, Köln's undoing was that they were perhaps a little too similar to Forest. Hindsight is a potent tool but sat on the bench that night at the Müngersdorfer was a 19-year-old Pierre Littbarski, who might have been able to produce that sorely absent piece of magic to make the difference for Weisweiler. Alternatively, had the Köln coach have still had the services of Elkjær at his disposal, then perhaps the impossible might have become possible.

Five weeks separated the second leg of the semi-final and the final, and for the second time in three seasons the European Cup was guaranteed to have a new name inscribed upon it. If Forest were surprise finalists, then Malmö's presence was a seismic shock.

Led by the former Hastings United midfielder and player-manager Bob Houghton, Malmö's run to the final was navigated without facing a European Cup-winning team. Yet they did defeat Monaco in the first round, while the scalp of Valeriy Lobanovskyi's Dynamo Kyiv in the second round was of the highest calibre imaginable.

Catching these considerable opponents when they did could not have been better timed. With the Swedish domestic season stretching from April to October, it meant that the first two rounds were played just as Malmö were within the eye of the storm that was the run-in to the end of the 1978 Allsvenskan campaign. That said, Dynamo Kyiv were also playing their Soviet Top League season to a similar calendar, which makes Malmö's achievement even more stunning.

Wisła Kraków were brushed aside in quarter-final played out in what was Malmö's domestic pre-season, meaning their semi-final against Austria Wien came just as the new Allsvenskan season was beginning.

Beneficiaries of some enormous helpings of luck along their way to the final, Malmö combined their good fortune with hard work and heavy degrees of percentage playing. They were a threat aerially so Houghton focused on his team's strengths. This was a project in pure pragmatism.

Going into the 1979 European Cup Final, Houghton's plans were thrown into chaos when deprived of the services of the assured Swedish international central defender Roy Andersson. This was compounded by the loss of the legendary midfielder Bo Larsson, Malmö's captain and a talismanic figure who had starred for his nation at three World Cups. Despite now being 35 years of age, Larsson was still the pivot upon which the team revolved. His absence was massive blow. To add to Houghton's pre-match headaches, Larsson's midfield partner and deputy as captain, Staffan Tapper, broke a toe on the eve of the game.

While Tapper would insist upon playing through the pain barrier, his involvement would be over before the first half was. It made for a patchwork quilt of a Malmö line-up which also included Anders Ljungberg, a player that was older than his manager. At the other end of the age spectrum Houghton also fielded a couple of teenagers, one of whom, Robert Prytz, would face Forest again in a Malmö shirt, in the 1995/96 UEFA Cup.

It wasn't only Houghton who had to make some difficult selection decisions. Gemmill had recovered from the injury that he had picked up in the first leg of the semi-final, but Bowyer had proved to be a man in form and retained his place in midfield rather than dropping back into defence. This meant that Frank Clark was able to bring the curtain down on his playing career on the highest stage imaginable.

Martin O'Neill too was struggling to prove his full fitness, and just like Gemmill, he too would have to accept a place among the substitutes. This meant a European debut for Trevor Francis, who Clough had brought in from Birmingham City, in the process making him British football's first £1m player.

UEFA's rules at that time stated that any new signing made beyond the start of the season would be subject to a three-month ineligibility for European competition, ruling Francis out of Forest's quarter-final and semi-final. Having never been part of a Birmingham team that qualified for Europe, the 1979 European Cup Final represented Francis's very first game in continental club competition.

At a packed Olympiastadion, Forest's supporters roughly outnumbered Malmö's by two to one, but they weren't to be served up a classic final by any means.

A better game than it has ever been given credit for, however, it had many similarities to Liverpool's victory over Brugge 12 months earlier. One team curling up into a protective ball, the other probing for a way through. It might have finished 1-0 but had Forest managed to pick off the extra couple of goals their endeavour deserved then it would arguably be viewed very differently.

Having thrived for so long upon being the underdog, the tag of favourites sat heavily on the Forest defence. For all the measured possession of Clough's midfield, and the potential for goals in attack, there were undeniable nerves at the back.

Birtles made the first attempt at goal, looping the ball on to the roof of the netting after receiving it from Robertson. This was soon followed by Burns almost gifting Tore Cervin an open invitation to score when a header he had sent back to Shilton did not have enough weight to comfortably reach his goalkeeper. If patience was required going forward, what Forest needed at the back was calm concentration.

More opportunities fell Forest's way. Robertson had a chance of his own at the back post and McGovern flashed an effort just wide. Shortly before Malmö lost Tapper, Bowyer shot low and straight at Jan Möller, but it was one that almost squirmed under the Malmö goalkeeper with the goal line perilously close behind him. In response, Cervin gave Shilton another scare via a fresh aerial attack.

Then came the decisive moment, on the stroke of half-time. Rather than in his favoured central attacking position, Clough had deployed Francis down the right, balancing Robertson on the left and Birtles through the middle.

Had Francis been positioned centrally then he probably would not have scored the goal. Drifting in from the right almost undetected while Malmö were busy being hypnotised by the sorcery of Robertson, when Francis got on the end of the cross it was converted with a certain sense of style and intelligence.

Directing his header into the roof of the net, Francis dramatically rolled across the stadium's shot put circle as he landed. The goal had been the first time that Malmö had allowed Robertson to reach the byline, and it had proved a costly mistake.

The second half drifted by with a selection of missed opportunities for Forest and a lack of punch for a Malmö side too in control of their emotions to experience the desperation of their situation. Despite a change in formation, which amounted to three up front, Houghton's side never compellingly tested Shilton.

Forest should have extended their lead, however. Birtles was wasteful with a volley when gifted vast quantities of space in the penalty area, Robertson hit the foot of the post after wonderful work from Francis down the right, while Woodcock looped one wide of the woodwork, the dropping ball just too high for Francis who was again drifting in to try and get there. Clough's side would have been worthy of a three- or four-goal

Real Madrid and Stade de Reims battle it out at the Parc des Princes in the inaugural, 1956 European Cup Final. The Spanish club would edge a close game, 4-3, and go on to win the next four finals.

Alfredo Di Stéfano scores Real Madrid's first goal in the iconic 1960 European Cup Final, to make it 1-1, against Eintracht Frankfurt. He and Ferenc Puskás would score all seven of their team's goals, during the 7-3 victory at Hampden Park.

Ângelo Martins defies Barcelona on the Benfica goal line, in the 1961 European Cup Final. The Catalans miss a glut of chances to hand Béla Guttmann's team the trophy, and it would be another 31 years before the Camp Nou outfit finally prevail in the tournament.

Benfica's José Torres causes concern for the Internazionale defence, during the 1965 European Cup Final, at the San Siro. The legendary Helenio Herrera leads the Italians to their second successive glory, although there are ambiguities over the fairness of their path to glory.

Celtic's Willie Wallace duels with Inter's Angelo Domenghini during the 1967 European Cup Final. Jock Stein's men are given little chance of success by their opponents prior to the game, yet they dominate in the Portuguese capital, to earn the name 'The Lisbon Lions'.

Brian Kidd leaps high into the air in celebration of scoring Manchester United's third goal, at Wembley, during extra-time in the 1968 European Cup Final, against Benfica. Matt Busby's team become the first English winners, ten years on from the Munich Air Disaster.

Rinus Israël is eager to get his hands on the trophy, as Feyenoord comprehensively outplay Celtic, at the San Siro, in the 1970 European Cup Final, to become the first team from the Netherlands to win the tournament. Their coach, Ernst Happel, would take three different teams to the final.

Johnny Rep and Arie Haan celebrate, as the Ajax number 16 opens and ends the scoring in the early exchanges of the 1973 European Cup Final, in Zagreb, against Juventus. The Dutch masters win the competition for the third successive time.

Leeds United's Peter Lorimer powers in what he and his team-mates believe to be the opening goal of the 1975 European Cup Final, only for it to be contentiously disallowed. Bayern Munich go on to win, 2-0, at the Parc des Princes, and riots ensue.

Kevin Keegan torments Borussia Mönchengladbach's Berti Vogts into conceding a penalty, in the 1977 European Cup Final, in Rome. It was to be Keegan's last game in a Liverpool shirt, before a big money move to Hamburger SV.

Trevor Francis salutes the Nottingham Forest supporters at the end of the 1979 European Cup Final, as the scorer of the decisive goal against Malmö FF, at Munich's Olympiastadion. Amazingly, it was the England international's European debut.

Nigel Spink is the unlikely hero for Aston Villa, when he replaces the injured Jimmy Rimmer during the early exchanges of the 1982 European Cup Final, against Bayern Munich, in Rotterdam. His heroics go a long way in Tony Barton's team lifting the trophy.

The Hamburger SV captain, Horst Hrubesch fights for the ball with Sergio Brio, on the way to lifting the European Cup, in Athens, in 1983, after he and his team rip up the script, in defeating Giovanni Trapattoni's mighty Juventus. Three years earlier, he had not been fully fit, when they lost as favourites, against Nottingham Forest.

There is only devastation at the 1985 European Cup Final, between Juventus and Liverpool, at the dilapidated Heysel Stadium. Thirty-nine souls, predominantly from Italy, yet also Belgium, France, and Northern Ireland, are senselessly lost. It is indelibly the tournament's darkest hour.

Helmut Duckadam is beaten in extra time, but Pichi Alonso falls foul of the linesman's flag. The 1986 European Cup Final struggles for quality, and stumbles its way to a penalty shootout, in Seville. Steaua București snatch the trophy from right under the nose of the big favourites, Terry Venables's Barcelona.

João Pinto, the FC Porto captain, lifts the trophy after a dramatic late comeback against the three-times winners Bayern Munich, in the 1987 European Cup Final. It is one of the best finals for a decade, but UK television opt not to broadcast the game live.

'The Curse of Béla Guttmann' strikes at Benfica yet again, as Ronald Koeman converts PSV Eindhoven's first spot kick in the penalty shootout in the 1988 European Cup Final. Many of Guus Hiddink's players went on to European Championship glory, with the Netherlands, a few weeks later.

Ruud Gullit opens the scoring in the 1989 European Cup Final, for Milan, against Steaua București, at the Camp Nou. Arrigo Sacchi's side run out 4-0 winners, during one of the finest team displays ever seen in the showpiece event. It is the club's third success, but their first for 20 years.

Olympique de Marseille's Chris Waddle finds his way forward is blocked by Red Star Belgrade's Ilija Najdoski and Slobodan Marović. The Yugoslavs play the percentages in the 1991 European Cup Final, in Bari, and claim the prize on penalties. A hugely anticipated game, it never matches the pre-match expectations.

The 1992 European Cup Final match-winner, Ronald Koeman, parades the trophy with Hristo Stoichkov, at Wembley, as Barcelona at long last break the spell, when defeating Sampdoria, in extra-time. It is the last final before the tournament is rebranded as the Champions League.

advantage but they were also still susceptible to being hit on the break. It made for an unlikely edgy end to a relatively one-sided final.

From Second Division misfits to champions of Europe in just two years, one of football's biggest mountains had been scaled by Clough and his players. McGovern being the Forest captain seemed entirely fitting given he had begun his professional career when walking off park pitches to follow his manager from Hartlepools United (as they were known when McGovern played there) to Derby, to Leeds, and then Forest.

After such a meteoric rise, where else was there for Forest to go other than an attempt to retain their hard-earned European Cup. If you reach the top of the mountain, all you can do is try to stay there.

Forest's 1979/80 defence began as the previous season's campaign had ended, with them being pitted against Swedish opponents. This time it was Östers IF in legs that landed within the same Allsvenskan campaign as the 1979 European Cup Final had.

Although winning 3-1 on aggregate, Forest had been far from convincing. Two Bowyer strikes beyond the hour, on what seemed set to be a frustrating evening at the City Ground, were followed a fortnight later by a nervous 1-1 draw at the Värendsvallen. Clough's side had been defensively vulnerable and they were reliant upon a late header from Woodcock to avert what might have been a fraught finale.

Next came the Romanian champions Argeş Piteşti, and with Liverpool having fallen to the mysterious eastern Europeans of Dinamo Tbilisi in the previous round, Forest could have been forgiven for entering this one with a mild sense of paranoia, especially with the second leg taking place behind the Iron Curtain.

Two early goals in both legs meant that it was a sedate passage into the quarter-final for the holders, and maybe the Nottingham public were becoming a touch too accustomed to being the champions of Europe all of a sudden. Almost 30,000 fewer spectators had converged upon the City Ground for the first two home legs of the 1979/80 campaign than had been the case for the same fixtures 12 months earlier.

Mitigating circumstances can be factored in, of course, and while European Cup football was no longer a novelty to Forest's supporters, Östers and Piteşti were never going to bring the numbers of travelling fans as Liverpool did.

By the time the quarter-final came into view, Woodcock had departed Forest for Köln, which handed Francis his favoured position through the middle alongside Birtles. To supplement the new pairing, Clough also swooped to sign the Queens Park Rangers maverick, Stan Bowles.

Another gamble, this one would ultimately backfire in the long run, even if the short-term gain was to win a second European Cup. In many respects, Forest would prevail in retaining their prize despite themselves. For differing reasons, neither Francis nor Bowles would take part in the 1980 European Cup Final.

As the quarter-final approached, however, all of this was an undetected drama somewhere over the Madrid horizon. Their next opponents were the shadowy BFC Dynamo, otherwise known as Dynamo Berlin, the East German team of choice of Erich Mielke, holder of the elaborately entitled position of the Deputy State Secretary of the State Secretariat for State Security. The infamous Stasi.

Domestically, Dynamo's success in the 1978/79 DDR Oberliga was not only their first league title but it was also to be the first of ten successive title wins. That achievement still provokes scorn and derision from some quarters. Suspicions of the dice being loaded in Dynamo's favour in East Germany were hardly eased by the sight of them failing repeatedly to make a substantial impact on the European stage beyond their debut effort, when the club came to within a penalty shoot-out of reaching the 1972 European Cup Winners' Cup Final.

Under the tutelage of Jürgen Bogs, Dynamo's route to the quarter-final had taken them past Ruch Chorzów and Servette without breaking sweat. As they headed to the City Ground for the first leg to take on the holders this was a game that represented the East Germans with a golden opportunity to prove themselves both on the continent and at home.

For Forest, it was a chance to break free of their increasing domestic difficulties. Four days prior to welcoming Dynamo to Nottinghamshire, Clough's side had travelled to Burnden Park, where they had lost to a Bolton Wanderers team convincingly propping up the rest of the First Division. Despite March having just begun, it had been only Bolton's second league win of the season.

Forest were seventh, ten points behind league leaders Liverpool, Paisley's side having started to get the upper hand on Clough's team by knocking them out of the FA Cup and beating them in the league at Anfield. In response, Forest had got the better of the Merseysiders in the League Cup semi-final to reach their third successive final.

Depending upon which version of Forest showed up, if they could build themselves a solid lead to take to East Berlin then their fragile-looking campaign might just be able to achieve some spectacular redemption. On an evening when Forest were forced to wear their away colours at home, Dynamo won 1-0.

With Forest struggling for inspiration and thrust in the final third, despite enjoying most of the possession, Dynamo were happy to frustrate their opponents, only pushing forward sporadically. On 63 minutes, Hans Jürgen Riediger broke the deadlock.

Stemming from Bowles's attempts play a quick one-two with Lloyd on the edge of the Dynamo penalty area, the East Germans were wonderfully swift in their counter-attack.

A raking crossfield pass found Frank Terletzki out on the left, and rather than take on Bryn Gunn he sent a searching cross over to Riediger. With a possible hint of handball, he controlled it and dispatched it low and into Shilton's bottom right-hand corner. The goal was met by a stunned initial silence but was soon followed by appreciative applause.

Riediger could have made it 2-0 as the clock ticked towards 90 minutes, but Forest breathed a sigh of relief and accepted the narrow loss.

With their reign as European champions sat upon the thinnest of ice, by the time Clough's team headed behind the Iron Curtain they had lost the League Cup Final to Wolverhampton Wanderers with what was a heavily self-inflicted goal. It meant that Forest's whole season was now balanced entirely on their return game against Dynamo, and they would be playing it without the suspended Burns.

As a validation of Clough's very public belief in his team's ability to turn around the most hopeless of situations, at Dynamo's Friedrich-Ludwig-Jahn-Sportpark, Forest departed the pitch for the half-time break armed with a 3-0 lead thanks to two goals from Francis and another from Robertson.

With one almost stumbled in and the other off the underside of the Dynamo crossbar, Francis's brace was added to by Robertson converting from the spot. Even then, the England international had tried his arm at attempting to persuade his team-mate to hand him the ball for the penalty, given the Scotsman had missed his last European spot-kick.

Francis was given short shrift and Robertson then rolled the ball into Bodo Rudwaleit's bottom-right corner with the Dynamo goalkeeper going the wrong way. Three away goals to the good, Forest would now have to concede three to be eliminated.

While Forest had built up a comfortable advantage, it was by no means one-way traffic with Dynamo breaking out of defence to spring a cluster of counter-attacks of their own. Within five minutes of the start of the second half, the East Germans had a goal back as Robertson, having converted a penalty, now gave one away. Terletzki powered the ball past Shilton, yet it was directed relatively centrally and the goalkeeper should have done better.

With Forest happy to sit on their lead, it was up to Dynamo to force the pace. This they did but to no avail. Clough's side were alarmingly vulnerable at set pieces and both Riediger and Wolf-Rüdiger Netz probably should have scored in the final few minutes. Just how this game might have ended had Dynamo bundled one over the line is anyone's guess, but it made for a fascinating spectacle which had many more layers than the scoreline might suggest.

An intelligent away European performance, this was Forest as a genuinely grown-up football entity and with some huge hurdles to clear before they retained their prize, inclusive of the eventual blow of the loss of Francis to absorb too, it was almost as if you could split their 1979/80 European Cup campaign into two defined halves. The uninspired chores of the early rounds had then given way to the need to come out fighting against Dynamo in the quarter-final after the first-leg loss at the City Ground. Heading behind the Iron Curtain to correct those errors was character-building.

This put Forest into a semi-final quartet alongside Ajax, Real Madrid, and Hamburger SV. It was a stellar line-up on paper, although one shrouded with caveats. The Dutch champions had struggled to hit the European heights since Johan Cruyff's departure for Barcelona, while almost a decade and a half had passed since Madrid had been the champions of Europe. In HSV, the biggest threat was arguably posed by the one team in the last four who had never contested a European Cup final before, let alone won one.

Forest were drawn to face the Eredivisie champions. A quite different Ajax to the one that had won a hat-trick of European Cups in the early 1970s, they were still led on the pitch by the familiar figure of Ruud Krol, yet he was essentially surrounded by a collective of faces new to the eyes of a British audience.

The first leg at the City Ground was the evening where Forest's status of European Cup holders seemed to sink in for their supporters, and perhaps for their manager too. Clough was bold in his team selection with Bowyer left on the sidelines in favour of fielding Bowles as an extra attacker. With Francis putting in one of his finest performances in a Forest shirt, Ajax were simply overrun by their hosts, for whom Anderson was given a roaming remit that the visitors struggled to cope with.

If Forest were left with any regrets, it was that they ended the game with only a two-goal advantage to take to Amsterdam. Shaking off the close attention of Ajax's smothering tactics, Francis bundled the first one over the line, while for the second his determination to keep the ball in play won his team the penalty Robertson converted.

Ajax, capable of moving the ball forward with great incisiveness down the flanks, seemed reluctant to commit the numbers centrally to prosper from such positions. It was a situation that they needed to remedy in the second leg at the Olympisch Stadium if they were to return to the final.

Armed with stubborn defending and admirable stifling tactics, which involved Bowyer returning in place of Bowles,

Forest had the measure of Ajax until the Danish international Søren Lerby made the breakthrough with 25 minutes still to play. Heading in beyond the back post from a Frank Arnesen corner, this was the culmination of some incessant Ajax pressure which included a compelling claim for a penalty that was waved away.

For a while Forest were rocking and potentially vulnerable to a quick second goal, and it took immense concentration and discipline to keep Ajax at bay. Leo Beenhakker's side were gifted plenty of the ball, yet as intricate as their build-up play was, actual sights of goal were rare with Shilton largely untested for most of the evening.

HSV, having pulled off a magnificent second-leg comeback against Madrid in the other semi-final, headed into the final as the sharper of the two teams. Or at least in theory they should have.

Forest had a 16-day gap between their last domestic game of the season and the 1980 European Cup Final, while for the West German champions it was a game that sat in between their last two Bundesliga fixtures, during a run-in in which they were locked in a battle with Bayern Munich for the title.

Four days before the final, HSV lost narrowly at Bayer Leverkusen, a result that handed Bayern the simple task of avoiding defeat on the final day of the season to reclaim the title for the first time in six years. At least subconsciously, Branko Zebec's side will have headed to Madrid psychologically wounded.

Having avoided facing Madrid at the Santiago Bernabéu, it had been with a sigh of relief that Forest had welcomed going up against HSV. While under no illusions that the soon to be deposed Bundesliga champions would be opponents of substance, Madrid's second-leg capitulation in the semi-final had at least drawn the sting from what would have been a massively partisan atmosphere for a team playing a European Cup Final on home soil.

Both teams had injury and absence issues going into the final. Forest were without Francis, who had succumbed to a badly timed Achilles tendon injury which also deprived him of the chance to take a place in the England squad for the European Championship finals. In reply, HSV's top scorer Horst Hrubesch was carrying an ankle injury that meant Zebec would only name him among his substitutes.

Adding to Forest's attacking woes, Bowles had refused to join Clough's squad, which had set up camp on Majorca prior to the game. The former England international had gone AWOL before, during a career blessed with the most outrageous of talents but not the focus and dedication to match.

Rather than call up an extra player, Clough opted to name just four substitutes, and it also meant that 18-year-old Gary Mills was drafted into the starting line-up to operate as an extra midfielder.

It was with pragmatism hanging densely in the air that Forest took to the final. They might have earned the same outcome, with the same scoreline as 12 months earlier against Malmö in Munich, but Clough's route to European Cup symmetry against HSV was quite different to what had transpired against Bob Houghton's team.

All the early possession belonged to HSV, who were technically superior and intelligent in their movement on and off the ball. With Forest's response being a five-man midfield, Clough's side were largely encamped within their own half for the first 20 minutes.

Forest were relaxed in their approach to the game while HSV were coiled like a tightly wound spring. The psychological impact of Robertson cutting in from the left to open the scoring against the run of play would have been seismic. It had been the first time in the game that Forest had retained any prolonged possession of the ball.

Felix Magath had not long since tested the resolve of a niggling calf problem that Shilton was carrying when forcing him into what would be the first of four vital saves. It had been an injury scare that had prompted the Forest goalkeeper to seek medical opinion on the afternoon of the game.

Uncompromising in their defending when they felt it necessary, Burns and Anderson both could have picked up early yellow cards due to their robust dealings with the HSV attack. Keegan, at the focal point in the absence of Hrubesch, felt the full weight of this approach, and at times opted for gamesmanship in obtaining free kicks around the edge of the penalty area, much to the ire of Bowyer in particular.

Within minutes of Forest taking the lead, HSV could have been level. After a panicked penalty box scramble Willi Reimann had the ball in the Forest net, but he was rightly adjudged to be offside. It was testament to the composure of their back line that none of the Forest defenders had been reluctant to step up to spring the offside trap, when natural reactions might have been to stay entrenched.

Before the interval, Forest had been forced into more desperate defending. Burns had been brandished a yellow card for a foul on Keegan and the impressive Jürgen Milewski had extended Shilton. As the first half came towards its end, however, Forest had become far more comfortable within their surroundings.

Zebec threw on Hrubesch for the beginning of the second half. Tall, barrel-chested and imposing, he was an identikit of John Toshack, thus the perfect foil for Keegan and wouldn't blink at the physical approaches of Burns and Lloyd. The problem was that in bringing a partly fit player on as a substitute when you are chasing a game essentially means you are operating with ten and a half players.

Hrubesch would arguably have been better off starting, to try and make the breakthrough, before being withdrawn early. This was a player who would go on to score the winning goal in the 1980 European Championship Final for West Germany and later captain HSV to success in the 1983 European Cup Final. His importance to HSV's hopes against Forest cannot be understated.

It was HSV who forced the pressure during the second half. Magath had a goalbound effort blocked by Lloyd, Manfred Kaltz hit the post, Peter Nogly provoked the best of Shilton, while the Forest goalkeeper overcame some late nerves to keep his sheet a clean one.

As the game meandered into its last 20 minutes, Forest started to retain possession for longer periods than at any other stage of proceedings, apart from the goal that ultimately decided the outcome. This coincided with the introduction of the veteran John O'Hare for Mills, which offered Birtles a little bit of respite at times. This was the role that Bowles would have likely been handed had he been present in Madrid.

Birtles' efforts had been tireless, foraging alone for almost the entirety of the game, and in the latter stages he was almost goading the HSV defence with his defiance. O'Neill also found himself available to alleviate the pressure occasionally and he drew the frustration of Nogly repetitively.

A yellow card went Nogly's way, and he was later fortunate to avoid a red. The game all but ended with Keegan chasing after the ball in his own team's corner. It had not been aesthetically pleasing, but it had undeniably been a tactical masterclass in containment from Clough and Taylor.

Two successive European Cups was a phenomenal achievement for a team that had only just risen from the Second Division, but as abruptly as they had announced their spectacular arrival in the tournament Forest made their exit.

In the 1980/81 first round, just as Liverpool had done in 1978/79 after their back-to-back European Cup successes, Forest were bundled out without ceremony. This time, CSKA Sofia were the culprits.

After the first leg in Bulgaria, Clough's team returned home with a 1-0 defeat that could have been far worse. Shilton had been in fine form, Lloyd had been in a stubborn frame of mind, while a belligerent referee was not in the mood to award the two penalties that CSKA had strongly felt they were entitled to.

Forest had escaped calamity, and the warnings that should have been heeded didn't seem to be. The first-leg scoreline was repeated at the City Ground and the European champions were out, beaten by the better team, on an evening when still without the services of Francis, and with their new signing Ian Wallace trying to find his feet, Clough's side were sadly lacking in creativity.

It was a noticeably clear end of an era for Forest and within weeks Birtles was a Manchester United player, where after two years of toil he would return to the City Ground, upon which he found a markedly different club despite the comforting and familiar surroundings.

Taylor retired at the end of the 1981/82 season, only to be coaxed the following season back to the Baseball Ground, and back into the employment of Derby. He and Clough were soon to fall out over Taylor's recruitment of Robertson.

It was to be a feud that was never resolved, and when Taylor died unexpectedly in 1990, Clough was devastated at not only the loss of his former partner but also that their bond was never repaired. It was a regret that Clough took to his own grave when he died in 2004.

Liverpool went on to reclaim the European Cup at the end of the 1980/81 season, but while Forest's flame was being extinguished, the Midlands was to prove the location of another rise in power. This time it came from the west and Villa Park.

First Division champions in 1980/81, Villa's consistency had held firm when going toe to toe with Bobby Robson's Ipswich Town for the league title. In a far too often downplayed success for Ron Saunders' team, the Portman Road outfit had been caught within the maelstrom of a chase for a treble.

While Robson's side would go all the way in the UEFA Cup, they were also beaten in the FA Cup semi-final. A flood of fixtures for the Suffolk club ensued and they fell short in the title race. The concept of Ipswich having fought on three fronts in 1980/81 has regularly been used as a stick with which to beat Villa's success in the league.

It's a disingenuous argument as while some league titles are won by a singularly dominant team, there are others that are won within a campaign where more than one team would have been worthy champions. The 1980/81 campaign just so happened to fall into the latter category.

As much as their title success had come as a surprise to most people, Saunders' Villa had been a compelling entity for many seasons. Picking up the manager's job at Villa Park in the summer of 1974, by the end of his first term in charge he had led the club not only back into the First Division but also to League Cup glory.

Two years later, harnessing the goals of Andy Gray and Brian Little, another League Cup was won in style, yet the following three seasons were beset by the type of inconsistencies that meant nobody saw their championship coming.

Had Villa been title challengers on the back of a fine 1976/77 season it would have been no shock whatsoever, but they were viewed as a quite different prospect in the summer of 1980 just as Forest were basking in the glow of their second European Cup success.

Despite the inconsistencies of the three seasons prior to winning the title, many of the components for the club's greatest glory were in place during this time. Most of them had been accumulated since their 1977 League Cup Final success, while the arrival of Peter Withe in May 1980 from Newcastle was to prove the catalyst for what was to soon escalate.

What was startling about the rise of Villa at the beginning of the 1980s was just how much it defied logic. Amid boardroom turmoil in 1979/80, the club had parted with what was effectively over £3.5m of talent. The sales of Gray, John Gregory, John Deehan, John Gidman, Frank Carrodus, and Joe Ward had accrued close to the £3m mark at a time when that represented double the British transfer record fee. Added to this, Saunders devastatingly lost Little to premature retirement.

Little had been an outstanding talent, breaking into the Villa first team before his 18th birthday and helping the club rise from Third Division to the top tier, winning an England cap and two League Cups. Only 26 when forced to call time on his career due to a persistent knee problem, not long beforehand he had almost moved to Villa's local rivals, Birmingham City, for a reputed £600,000, only for the transfer to fall through, due to failing the medical for reasons unrelated to the eventual injury that caused his retirement.

It meant that the 1980/81 Aston Villa should have been a dysfunctional entity, mixing youth products with responsibly sourced new or relatively recent arrivals. Going into their title-winning campaign Saunders did not spend a further penny beyond the £500,000 on Withe, which had effectively been paid out as the previous season ended.

Crucially, at the centre of this rehashed Villa team was the metronomic Dennis Mortimer, a midfielder and captain of utter dependability and immense purpose, who was one of the finest players ever to evade an England cap. Alongside him sat the skilled visionary and combative Gordon Cowans, with the added assistance of Des Bremner, who offered speed and tenacity, along with no shortage in ability of joining or instigating attacks.

They made a triumvirate that offered a balanced conduit between defence and attack and gave the outrageously gifted Tony Morley all the freedom in the world to effectively make the partnership of Withe and the talented Gary Shaw a front three when in full flow. Together, Withe, Shaw, and Morley scored 53 of their team's 72 league goals in 1980/81.

In goal was the reliable Jimmy Rimmer, a European Cup winner with Manchester United in 1968 as an unused substitute, the marshal of a solid back four of Kenny Swain, Gary Williams, Ken McNaught, and Allan Evans.

Incredibly, Villa used just 14 players during their title-winning campaign, with the supporting acts being supplied by Eamonn Deacy, Colin Gibson, and David Geddis.

In the summer of 1981, Coventry City midfielder Andy Blair was the only recruit to command a transfer fee, and he would remain on the periphery of the side for most of the season, struggling not only to break the trio of Mortimer, Cowans, and Bremner but even to usurp Gibson from the role of the primary back-up.

The domestic harmony of 1980/81 would evaporate the following season, both on and off the pitch, as Villa limped through the defence of their championship to finish in a disappointing 11th position, while their involvement in the FA Cup ended in the fifth round and the League Cup at the quarter-final.

A first European Cup campaign would offer comfort, however, and Valur of Iceland were easily overcome 7-0 on aggregate in the first round.

It was only Villa's third voyage into European competition. Their debut effort had ended at the first hurdle of the 1975/76 UEFA Cup, although two years later they fared far better when in the same tournament they were narrowly ejected by Johan Cruyff and Barcelona in the quarter-final.

As if to demonstrate Villa's mood swings of 1981/82, in the second round, Saunders' side travelled to East Berlin for the first leg, where they would win against Dynamo, only to struggle at home in the second leg.

Taking the ball on the volley and dispatching it into the bottom-right corner, Morley had benefited from a headed clearance that dropped invitingly for him just inside the penalty area. It had been a wonderful finish at the end of a move that flowed through Mortimer, Shaw, and Bremner and a crucial away goal had been gained within five minutes of the start.

An incensed Dynamo went into all-out attack mode and Rimmer had to be alert to the dangers posed. Just as against Forest 18 months earlier, Netz provided much of the creativity for the East Germans and he could have levelled the scores before the break, as could Bernd Schulz with a venomous effort that the Villa keeper did well to stop. Incessant in spells, even the Dynamo defence were stepping up as both Norbert Trieloff and Michael Noack came close.

Villa themselves absorbed the pressure and would spring on the counter-attack. Dynamo, meanwhile, were the team with the balancing act to perfect as although there was a bold method at play, they were also vulnerable to the speed and skill of Morley and Shaw.

Riediger should have scored when ploughing through a gap that was offered by Evans and Williams, while Brendan Ormsby did exceptionally well to stop the same player forcing the ball in almost on the goal line. Just as Villa were able to harbour thoughts of making it to the interval unscathed, Ralf Sträßer hit the post.

It was only to be a temporary reprieve and five minutes into the second half, Riediger was at the back post to head in the equaliser past a helpless Rimmer. A Sträßer free kick swung in from the left beat the Villa defence and there was Dynamo's most potent weapon to meet it.

It could have then all gone horribly wrong for Villa. By now into the second half of October, Saunders' team had only just secured their first home win of the season, and the psychology of being the defending First Division champions was resting heavily on the collective mind. Behind the Berlin Wall, this was the evening where Villa had the choice of carrying that poor domestic form into Europe or separating the two platforms and cocooning the European Cup as a joyous respite.

It was an inhospitable environment in which to make such a choice. The Friedrich-Ludwig-Jahn-Sportpark sat so uncomfortably close to the Berlin Wall that border guards were able to see into the stadium from an ominous nearby tower. More of an unsettling atmosphere than a hostile one, it was as if the home support had had to obtain state approval to attend.

In the 81st minute the game looked to have turned Dynamo's way when Villa substitute Ivor Linton was adjudged to have brought down Netz. Certainly caught napping, Linton was slow to respond to the threat, but did seem to redeem himself with a well-timed tackle rather than the foul he was accused of.

Up stepped Arthur Ullrich, who sent Rimmer the wrong way only to see the ball rebound off the right-hand post and straight towards the Villa goalkeeper, who instinctively stuck out his left foot. The ball hit the studs of his boot, rolling back into the direction of the penalty taker, who was now loitering close to the six-yard line.

Rimmer, back to his feet in a flash, made himself as big and imposing as possible, not an easy thing to do when he was a rarity at under six feet tall. As Ullrich made contact with the ball again he was foiled once more by the former England international, as he somehow managed to stick out his left leg, deflecting it up and over the crossbar.

It was utterly pivotal and within four minutes Villa had the lead again, springing to counter from a Dynamo corner. Withe, back in his own penalty area helping with the late rearguard action, started the move with a powerful clearing header that the onrushing Shaw and Roland Jüngling looked set to contest.

Shaw and the Dynamo substitute totally misread the bounce of the ball, however, reaching the landing spot half a second too late only to see it loop over their heads and into the path of the outrushing Morley, who after evading one desperate challenge was away to run half the length of the pitch before coolly dispatching his shot beneath the advancing Rudwaleit.

Rapturously celebrated both on the pitch and on the terraces by a healthy travelling contingent of Villa supporters, and perhaps a few locals to have found a way through the turnstiles too, it was a magnificent result for Saunders and his team.

Two weeks later, Villa's nerves were tested to the limit. Home form was still proving problematic and four days before the visit of Dynamo, Saunders' side had seen a 13-game unbeaten run come to an end at Villa Park against their title rivals from the previous season, Ipswich. Indecisive in defence and blunt in attack against Bobby Robson's team, Villa could have been forgiven had they took a sense of foreboding into the visit of Dynamo.

Villa were defeated 1-0 on the night by Dynamo, the same scoreline that the East Germans had won by at the City Ground, against Nottingham Forest, yet it was enough to see Saunders' side through to the quarter-final on the away goals rule.

With the outcome on a knife-edge to the final whistle, there was this time more to Villa's loss than the result suggests. Going all out for goals, they were denied by a succession of outstanding saves from Rudwaleit, and on the occasions that the 6ft 7in goalkeeper was beaten, there was a team-mate on the goal line perfectly positioned to make the block.

Morley was in inspired form down the left, and with Withe showing his often-underappreciated ability with the ball at his feet, on any other night Villa probably would have won with ease. Yet Dynamo were full of danger themselves, especially after taking a 14th-minute lead when Terletzki drove a low and powerfully struck effort through a forest of legs and beneath a shocked Rimmer after the ball was laid off to him by Schulz.

Still Villa came with wave after wave of attacks but with Dynamo determined in defence and incisive in their breaks, it made for a fascinating battle. Joining Morley and Withe on the front foot, Shaw and Cowans also made their presence felt, and it was Dirk Schlegel who performed the first goal-line clearance, from Williams.

On it continued in this inexhaustible theme. A disallowed goal here, the frame of the goal hit there. Rudwaleit frustrated Morley when stretching his left foot to a goalbound effort and then also made an incredulous stop from Cowans. Added to this barrage, there was an excellent save from a 30-yard drive by the Villa winger.

In shades of Jan Tomaszewski and Poland against England in 1973, Rudwaleit and Dynamo seemed to defy all the physics of football to keep themselves a clean sheet. The most ridiculous stop of the collection was an instinctive double goal-line clearance by Trieloff, from both Withe and Cowans.

At the other end, late in the game, Dynamo almost snatched the quarter-final berth, firstly when Rimmer pushed a venomous Riediger effort on to his left-hand post and then denied the same player when hooking away the last chance of the evening.

After a magnificently entertaining game, both sides deserved huge credit for their approach. For Villa's players, when they made their exit from the pitch, they could never have imagined just how much the landscape of not only their club but football across the second city would have altered by the time they took to the field for the last eight four months later.

By the time Villa headed to the heavily disputed city of Simferopol, which sits provocatively upon the Ukrainian and Russian border, Saunders was no longer their manager. Villa were going into the first leg of the quarter-final away to the dangerous Dynamo Kyiv but Saunders was the manager of Birmingham instead.

Stubbornly in disagreement with the Villa board of directors over funds for restrengthening his squad, and alterations to his contract, Saunders had resigned during an explosive telephone conversation with his chairman, Ron Bendall.

Saunders' success in landing Villa their first league title in 71 years, alongside what he had already achieved, had led to Manchester United seeking out his services in the summer of 1981, when they were in search for a replacement for Dave Sexton.

Flattered but with every intent upon seeing out his career at Villa Park, Saunders turned down the opportunity, just as he had knocked back an approach from Leeds United three years earlier.

With an eye on regenerating his team while still champions, despite their continued involvement in the European Cup and still being in the FA Cup, Saunders had been alarmed by the poor nature of Villa's defence of their First Division title. Sat in 15th fresh off the back of a 4-1 defeat at Old Trafford, he had wanted to act in the transfer market in order to make another run at glory in 1982/83.

Viewing things very differently, the Villa chairman and his board of directors were of the mind that belts needed tightening rather than loosening. From their perspective, with a wage bill in excess of £1m a season already, the last need of the club was to send that figure soaring upward.

This clearly jarred with a manager who two years earlier had effectively seen more than £3m of talent drained from his squad. Saunders must have wondered how much value the Villa hierarchy had attached to him winning the league title and delivering a European Cup quarter-final. Perhaps it had all been a glorious inconvenience.

His assistant, Tony Barton, was the man to fill the void. Twenty-four hours after the resignation of their manager, Villa's players put in a spirited performance in a 1-1 draw at home to a Southampton side who were one of a cluster of teams with designs on succeeding them as champions. Outbreaks of vocal discontent on the terraces were aimed in support of Saunders, while the head of the chairman was called for. The club's former supremo, Doug Ellis, was an interested observer of what would escalate into a power struggle that eventually saw him back into the ultimate position of power at Villa Park.

After being knocked out of the FA Cup at Tottenham Hotspur, although on a day when Villa's players again seemed up for the battle, the situation escalated with a supporters' action group formed and a petition for Saunders' reinstatement launched.

Within days, the mood had altered dramatically when Saunders was unveiled as the successor to the sacked Jim Smith at St Andrew's. Incredibly, the first game beyond his appointment at Villa's biggest rivals was the derby between the two clubs.

Saunders watched on from the stands and would not take charge of Birmingham until their next match. He saw Villa go away with a narrow victory, and with their travelling support having turned on their old manager. It was an electric footballing pantomime that galvanised Barton and Villa for the remainder of the campaign to come, inclusive of intimations from some observers that their players' upturn in effort was a product of Saunders no longer being at the club.

After a sad end to a glorious union, both the fortunes of Villa and Saunders would regress during the seasons ahead, but for now, at least in the short term, European Cup glory sat upon the horizon at Villa Park, while over at St Andrew's Birmingham would avoid relegation.

Eleven days beyond the drama and pantomime of the Birmingham derby, Villa made their trip to Simferopol, 350 miles south of Kyiv, for the first leg of the quarter-final, which had been moved there for the promise of milder weather. Barton's team had only been handed the news of the switch the week before the game.

Whether gamesmanship or pure commercial opportunism, even the time of the game was brought forward by two hours from its original kick-off time in order to satisfy the audience of the live televised coverage.

With the Soviet Top League campaign yet to begin, the legendary Valeriy Lobanovskyi took his team to Switzerland for a rapid series of friendlies to sharpen them up away from the studious and prying eyes of Barton, who instead had to do all of his research by getting hold of the most recent video tapes of Kyiv in action.

Classically going into the unknown to a degree, the Soviet Union would take eight Kyiv players to the 1982 World Cup, seven of whom were on duty for the first leg, including the iconic Oleg Blokhin. It meant that Villa were faced with the most difficult challenge that eastern Europe could offer a team from the west.

With a maturity beyond the remit of their previous European experiences, Villa contained and tested Kyiv in a manner that had largely been expected to be played out in reverse on the occasion of Kyiv's 70th game in European club competition. They had won the European Cup Winners' Cup in 1975, following that up by beating Bayern Munich in the European Super Cup a short few months later and going on to reach the semi-final of the European Cup in 1977.

Up against opponents of repute and achievement, the last thing Barton needed was to lose one of his central defenders on the morning of the game. Evans, carrying a shoulder injury, was ruled out after a fitness test, and rather than bring in one of the lesser experienced options, Bremner was asked to drop back to partner McNaught, with Blair brought in to cover in midfield.

The adjustments worked perfectly, apart from an early scare when Blokhin beat Bremner for pace and struck the Villa post. With Morley enjoying the freedom of the wings and Mortimer dominating midfield, both teams did no more than flirt with scoring due to Withe and Shaw being heavily man-marked, and Blokhin being inclined to go for goal rather than lay in his team-mates.

A disallowed Vadym Yevtushenko strike was as close as anyone came and losing Volodymyr Bezsonov to an early injury seemed to unsettle Lobanovskyi's side. All Villa were shy of was the away goal to ease any potential anxieties of conceding one themselves back at Villa Park a fortnight later.

For Barton, Evans was fit once again and in timely and imperious form, putting in a display that went a long way towards winning him a place in Jock Stein's Scotland squad for the 1982 World Cup, the former Celtic manager being an interested observer in Villa's directors' box. In comparison, Kyiv had to cope without Bezsonov and his absence told very quickly. Lobanovskyi also lost Buryak shortly before kick-off, a victim of the Villa Park surface.

On a heavily sanded pitch, Shaw opened the scoring after just five minutes, picking up a loose ball after Cowans had been blocked and powering his way to the left of goal from where he struck from an acute angle to embarrass Kyiv goalkeeper Viktor Chanov.

After days of rain and struggles to construct a cover for the pitch, there had been genuine fears that the game would not go ahead, but now it had there was only one likely winner as soon as Shaw made the early breakthrough.

After further early opportunities were squandered, Villa could easily have led 3-0 within half an hour, with Morley again the chief tormentor. Meanwhile Viktor Khlus could count himself lucky to remain on the pitch after he ploughed into a late challenge on Mortimer when already in possession of a yellow card.

Seemingly weathering the storm, Kyiv began to come out of their shell but before the break they were dealt a double blow as they lost another midfielder in the shape of Volodymyr Veremeyev, and then followed this by conceding a second goal. McNaught was the unlikely hero when he got up highest at the back post to get on the end of a Cowans corner.

There were no further goals in the second half, but there were chances. Cowans almost gifted Blokhin the opportunity to get his team back in the game while Shaw and Morley both missed when well positioned.

Villa saw themselves comfortably into the semi-final but at the expense of injury to Mortimer, who dislocated an elbow when landing awkwardly from a fair tackle.

With Liverpool having surprisingly been knocked out earlier in the day in Bulgaria against CSKA Sofia, amid much frustration and a horrendous error from Bruce Grobbelaar, the dismissal of Mark Lawrenson, and claims that one effort by Paisley's team had actually crossed the line, suddenly Villa were front and centre of English football's attempts to retain possession of the European Cup for a sixth successive season.

Pitted against the European pedigree of Anderlecht in the semi-final, with the first leg at home, Barton, by now five days beyond having been handed the manager's job on a permanent basis, had a full-strength side at his disposal, albeit one in which Mortimer could still be classed as being of the walking wounded.

Mortimer's midfield colleague, Bremner, had also picked up an injury against Kyiv, and was another who was only just returning to the team in time for what was being billed as the most important game in Villa's history.

Both in terms of the prestige of standing only one step away from the biggest club game in European football, and in hope of generating the type of funds that would slash into what were increasingly uncomfortable debts, this was an evening of massive significance for Villa.

This was an era before television money made a major impact upon English clubs. Shirt sponsorship was still in its infancy, and the prime source of financial prosperity was supplied by the supporters who clicked through the turnstiles, and benevolent local businessmen done good. During what were times of great hardship for the working classes, many of whom had flooded away from the game to be able to make ends meet at home, it was an intolerable situation for all clubs no matter their historical standing.

Anderlecht, deployed defensively by their coach Tomislav Ivić, set out to frustrate Villa. This they succeeded in doing for long stretches of the game, fielding a five-man back line and even omitting one of their most potent attackers, Willy Geurts, who would be unfortunate to miss out on a place in the Belgium squad at the upcoming World Cup in Spain.

Shackling Withe, and Shaw very effectively, Ivić's tactics centred around inviting Villa to push forward as much as they dared, from where Anderlecht would strike with speed on the break. In effect, however, facing the Dynamos of Berlin and Kyiv had been the perfect preparation for taking on the Belgian champions.

Conversely, Anderlecht had faced their own set of unenviable challenges to reach the last four. Widzew Łódź, Juventus and Red Star Belgrade had all been dispensed with convincingly and, if anything, Ivić, or at least his players, might have felt a little overconfident in facing Villa, when in the other semi-final sat Bayern Munich and Liverpool's conquerors, CSKA.

With Villa Park bouncing, Shaw missed an early opportunity to open the scoring when the Anderlecht goalkeeper Jacques Munaron found the ball to be marginally out of reach as he attempted to beat the Villa striker to it around eight yards from goal. It was an ambitious attempt to clear the danger and Shaw looped a header which just dropped the wrong side of the crossbar, and on to the roof of the netting.

Morley should then have done better when Bremner set him free on the left, only to be wasteful with the chance. In a game of cat and mouse, Juan Lozano struck a volley from just outside the penalty area that Rimmer did well to deal with as it bobbled along the unpredictable surface.

Next, Mortimer tested Munaron with an excellent dipping effort before McNaught gifted Anderlecht their best opportunity of the evening when caught in possession in the centre circle, from where the visitors broke swiftly into a four on one situation. Evans did his best to shepherd Franky Vercauteren into being the only option for the pass, in turn giving Rimmer a 50/50 chance to make the save.

Rimmer did just that as Vercauteren poked the ball towards goal with an awkward shot with the outside of his left foot, and Villa breathed a sigh of relief. Apart from this potentially damaging punch to the gut, the game so far had been one of bobbing and weaving, of landing exploratory jabs rather than swinging haymakers.

Unsurprisingly, it was Morley who finally made the breakthrough in the 28th minute when latching on to the ball after some wonderful link play down the left between Cowans and Shaw. After a magnificent through ball from the former, the Villa number 11 was clinical in mood as he advanced into the Anderlecht penalty area, sending his shot across the face of Munaron and in off his left-hand post.

An explosion of sound flooded Villa Park, and Cowans did well to restrain Morley's celebrations as at one point he was seemingly carried across the turf and sand by the goalscorer. It was not to be the catalyst for more goals, however.

Ivić's tactics remained steadfast throughout the second half with defensive strangulation, offset by the occasional breakaway. Yet an away goal was not sought at the risk of conceding again.

Ivić had proved before that he had a penchant for cautious football and was a man very much cut in the cloth of the pragmatist. Even at Ajax, an environment steeped in expansive football, he took them to the 1976/77 Eredivisie title by playing the percentages and via an average of goals per game set at under two. In a notoriously high-scoring league, PSV Eindhoven had won it the previous season with 27 more goals.

With Barton having made Villa's defence harder to penetrate, they headed to Brussels on the back of four clean sheets, while Anderlecht had contrived to lose four of their last five games. The goalless draw that unfolded should have come as a surprise to nobody.

Yet this was an Anderlecht line-up that suggested they were capable of goals, with Ivić recalling Geurts, fresh off the back of him throwing in a transfer request. For added attacking emphasis, there was also a place in the team for the Danish international striker Kenneth Brylle. Meanwhile, Wim Hofkens was back after suspension to bolster the midfield.

There were no injury problems for Barton, and apart from Bremner recovering from a neck issue sustained a few days earlier during an afternoon nap on his own sofa, the biggest concern for Villa were the crowd disturbances at the Stade Émile Versé that erupted an hour before kick-off.

With extraordinarily little in the way of police presence in the stadium until 20 minutes prior to the start of the game, it made for a foreboding preview of the lack of control and the tragedy to come three years later in the very same city.

The trouble was centred behind the end that Rimmer was defending in the first half, with initial scuffles swiftly escalating during the game, which were responded to by the enthusiastic baton charges of the local riot police.

Before long, a spectator had been dragged off the terraces and on to the pitch, from where a cluster of officers had attempted to spirit him away along the touchline, only to drop him then seemingly trample on him. While this was occurring, Rimmer was behind his netting, trying to diffuse the violent situation. With reinforcements called upon, the game was then delayed for seven minutes until a modicum of sanity could prevail. Yet once proceedings resumed, so did the fighting too.

Whether dictated by events off the pitch, on it matters were infinitely more sedate as Villa shepherded the game through

90 goalless and comfortingly unremarkable minutes to claim their place in the 1982 European Cup Final.

An incensed Anderlecht opted for the opportunism of lodging an appeal to UEFA in a bid to expel Villa from the final, covering the unlikely event of this demand working with a lesser appeal for the second leg to be replayed. Kept waiting on news of their punishment for nine days, Villa were eventually fined £14,500 and ordered to play their next home European tie behind closed doors.

While Anderlecht had a valid point that they had been on the attack when the pitch was invaded, Villa's riposte had been that none of those arrested in Brussels had been a member of the official travelling party, and that Anderlecht's poor ticketing, policing, and stewarding had been heavily responsible for the outbreak of violence. In terms of English supporters on their European travels, it was an increasingly familiar piece of football bureaucratic pass the parcel.

As April turned to May, Villa still had five league games to navigate. Having won two, drawn one and lost two, as far as their European Cup Final opponents were concerned, Bayern Munich will have viewed Barton's side as something of a riddle.

Bayern's general manager, the iconic Uli Hoeneß, had been an interested observer when in the Villa Park crowd to watch Barton's side ease to a 3-0 victory over an understrength Swansea City, on the Friday evening prior to the final.

Five days prior to the big night, only Shaw was missing from what would be the starting line-up in Rotterdam. Maybe beginning to feel the weight of the occasion that lay beyond the Swansea game, Villa corrected themselves from an unconvincing start in which Bob Latchford twice hit the post for John Toshack's side. They were eventually overpowered by goals from Morley, Bremner, and Withe, but had it not been for Swansea's 19-year-old goalkeeper Chris Sander then Villa might have threatened double figures.

Exactly what Hoeneß made of it all is open to debate as Villa offered him a microcosm that was akin to something of a visual tapas of the good, the bad, and the ugly of what had been the defence of their First Division title.

Dethroned as Bundesliga champions, Bayern had at least put up a stronger defence of their league title than Villa had. Also on the plus side, Pál Csernai's team had prevailed in winning the DFB-Pokal, thus ensuring a minimum of Cup Winners' Cup football for the following season.

For Villa it was a case of win or bust. Not only did the European Cup represent their only chance of a silver-lined end to their troubled campaign, but it was also their only route back into European competition for 1982/83.

After just nine minutes Villa's hopes had taken a massive blow when Rimmer's game came to a premature end. Having aggravated a persistent shoulder injury in the build-up to the final, he had added to the discomfort by injuring his neck when heading a ball in training. Thrust into the heat of battle was the inexperienced former Chelmsford City goalkeeper, Nigel Spink.

With little in the way of thinking time, Spink slotted in seamlessly. Although Villa's winning goal would not materialise until midway through the second half, it was arguably between the departure of Rimmer and half-time that the 1982 European Cup Final was won and lost.

Bayern, having set out to test the nerve and capabilities of Villa's reserve goalkeeper, had found themselves hitting their head against a brick wall. Both Bernd Dürnberger and Karl-Heinz Rummenigge cut a ruthless swathe past Swain and McNaught when hammering through down the Bayern left to sting the hands of Spink.

Soon after, a collective sigh of Villa relief was exhaled when a Rummenigge bicycle kick flashed past Spink's left-hand post after wonderful work on the right by the legendary Paul Breitner. In response, Morley was regularly making Wolfgang Dremmler sweat down the Villa left in a bid to relieve the pressure.

In a fascinating game of attack vs defence, Dieter Hoeneß was another threat to the resolute Villa back line, while Klaus Augenthaler was always eager to step forward from his sweeper duties in order to join the raids.

With dangers approaching from a myriad of directions, this was a free-flowing and free-scoring Bayern side who had scored 20 goals on route to De Kuip when accounting for the scalps of Östers, Benfica, Universitatea Craiova, and CSKA.

Conversely, beyond the seven goals Villa had put past Valur in the first round, they had scored only five further times across the span of the next six games to reach the final. This was, however, offset by the fact that when they arrived to face Bayern, it was off the back of four successive European Cup clean sheets, all accumulated under Barton's reign. The new manager's keen eye for detail and intense preparation cannot be undersold.

By the time Rummenigge saw an effort deflected wide for a corner that his team were given no opportunity to take, there was a clear sense of Bavarian frustration in the air. Still, when Csernai sent his team out for the second half, he could do no more than implore them to continue with what they had been doing in the first 45. A goal would surely come.

After the restart, Augenthaler was the first to stride into a dangerous position. Allowed to plough forward, after evading the lunge of Bremner he went unchallenged into the Villa penalty area thanks to an untimely slip from Evans. Once there, he slashed his shot harmlessly across goal and out for a goal kick when Hoeneß had been well positioned for a pass, or alternatively Spink was there to be shot at.

It was largely one-way traffic and seemingly only a matter of time before Bayern would breach the Villa barricades. Augenthaler was again the key to a move which ended with Dürnberger forcing Spink into a save low to his right.

All the time, however, the stubbornness of Villa's unlikely hero was growing by the minute, and on the one occasion when he was beaten by the ball, Augenthaler's brilliantly directed header was cleared off the line by Swain.

Spink made another fine save when claiming the ball at the second attempt after Hoeneß tried to prod it home during another excellent Bayern attack. By now, a lesser team than Villa would have been 4-0 down.

As the Bayern chances came and went, the more the likelihood of a Villa sucker punch increased. The final essentially condensed itself into a 30-minute game of football and Morley sent out a warning with a shot from distance that went high and wide.

It was not that Morley's effort was even remotely close to the target, it was more the symbolism in which Villa were reminding Bayern that at 0-0, they were still very much a part of the reckoning.

Then came the moment. Mortimer, starting the move, fed the ball to Shaw, who ignored the advancing Williams down the left, instead evading his marker Dremmler to play in Morley in the left-hand channel. The Ormskirk-born magician twisted and turned Hans Weiner before rolling the ball into the possession of the criminally unmarked Withe. From five yards, the former Forest man scored the only goal of the game, possibly off his shin or maybe off his ankle, but certainly off the inside of the post. With incredulous emotion on the pitch from their players, Villa's supporters in De Kuip were delirious.

A stunned Bayern began to unravel. Villa, rather than opting to put everyone behind the ball, sought out more possession, and pressed their opponents for more mistakes. Cowans tested Manfred Müller from distance.

Still Bayern remained a threat, however, and never more so than when Hoeneß had the ball in the Villa net only to be adjudged as offside. It was a borderline decision that on one camera angle looked the correct call and on another was altogether less convincing. The biggest help to Barton's players was that the linesman was perfectly positioned to make his decision.

With Bayern's spirit and energy draining during each passing minute, the West Germans had travelled the distance from a team who looked likely to score every time they ventured forward to one who would not have scored had they played another 90 minutes.

Villa saw themselves over the line in relative comfort for a success that is entirely comparable to that of Forest's against HSV in the 1980 final. In many ways the successes of both Midlands clubs in the European Cup, and domestically, are inextricably linked.

While Forest's rise from Second Division middle-of-the-roaders to double champions of Europe in just four seasons is quite rightly celebrated and respected by the wider breadth of football as an achievement that will never likely happen again, Villa's path from Third Division football to European Cup winners within a decade often unfairly slips beneath the radar.

For Villa, it was a truly incredible achievement to climb that arduous European Cup-winning mountain with a team pieced together to win the First Division title, off the back of an exodus of key players, and then to shake off the blow of their manager resigning and resurfacing at bitter cross-city rivals.

Having overcome Beşiktaş behind closed doors, and then the future European Cup semi-finalists Dinamo Bucharest, Villa's defence of their European Cup ended in the quarter-final in 1982/83 against Juventus, a team under Giovanni Trapattoni who were at the peak of their powers and basking in a first-season glow of their new number ten, Michel Platini. Liverpool aside, they were the one team everybody wanted to avoid.

Solace was found, however, in defeating Barcelona in the European Super Cup, yet this was the end of the road for not only Villa and Forest in the European Cup but the Midlands in its entirety. It was the end of a stunning rise in prominence that stretched for five seasons, three of which ended with success.

It was a rich era in which the Midlands had usurped London as English football's alternative power base to the north-west and then made its imprint on the European Cup too, something that would always be beyond the hopes and dreams of the capital city.

11

With or Without Keegan

STUNG BY the loss of the 1980 European Cup Final, a pain that was accompanied by the departure of Kevin Keegan the very same summer, it would have been completely understandable had Hamburger SV's European Cup aspirations ended there and then.

Other clubs of purpose had flirted with European Cup glory only to regress once the trophy had been picked up by another team. In the previous decade alone, Panathinaikos, Atlético Madrid, Leeds United, AS Saint-Étienne, Borussia Mönchengladbach, Club Brugge and Malmö FF had all reached a final having neither won nor contested the showpiece occasion before.

Not one of them returned to a second final, although Atlético did contest Champions League Finals in 2014 and 2016. HSV did reach another European Cup Final, though, and against the odds they won it. Beaten as favourites in 1980 by Brian Clough's Nottingham Forest, HSV prevailed as underdogs three years later in Athens against a star-studded Juventus, whose pre-match entitlement to the prize was utter and complete.

HSV's two finals were all about the expected outcomes being turned on their heads. During their 1980 run they had defeated Liverpool's convincing vanquishers, the iconic Dinamo Tbilisi, even winning the away leg in Georgia where Bob Paisley's First Division champions had been ruthlessly picked apart by the frightening speed and skill of Vladimir Gutsaev, Ramaz Shengelia, and Aleksandre Chivadze. Tbilisi would go on to win the European Cup Winners' Cup the following season, to validate the danger that they unequivocally were.

Holding off the stirring fightback of Hajduk Split in the quarter-final, where HSV's 3-0 aggregate lead was levelled with four minutes remaining of the second leg only for them to sneak through on the away goals rule, Branko Zebec's side destroyed Vujadin Boškov's Real Madrid in the second leg of the semi-final at the Volksparkstadion, in a meeting of Serb and Croat footballing minds.

Madrid had won the first leg 2-0, setting themselves up nicely to strike through to a final that was being played at their own stadium. Yet the return game was to torment Boškov and his players, who swiftly hit the self-destruct button from the very moment they gave away an entirely needless penalty within ten minutes, which was converted by Manfred Kaltz.

With their aggregate lead wiped out seven minutes later when Horst Hrubesch powered home a diving header to make it 2-0, Madrid had gifted HSV all the space they could possibly want down the right and in the penalty area for the goalscorer to swoop. It was a reckless and careless way to throw a hard-earned advantage away.

Even when HSV returned the compliment, handing Laurie Cunningham an away goal on the half-hour, before the interval had arrived Kaltz and Hrubesch had scored another goal apiece, the former from distance and the latter another towering header. Caspar Memering added a fifth in the 90th minute.

It was this determined, skilled, and balanced side that made HSV the favourites to win the 1980 final, and it defied footballing gravity that they did not do so in a game that was set up to be Kevin Keegan's symmetrical parting gift, to match the way he departed Liverpool in 1977.

Seasoned campaigners in Europe, HSV had been European Cup semi-finalists as far back as 1960/61, three seasons before the launch of the Bundesliga, during a time when West German club football was still on at least a notional amateur footing. Beaten by Milan in the 1968 Cup Winners' Cup Final, HSV were winners of the tournament in 1977, a year after a run to the semi-finals of the UEFA Cup.

They were Bundesliga champions again in 1981/82 and were also beaten in the UEFA Cup Final. Just as two years earlier, they had gone into a major European final as the favourites only to see it all go so wrong, this time against a youthful Sven-Göran Eriksson's IFK Göteborg.

In an era of pleasure and pain, by the time the 1983 European Cup Final rolled into view, HSV were locked within a closely fought duel with Werder Bremen for the defence of their Bundesliga title with two games to go.

In comparison, while the latter stages of the Coppa Italia were still to be played out, Juventus's Serie A season had ended with them as runners-up to Roma ten days before the game in Athens. With Italy's domestic cup competition something of an afterthought, all of Giovanni Trapattoni's focus was locked upon breaking the European Cup curse blighting I Bianconeri.

With Zebec long gone, the man at the helm of HSV's rise to a second final was Austrian Ernst Happel, who had taken Feyenoord to glory in 1970 plus Club Brugge to the 1978 final, and also the 1976 UEFA Cup Final.

In an unlikely combination, Happel and the HSV general manager Günter Netzer harvested the most successful era of the club. Netzer's move into the powerful position at HSV was probably as much a shock to him as it was to the wider span of football. Notoriously anti-authoritarian, often as explosive off the pitch as he was on it, the irony of the former Mönchengladbach legend becoming part of the mechanics and administration arm of the game would not have been lost on figures such as Helmut Schön and Hennes Weisweiler, his national and club managers, who struggled to balance the skill and the mentality of Netzer the player.

Yet Netzer the general manager proved to be as visionary off the pitch as he was on it. Under his direction the Zebec and Keegan years, which delivered a Bundesliga title and a European Cup Final, were eclipsed by the Happel years which went one step further in winning the biggest prize of all to sit alongside back-to-back Bundesliga titles.

Between 1978/79 and 1983/84, HSV never finished outside the top two in the Bundesliga. This was the eye of the storm, the greatest era throughout the entire history of the club. On the back of such a basic outline of their late 1970s and early 1980s appetite for success, it seems odd to suggest that anybody should have viewed them to be convenient fall guys to the coronation of Juventus. Except that is exactly how Happel's HSV were viewed.

With Bayern Munich remaining the ominous shadow which cast itself across the Bundesliga, while there was a degree of overlap, HSV essentially picked up the baton as the Bavarians' primary thorn in the side from Mönchengladbach, with honourable mentions to 1. FC Köln and VfB Stuttgart.

Having supplied four members of Jupp Derwall's squad for the 1982 World Cup finals, three of HSV's 1983 European Cup Final line-up would go to Mexico in 1986 with Franz Beckenbauer, who himself was a HSV player during the twilight of his playing career. It was an association that ended with a bit-part role in their 1981/82 Bundesliga success, before he headed back to New York for a second spell at the Cosmos.

It was under all of this positivity that HSV really should have been taken far more seriously than they were by the watching world. Yet Juventus were Juventus, and at this time it was classed as a far bigger anomaly that the Turin giants had not won the European Cup than it was for Barcelona.

Trapattoni's line-up in Athens contained six World Cup-winning players in Dino Zoff, Gaetano Scirea, Claudio Gentile, Antonio Cabrini, Marco Tardelli, and Paolo Rossi.

This core of Enzo Bearzot's team from just a year earlier were complemented by the legendary Roberto Bettega, the dependable Sergio Brio, and Massimo Bonini, plus the not inconsiderable and imported talents of Michel Platini and Zbigniew Boniek.

It was a collective of footballing villains and artisans, those who broke the game and their opponents down into their simplest and most subjugated of forms, respectively, and then handed them to the freethinkers to turn into goals and trophies. At the helm stood Trapattoni, the master tactician, funded and supported by the Agnelli family. HSV were taking on an entire empire.

In a classic first-round clash of West Germany vs East Germany, HSV outwitted Dynamo Berlin, returning from behind the Wall with a valuable 1-1 draw before seeing out the job with a 2-0 victory back at the Volksparkstadion.

It was not as easy as the aggregate scoreline might indicate and HSV had played on the break in the first leg, with a powerful Jürgen Milewski run and finish cancelling out Hans Jürgen Riediger's opener. In the return it was HSV's pressing game that reaped the rewards, although the nerves were only eased thanks to Hrubesch heading home the second goal with just two minutes remaining.

Olympiacos then proved stubborn opponents in the first leg of the second round, restricting Happel's men to a narrow 1-0 lead to take into a second leg that was played out in front of over 75,000 hostile locals at the Olympic Stadium.

However, the story of the second leg was surprisingly that the Greek champions struggled with the weight of expectation rather than HSV struggling with the intimidation. Felix Magath silenced the Olympiacos supporters with a long-range effort midway through the first half before Hrubesch, Wolfgang Rolff, and the Danish international Lars Bastrup ran riot in the second period.

Victories picked off during a metronomic run between January 1982 and January 1983, within which HSV went unbeaten in the Bundesliga, meant that they were set up nicely for the quarter-final in March.

They were sent to Tbilisi to take on Dynamo Kyiv in another game moved in the name of milder weather, and after an arduous journey via Moscow, HSV's response was spectacular. A Bastrup hat-trick brushed the Ukrainians aside with an almost obscene ease; it was an empathic result that rendered HSV's 2-1 second-leg defeat on home soil inconsequential other than in terms of a mildly bruised ego.

It set up a magnificent brace of semi-final encounters with Real Sociedad, the first ending in a 1-1 draw at the rustic yet atmospheric Atotxa in San Sebastián on an evening when Rolff's wonderful looping header eluded the desperately back-pedalling Luis Arconada.

Agustín Gajate's equaliser might have initially seemed no more than a likely consolation, but what it instigated was an evening of unnecessary nervousness at the Volksparkstadion a fortnight later as a clearly superior HSV missed a succession of excellent chances to ease anxieties in a game that stalled at 0-0 until 15 minutes from time.

Although they were heading through on away goals as the scores stood, a towering Ditmar Jakobs header broke the deadlock when had the reactions of Arconada been slower the ball might well have been cleared off the goal line by Julio Olaizola.

Arconada got a hand to the ball, however, which was not strong enough to keep it out of his net but was strong enough to deflect it past the stooping Olaizola.

In a way, the goal did HSV no favours, as all it did was provoke a swift Sociedad response which took the tie to the brink of extra time when José Diego powered the ball into Uli Stein's top-left corner in the 80th minute.

Up until that point, Sociedad had been heading down a series of frustrating dead ends in their attempts to find the goal they needed to send them through to the final, or at least to elongate the game to a further 30 minutes. Diego's strike kick-started a wild ride to the final whistle.

Within three minutes HSV had the lead again with a contentious Thomas von Heesen winner, which possessed at least a vague hint of offside. Yet within seconds of the restart their influential midfielder William Hartwig had picked up a second yellow card which meant he would be suspended for the final. It was just one component in an ill-tempered crescendo to the game.

Despite the excellent form Happel's side had shown throughout their run, suffering only one reversal, Juventus, themselves unbeaten on the road to Athens with Rossi and Platini sharing 11 their 19 goals on route to the final, were fully anticipated to be a bridge too far for HSV.

Impressively invaded by expectant Italian supporters, Athens was awash with black and white stripes, lending a Latin aura to the city in the days leading up to the final. The idea that this post-Keegan HSV could have the temerity to upset the apple cart was largely dismissed out of hand.

Yet there were parallels between the two teams. Neither had won the European Cup before, losing one final each, while both had won only one major continental honour – coming in the same year, 1977, when HSV lifted the Cup Winners' Cup and Juventus took the UEFA Cup. Both clubs also had players involved in the 1982 World Cup Final, although given the outcome of that game it was deemed that the 1983 European Cup Final would naturally follow suit.

All signposts led the watching world into believing that the European Cup would be heading to Turin rather than Hamburg. Juventus even had footballing romance on their side as both Zoff and Bettega were about to retire, projected to sign off by fulfilling the prophecy of turning I Bianconeri into the champions of Europe.

Subtly differing in formation yet both deploying a sweeper system, Happel and Trapattoni had to factor in a suspension each as to balance HSV's loss of Hartwig, Juventus were denied the services of the future Italian national coach Cesare Prandelli.

Prandelli was by no means a regular starter but his importance from the bench in assisting to close out results was crucial to Trapattoni's game plan. While Bonini was the main defensive midfielder, as the insurance policy alongside the more expansive figures of Platini, Tardelli, and Bettega, losing the option of Prandelli as extra steel if required meant that a compelling Plan B was not available. Essentially, for Juventus to win the final, Plan A would have to work to perfection.

Hypnotic on their way to the final, particularly against Aston Villa in the last eight, there was little pre-match reason to suspect Plan A would not work to perfection, however. Either side of Villa, Standard Liège and Widzew Łódź had been dealt with efficiently, yet while brushing Hvidovre IF aside in the first round, Trapattoni's side had potentially displayed an alarming ability to believe in their own hype.

Neither the victories over Liège nor Łódź work well in contemporary translation, but at the time they were significant opponents. In the autumn of 1982, Liège were less than six months beyond having contested the 1982 Cup Winners' Cup Final against Barcelona at the Camp Nou, while Łódź had knocked Liverpool out in the last eight before facing a Juventus side to whom they had sold Boniek the previous summer.

In comparison, Hvidovre, the Danish champions in 1981, had unsurprisingly been comfortably beaten 4-1 in Copenhagen in the first leg of the first round. Yet at 2-0 down in the return game with only 12 minutes left to play, they ended the encounter with a wild 3-3 draw, managing to score three times within an eight-minute span.

That was perhaps something of an anomaly for Juventus watchers, but from HSV's perspective it gave them hope that Trapattoni's players could sleepwalk their way into the final if the Italians were to be of the mind that they merely needed to show up to claim the prize.

And nine minutes into the final, HSV had obtained a 1-0 lead that they would not relinquish. It was no smash and grab mission either as Happel, perhaps having absorbed the lessons from his approach to the 1978 final with Brugge against Liverpool, on an evening when he opted for guarded caution, it was a case of attack, attack, and attack again for the West German champions.

Happel had also had the measure of Trapattoni before, in the 1978 semi-final. It was as if the Austrian could see through Italian football, as his successful 1969/70 European Cup-winning Feyenoord side had seen off the Trapattoni-captained Milan in the second round too.

Magath the conductor, backed up by a wonderfully stubborn defence, scored the only goal of the game four minutes after a Bettega diving header had tested the resolve of Stein.

Coming at the end of an almost uncomfortable period of keep-ball for HSV, after seemingly having clumsily dispossessed Kaltz, his own team-mate, of the ball, Rolff rolled it to Magath, who looked up and dipped his shoulder to feint for a shot from distance that he never took, causing Bettega to jump in expectation of an effort to block, before the West German international took another three or four steps to the edge of the penalty area from where he unleashed his genuine attempt for goal.

This flew into Zoff's top-left corner, taking the legendary goalkeeper by complete surprise. Barrell-chested and already looking drained of energy, Magath accepted the shocked congratulations of his team-mates before imploring them to retake their positions and to focus.

With their discipline and shape lost, a punch-drunk Juventus struggled to comprehend what had happened to the script. Before the interval had arrived they were fortunate not to give away a couple of penalties, benefiting from the lenient refereeing of Romanian Nicolae Rainea, the man who had blithely permitted Gentile's brutal treatment of Diego Maradona at the 1982 World Cup.

HSV would have been forgiven for falling back in order to protect their early lead, yet forward they went to such an extent that Rossi was in his own penalty area making untidy clearances, while Boniek was forced into making a desperate goal-line block from a wonderful curling effort by Kaltz.

Juventus eventually began to find their senses once again, with Platini, and Cabrini being denied by Stein. These were timely reminders to HSV that this dream performance would also contain dangers. Yet Rolff then had what appeared to be a perfectly legitimate goal disallowed when put in by the criminally under-observed Magath.

After another strike was disallowed on a marginal call in the second half, this time from Milewski, Magath was soon testing the ever-increasing Juventus nerves with a dipping half-volley that only just went over the crossbar. In response, Boniek was high and wide for Trapattoni's side.

At times, with Tardelli left to try and pull the midfield strings on his own, Gentile was often pulled out of position when compelled to assist his team-mate. Serie A's most notorious of hatchet men, his biggest contribution to the game was to ensure that Bastrup departed the pitch shortly before Juventus's main goal threat with what turned out to be a broken jaw.

Frustrated and isolated, Rossi was withdrawn from the fray after less than an hour, replaced by an extra midfielder as Trapattoni tried to wrest back the advantage of the centre ground. In the absence of Prandelli, it was left to Domenico Marocchino to attempt to make a difference.

As the second half wore on, the reality of the situation escalated for both teams. For HSV a natural air of self-preservation kicked in, while for Juventus the desperation of the chase for an equaliser took hold. Platini tried to loop the ball over Stein unsuccessfully, falling to the turf theatrically and unconvincingly in search of a penalty.

In retaliation, HSV occasionally threatened on the break where an excellent exchange of short passes produced a chance for Jürgen Groh, only to shoot straight at Zoff. This was followed by Magath passing up on a golden opportunity to snatch his and his team's second goal.

Running out of both ideas and steam, the final seconds of the game were almost met with resignation by Juventus, the heat perhaps counting them out as much as the determination of HSV.

The second Bundesliga team to win the European Cup after Bayern, HSV succeeded where Mönchengladbach failed, yet the team Netzer was the general manager of strangely remain a less heralded entity than the team that Netzer played for, despite overcoming one of the biggest favourites a European Cup Final has ever offered up.

They might have come away from Athens with a narrow winning margin to go alongside the trophy, yet this was a game that HSV truly dominated on a night when Juventus were made to seem blunt and unimaginative going forward. Trapattoni's team ambled into the final and were ambushed by a well-prepared and hugely motivated unit, who were still within a section of their season where they could not afford to break stride.

Yet, strangely, this success represented the end rather than the continuation of an era of prosperity for HSV. Despite this, their place as the European Cup's best-winning secret remains an indelible one.

12

Heysel

EVERY SINGLE glorious thing that happened in the European Cup prior to 29 May 1985 was brutally swept away with 39 innocent and lifeless bodies, along with the rubble and the debris of the negligently decrepit Heysel Stadium in Brussels.

The reputation of one of the tournament's most successful clubs was irrevocably stained and the future landscape of the game would soon alter exponentially because of plans drawn up while English clubs sat in self-isolation, cast into a half-decade long exile. Football, its supporters, the clubs themselves, and the entities which governed it were all complicit in varying degrees of dragging the sport to its most violent low.

Much is made of how the 1960s swung, and how savage the 1970s were, yet the 1980s took ingredients from both decades, baked them, and smothered the results with neon and multicoloured icing. Like most things that the '80s offered up, its football was tinged with liberal helpings of beauty and ugliness.

Juventus vs Liverpool in the 1985 European Cup Final was massively anticipated, despite neither team having enjoyed a particularly vibrant domestic campaign.

Liverpool, the defending European champions, had started the 1984/85 season sluggishly, struggling to absorb the loss of their metronomic captain Graeme Souness to Sampdoria. Joe Fagan's side had laboured in the early months, unable to settle upon a new midfield balance while also nursing the blow of being without the injured Ian Rush and suffering the fluctuating performances of Bruce Grobbelaar.

Three successive league title-winning campaigns had created something of a physical and mental exhaustion at Anfield, particularly for the steadily ageing members of the squad. The latter of this hat-trick of league titles had been achieved as part of a treble of First Division, League Cup, and European Cup, and while many outside observers will have expected the new season to offer more of the same, the early tell-tale signs were not promising.

Beaten by Everton thanks to a Grobbelaar own goal at Wembley in the Charity Shield, then held to a 3-3 draw at Carrow Road on the opening day of the defence of their league title, by the latter half of October 1984 Liverpool had just lost at Anfield to the blue side of Merseyside for the first time in almost a decade and a half. It was a reversal that left them sat in 17th position with over a quarter of the season already completed.

It was a result that meant that Fagan's team had failed to win any of their last seven league games and had picked up only two victories in their opening 11 First Division fixtures. While that run would be halted in the next game, away to Nottingham Forest in front of a live terrestrial television audience, within days of that boost Liverpool had relinquished their four-year grip on the League Cup when defeated by Tottenham Hotspur at White Hart Lane.

With Jan Mølby initially struggling to adapt to his new surroundings after his arrival from Ajax, Sammy Lee suffering a dip in form, and Craig Johnston often falling foul of Fagan's search for the right midfield chemistry, there was an unusual turbulence at Anfield which was added to when the Liverpool manager informed his chairman, Sir John Smith, and the board of directors, that he intended to retire at the end of the season.

Aged 62 when he took the job in succession to Bob Paisley, Fagan was only two years younger than his predecessor when taking the helm and already older than the age Bill Shankly was when the Scot resigned in 1974. Fagan was never a long-term option but the club had at least hoped that they might get another season or even two out of him in order to bide their time to plan a new path forward.

Despite the problematic start to Liverpool's season, they did eventually find some rhythm, aided by the return of Rush and the form of John Wark. They would lift themselves up the First Division table to finish a distant second to Everton and embrace their best FA Cup run in five years when making the semi-final, where they lost out to their bitter rivals Manchester United in a Maine Road replay, after an explosive first encounter at Goodison Park.

Liverpool had essentially gone back to basics; Fagan's side had resorted to doing the simple things well. The reward was a place in a fifth European Cup Final, breathing a sigh of relief in getting past Benfica for a second successive season, this time in the second round, yet making light work of Lech Poznań, Austria Wien, and Panathinaikos.

For Trapattoni and Juventus, their Serie A campaign had strikingly similar overtones to Liverpool's First Division travails. They too won just twice during the first two months of the new season, and a loss in the Turin derby against Torino had left I Bianconeri severely lagging in their defence of the title.

Form and fitness blighted Juventus too. The usually prolific Paolo Rossi had seen the goals dramatically dry up, scoring only three in the league, while his partner Zbigniew Boniek fared not much better. Added to this, their goalkeeper Stefano Tacconi had struggled to maintain the high standards he had initially shown in the wake of Dino Zoff's retirement. He was often left out in favour of Luciano Bodini, creating an ambiguity all the way up to the eve of the final over which of the two would play.

Like Fagan with Liverpool, Trapattoni went back to basics and Juventus climbed the Serie A table, where they marginally missed out on UEFA Cup qualification. Fresh off the back of leading his nation to European Championship glory the previous summer, French ace Michel Platini was in imperious individual form.

Again, just like Liverpool, Juventus had found solace in the European Cup. While there was to be an almighty scare in the semi-final against Bordeaux, their run up to that point had been all too easy when brushing aside the challenges of Ilves of Finland, the Swiss champions of Grasshopper Club Zürich, and the potentially tricky Czechs of Sparta Prague.

Both teams had encountered moments where fate might have intervened to keep them away from Heysel.

For Liverpool, that was the second leg of the second round in Lisbon where Benfica came to within one goal of eliminating the holders on an evening when Kenny Dalglish was the recipient of an exceedingly rare red card, for retaliation, and Fagan's team had to navigate half the game with ten men, having conceded the only goal in the fifth minute.

For Juventus, fate blinked in the second leg of the semi-final against Bordeaux, when the French champions almost completed an incredible fightback from a 3-0 first-leg defeat. A late save by Bodini from a Jean Tigana effort stopped Bordeaux taking the game and their clear momentum into a period of extra time.

While virtually every European Cup finalist can point to their moment of jeopardy during a run to the decisive evening, these instances for Juventus and Liverpool seem to be ever-increasingly haunting examples. As futile as 'what ifs' are, it is hard not to imagine that the 1985 European Cup Final might have had a markedly different outcome had either club not contested it.

There was a wide-ranging cause and effect to the Heysel Stadium disaster. Supporters in the name of Liverpool Football Club pulled the trigger yet the bullets were loaded by not only themselves but also by the Belgian authorities, UEFA, and a simmering tension caused by the violence Liverpool's followers had endured in Rome 12 months earlier after the 1984 final.

In an era of expected violence at football matches, Heysel was the nadir. Yet it was an entirely unnecessary and preventable war zone.

When discussing a topic where irony is not welcome, it is ironic that the blood of Heysel ended up on the hands of Liverpool. Of all the English clubs to traverse Europe on a regular basis, their supporters were among those to cause the littlest damage.

Cross-channel ferries went unscathed, and the concept of expulsions, bans, games behind closed doors, or being made to play home fixtures hundreds of miles from base were the preserve of other clubs. They were not always angelic by any means, but for the majority, following Liverpool in Europe was all about broadening horizons, travelling to new places, enjoying the local wine, women, and song, and of course the football.

As a city, Liverpool is one which looks out to sea for its experiences, influences, and often for its allies too. It does not look inland, toward the hills; it is not a city that starts fights but will stand up to end them.

This is what makes the events of 29 May 1985 so bewildering.

I hate the way that the number count of a disaster tells you everything and yet nothing of the human loss. Thirty-nine souls extinguished in the name of a football match is utterly sickening.

Thirty-nine families were left bereft, unable to fill the void that was left by the cruel death of a much-loved father, mother, sister, or brother. School and work desks were left empty as friends who went off in the hope experiencing one of the best days of their lives encountered what proved to be the last day of their lives.

As a Liverpool supporter who was 11 at the time and watched it unfold from the comfort of their own home, having been pensive ever since the semi-final that our unbeaten record in European Cup finals might be set to end only for all football considerations to be made to feel so very insignificant, over three and a half decades on it still makes for an uncomfortable lack of sense.

In the 1980s, one disaster or another was never far from our television screens. In an era prior to rolling news channels they were ratings gold for the TV companies, who would interrupt our regular viewing with an announcement of one grotesque event or another. A news flash would cause the heart to skip a beat and immediately draw attention to the corner of the room where the images and words would be seared on the psyche and the memory forever.

Lockerbie, Air India, Hungerford, Zeebrugge, the Marchioness, Piper Alpha, and the Manchester air disaster to name but a few. Shocking events, even but more so when broadcast live, as was the case with the Challenger shuttle disaster. The nation almost became desensitised to it all. Shocked, but not shocked at all, we had sat and watched

Tommy Cooper die live on prime-time television. Life seemed cheap.

In terms of football, 1985 was abysmal off the pitch. Millwall supporters ripped Kenilworth Road apart when there for an FA Cup quarter-final and a 15-year-old Leeds United supporter, Ian Hambridge, died during rioting at St Andrew's in a tragedy that happened on the very same day that 56 fans perished at Valley Parade, Bradford.

Frighteningly, the bottom of the barrel was yet to be reached. Two and half weeks later came Heysel. Football was eating itself, and before the year was over we had seen the breakdown in the relationship between the English game and television, plus the death of Jock Stein played out on a shocking evening in Cardiff during an increasingly rare live televised match.

Symptomatic of societal trends, civil unrest came in a variety of guises. The UK miners' strike escalated to the violent Battle of Orgreave, while selected big cities were allowed to decay, no more so than when the managed decline of Liverpool was effectively put into operation, provoking the rise of political militancy.

Poverty, deprivation, and racial subjugation brought about the Toxteth and Brixton riots, while there were other epicentres in Birmingham, Dewsbury, Leeds, and Manchester. The entire decade was mapped by division between the haves and have nots. We were all advised to desert the north and move to the prosperous south-east, as if huddled refugees.

It was not just a working-class call to arms either, as the middle classes boosted the cause of CND protests over nuclear missiles at Greenham Common. Soon the Poll Tax would bring people to the streets. It was a creative, vivid, sometimes vulgar, but often angry decade, where the name of the upwardly mobile game was not to help others up the social ladder but to kick them back down it as you scrambled as high as you could.

Football became escapism for thousands upon tens of thousands of disenfranchised people. In Liverpool, particularly at Anfield but also over Stanley Park at Goodison for a while, this was where a besieged and increasingly isolated way of life unfolded, yet in the most successful manner imaginable.

It might have been the avalanche of success that made Liverpool's football supporters that little bit more laid back than in other parts of the country. They could and would rise to a fight when required to do so, but they were not renowned instigators.

Unlike other clubs, while there was always an element ready to swing the punches at a moment's notice, despite short-lived attempts Liverpool had no long-lasting splinter groups adorned with a notorious and what was perceived to be threatening name. There were no Headhunters; there was no ICF. Laying waste to picturesque town squares in mainland Europe or running wild across the terraces of concrete bowl stadia, amid plumes of tear gas was not a Liverpool thing. It was seen as the Neanderthal-like behaviour it was, and in the emerging fanzine culture within the city it was roundly mocked.

Brussels was different, however.

The experiences and stories of Rome were still raw. Liverpool supporters had been attacked before the 1984 European Cup Final, yet it was afterwards that the horrors really kicked in. Within the slipstream of the most painful of defeats for Roma, on their own pitch, coach drivers left their visitors to fend for themselves, hotel owners locked their doors to their paying customers, and the police purportedly turned a selective blind eye to proceedings. Many were forced to seek sanctuary in the British Embassy.

Little to no attention and scrutiny on the events of Rome was given by the British media. There was a lingering anger in the blood of a lot of Liverpool supporters who made the trip to Brussels for the 1985 final, and instead of it being diffused it was to be channelled in the most destructive of ways.

Yet the afternoon of the game passed off peacefully; pockets of supporters mingled without incident. As the sun began to dip, the mood altered and aggression escalated. Many core Liverpool supporters were ready for any Italian threats, which created a hair-trigger situation, despite them being heavily outnumbered by Juventus supporters.

It might have been cast within the shadow of the iconic Atomium, but there was nothing futuristic about the Heysel Stadium.

There was a perimeter wall made of crumbling cinder block which could be too easily dislodged, and it was topped with barbwire. Inside the stadium the terraces were littered with loose rubble and rotting crush barriers, while some of the dividing fences were held together with handcuffs. This was a stadium that was younger than most of its European Cup Final-hosting contemporaries.

Run your finger down the list of European Cup Finals and check out the venues; 1985 and Heysel stands out like the sorest of thumbs. A stadium set for demolition and rebuilding, just what UEFA's thought processes were in awarding it another major final remains mystifying.

Five years earlier, Arsenal had raised concerns about the safety of the ground when they contested the 1980 Cup Winners' Cup Final. Even when Heysel had hosted its third European Cup Final in 1974, it seemed at odds with the venues of the finals to have been played out since it had previously been the host, in 1966.

Lisbon's Estádio Nacional, Wembley, the Santiago Bernabéu, the San Siro, De Kuip, and the Red Star Stadium had all been safe, secure, and sensible choices, speaking of a new way of thinking and an acknowledgement that Europe's biggest football match needed to be played out within the continent's grandest arenas.

Heysel's predecessors, from a 1985 perspective, had been entirely fitting both in terms of stature, safety, and comfort: Rome's Stadio Olimpico, the Olympic Stadium in Athens, De Kuip, the Parc des Princes, the Santiago Bernabéu, and the Olympiastadion. They were stadiums of purpose that would go on to host major European finals and international tournaments long into the modern age.

Sending the 1985 European Cup Final to Heysel was akin to sending royalty to the roughest bar in town, and it smacked of backs being scratched in the corridors of power. Blessed, or maybe cursed, by foresight, Liverpool secretary Peter Robinson and the president of Juventus, Giampiero Boniperti, both voiced grave concerns about the choice of Heysel. They were ignored by UEFA.

UEFA's inspection of the stadium prior to agreement of its right to host the game reportedly lasted for no more than 30 minutes.

On one hand, had Liverpool not reached the final, or had they not been up against Italian opposition, then the disaster would have never happened. Alternatively, on the other hand, had Liverpool faced Juventus at the Olympic Stadium in Athens, De Kuip, the Parc des Princes, the Santiago Bernabéu, or the Olympiastadion, then equally it wouldn't have occurred.

None of this came to pass, however. Instead, access to the stadium was criminally lacking in security. Staff sat at tables to check tickets but supporters without tickets could stroll straight through, while many ticket holders returned home without their tickets ever having been checked. There had also been a heavy trade in counterfeit tickets in the city centre in the days leading up to the game.

As recipes go, this one was rotten to the core.

With two curved banks of terracing behind each end, Juventus supporters filled sections M, N, and O, while at the other end, separated by the seated stands to the sides of the pitch, Liverpool fans had occupied only sections X and Y, with the remaining tickets in the fateful section Z sold to neutrals. Most of these ended up in the hands of Juventus followers, with only a small and poorly policed no-man's land in between sections Y and Z.

There was an outbreak of baiting between rival supporters, and projectiles were thrown in both directions. According to the journalist and author Tony Evans, when recounting his experiences at Heysel in *The Times* prior to Liverpool facing Juventus in the 2005 Champions League quarter-final, it was an exchange of missiles that was no worse than anything he had seen before.

Ill feeling was undeniably mutual, and it was not solely located to sections Y and Z. An hour or so prior to the scheduled kick-off, Alan Hansen and the injured Alan Kennedy were among Liverpool players to take a walk around the stadium, only to become the targets of a barrage of what seemed to be bricks. Rather than objects smuggled on to the terraces, they were shocked to realise it was instead lumps of the stadium itself.

Back in sections Y and Z, with the anger of events in Rome festering, down came the flimsy segregating fences, and while the police were overwhelmed, some officers simply vacated the scene until reinforcements belatedly arrived.

By then the damage had been done, the situation exacerbated by the Liverpool supporters who did make incursions into section Z not restricting themselves to one charge forward. They were allowed to regroup and have time to consider options before venturing forward again. This was a lull in which the Belgian police should have gained control.

With section Z not only populated by core Juventus support but also by families and indeed neutrals, and even a small collection of Liverpool supporters, in the panic that ensured there was a crush towards the far corner that resulted in the collapse of an unstable wall. The falling of the wall was not what killed the 39; it had been the crush.

Witnessing the carnage from the opposite end, some Juventus supporters made their way down to the Liverpool end and chaos reigned, during which one Italian was pictured with a starting pistol in his hand. With their path barred by a now increased police presence, a running two-hour battle ensued between Juventus supporters and this thin, baton-wielding, blue line.

Pleas for peace from both Fagan and his captain Phil Neal went ignored. Just what the Juventus and Liverpool players did and did not know when they eventually took to the pitch has long been discussed and disagreed upon. Much of this conjecture surrounds Juventus, and particularly Platini, due to the way he led his team's celebrations at the end of the game. It is something that added to the distress of the families of the victims.

On the morning after the final, Platini freely admitted that he knew the full extent of the disaster as he led his team on to the pitch, while decades later, when gaining traction in his bid to become the president of UEFA, he claimed the complete opposite.

In the stands there was a lack of knowledge. Many Liverpool supporters had no idea of the human toll until boarding ferries home. In an interview with the *Liverpool Echo* in 2015, marking the 30th anniversary of the disaster, Peter Hooton, the lead singer of The Farm, was unequivocal over just how much in the dark he was.

In April 1989, 14 Liverpool supporters were convicted of involuntary manslaughter for their parts in the disaster. In belated concessions for their respective failings in organisation and policing, Albert Roosens, the general secretary of the Belgian Football Association at the time of the final, received a six-month suspended sentence, and Johan Mahieu, the police officer who was responsible for section Z, was given a nine-month suspended sentence, plus a derisory 500 franc fine, which amounted to around £8.50. Mahieu's suspended sentence was eventually reduced to three months.

Further down the line, some of the families of the victims of Heysel took out largely unsuccessful private prosecutions on Jacques Georges, the former president of UEFA, along with the former UEFA general secretary Hans Bangerter, plus the former Brussels mayor Herve Brouhon, the former Brussels chief of police Major Michael Kensier, and Vivienne Baro, a former Brussels councillor for sports.

A series of unsatisfactory acquittals were reached, although Bangerter was later handed a three-month suspended sentence and a fine of 30,000 francs, roughly £500. He essentially took the public fall for UEFA, with Georges remaining unscathed, despite a trial to establish who was responsible for the organisation and safety of the game finding that it had been the duty of the governing body.

For his part, Brouhon was criticised for his response in the days after the disaster, when praising a clearly inadequate Brussels police force and even later in refusing calls for a memorial at the stadium dedicated to those who died.

Chillingly, it was disclosed during the trial that Baro had assured UEFA and the Belgian FA that the Heysel Stadium would be renovated in time for the final, which it plainly was not.

Mahieu's superior, Kensier, was identified as being the man responsible, in principle, for safety at the stadium, yet he too walked away without sanction. In fact, no individual or organisation was ever found to be legally responsible for safety at Heysel.

Blind eyes were poked, yet, unsettlingly, Georges remained at the helm of UEFA until 1990, ironically the year that English clubs began to make their first steps back into European competition after a ban that stretched to five years for all clubs other than Liverpool, who served a sixth.

With Heysel becoming the disaster that should not be mentioned, in far too many respects, it took Liverpool Football Club a long time before they even relented to placing a plaque of respect at Anfield, while Juventus themselves tried to move on with an unseemly haste. Within a year of the disaster they had come to an agreement with Liverpool to sign Ian Rush, who was rapturously welcomed upon his arrival in Turin before a season of toil and a swift return to Anfield.

Having been rightly pilloried for the events of Heysel, it was the supporters who took it upon themselves to attempt bridge building. A group of Juventus supporters were invited to Liverpool in August 1985, a prominent leader of the ultras among them, and a year later a collective of Liverpool followers made the return journey. Yet those initially positive experiences were never really advanced into anything lasting.

Time has not been a healer, and nor should anyone expect it to be. When Juventus supporters made the trip to Anfield in 2005 for the first leg of the Champions League quarter-final, a presentation and show of friendship went unaccepted by many, who turned their backs. The clubs faced one another again eight days later in Turin, and Liverpool went on the lift the trophy at the end of the season. They have never crossed paths since, although had the proposed Super League have come into being then regular fixtures between the two would have been unavoidable.

Liverpool supporter aggression due to previous events that had nothing to do with Juventus fans, a stadium not fit to pass a basic safety certificate, a complete lack of organisation from UEFA, and an acknowledged criminal negligence from the Belgian authorities; there was a defined cause and effect to the Heysel Stadium disaster, of which the removal of any one of the above ingredients would have meant it likely would never have happened at all.

A sadness and a shame that will reverberate through eternity.

13

The Years of the Ban

REGENERATION, RESTORATION and redemption of the European Cup came via sleight of hand. In the absence of English clubs, a hat-trick of unexpected winners emerged in the shape of Steaua Bucharest, Porto, and PSV Eindhoven, before Arrigo Saachi's Milan made the competition stylish once more with back-to-back successes in 1989 and 1990.

Despite the ban on English clubs, there were still British elements at the 1986 European Cup Final, the last one to be broadcast live on television in the UK for five years.

Terry Venables was the surprise choice of the Barcelona hierarchy to be the successor to César Luis Menotti in the summer of 1984. As the Queens Park Rangers manager arrived, Diego Maradona, the world's most talented footballer, complained bitterly, and agitated his way into a transfer to Napoli. Replacing him in the number ten shirt at the Camp Nou was Tottenham Hotspur's Scottish international Steve Archibald.

It all seemed so surreal, yet by the end of his first season in Catalonia, Venables had led Barcelona to what was their first La Liga title in 11 years and only their second domestic title for a quarter of a century. A World Cup-winning coach and the best player on the face of the planet, replaced by the co-creator of the 1970s television series *Hazell* and a former East Stirlingshire and Clyde striker.

Swiftly easing any doubts about their arrivals, Venables bravely proffered words in Catalan at his Camp Nou unveiling, while Archibald would end the 1984/85 campaign as the club's top scorer. Barcelona were comfortably champions, finishing an impressive ten points clear of Atlético Madrid, while even the notoriously volatile Bernd Schuster seemed to enjoy a new lease of life.

Within what was to follow at Barcelona under Johan Cruyff, the era of Venables became somewhat smudged by later failures. The fork in the road was their 1986 European Cup Final defeat in Seville, when just as with Juventus three years earlier, it had been an evening when a coronation rather than a football match had been expected.

Instead, widely disregarded opponents won the honours, except this time, unlike Hamburger SV's 1983 success, it did not come tinged with fine football. It was a victory that was chiselled out at the end of 120 soulless minutes of football thanks to the most stunning of penalty shoot-out capitulations imaginable.

A wounded Barcelona limped away from the 1986 European Cup Final riven by internal disagreement, on an evening when their biggest name was substituted in the 85th minute and did not take up a place on the bench, instead exiting the stadium and returning to the team hotel under his own combustible steam.

With his dirty linen pinned up in a very public manner, Schuster would lose a year of his career. Barcelona were neither willing to release him from his contract nor to allow Venables to select him, and they would stumble towards the end of an elongated title race in 1986/87, handing their despised rivals from the Santiago Bernabéu another success.

In the same season as a numbing UEFA Cup quarter-final exit at the hands of Dundee United, even the added presence and goals of Gary Lineker would have benefited from the midfield class of Schuster and could have helped Barcelona master the fine lines of a painful campaign.

By September 1987, Venables had gone, soon to resurface at White Hart Lane. Yet in May 1986, just 16 months prior to his exit from the Camp Nou, he really was upon the cusp of being canonised in Catalonia.

Already the talk of the potential arrival of Lineker was circulating, while an agreement to sign the Spanish international goalkeeper Andoni Zubizarreta from Athletic Bilbao had been sealed. Upon the eve of the 1986 final, everything was pointing toward an idyllic end to a difficult season.

After missing almost two months of football due to hamstring and groin problems, Archibald had also provided a pre-match boost when Venables stunned the congregated journalists, by naming him in his line-up at Barcelona's last press conference before the game. It was a bold move, with cards expected to be played close to Venables' chest until shortly before kick-off.

There was method in the madness and it had been a revelation designed to cause a stir. Theoretically, Venables, in one swoop, had emboldened the dreams of the Barcelona faithful and given opponents Steaua Bucharest extra food for thought.

Football in the form of poker, this was Venables at the card table, and possibly struggling privately with his thoughts and fears of failure in what was both the biggest game of his career and in the entire history of Barcelona.

Barcelona had not played for 11 days, and their last outing had been a 1-0 defeat to Real Zaragoza, in the final of the

Copa del Rey. Six days before this, they had ended their laboured defence of the La Liga title with a 5-3 loss in the derby against Español at the Estadi de Sarrià, the venue where Italy and Brazil had played out their iconic clash at the 1982 World Cup.

It was as if Barcelona had taken their foot off the accelerator after navigating their stunning second-leg fightback in the semi-final against the dangerous IFK Göteborg. Trailing 3-0 from the first leg, a hat-trick from Archibald's replacement Pichi Alonso had levelled the aggregate scoreline, and with the fervent backing of a 120,000 sell-out crowd at the Camp Nou, the Swedes were unnerved on penalties when handed one last kick to put themselves into the final.

From the frame of the goal being hit to a disallowed goal, Göteborg had passed up on a succession of gilt-edged opportunities to take themselves through long before wasting the chance to do it from 12 yards.

One of the most hazardous of European entities throughout the 1980s, within a year Göteborg had won a second UEFA Cup. Back in 1986, however, given that Anderlecht lost the other semi-final, the opportunity of one of the most hipster-centric finals of the European Cup imaginable had slipped through the fingers of football history.

Undeniably, Venables had been blessed with a heavy slice of luck, but then you must put yourself in the right place at the right time to make the most of your own fortune.

There was more to Barcelona's run to the final, however. Belligerence was at play. Sparta Prague and Porto were beaten on away goals in the first two rounds, dealing with tricky opposition from behind the Iron Curtain in the first instance then showing massive character in the face of a second-leg fightback from the team who would win the European Cup the following season.

Then in the quarter-final came what many viewed to be the de facto final and a tie with Giovanni Trapattoni's Juventus, the tormented holders, against whom Venables arguably enjoyed his finest hour as a manager away from trophy-winning occasions.

Restricted to a narrow 1-0 victory in the first leg at the Camp Nou, it was a wild night during the return game in Turin in which Barcelona eliminated the holders and favourites. A 1-1 draw against the odds was garnered thanks to an excellent back-post header from Archibald against the run of play; whereas Venables' team were ruthless with their first serious half-sighting of goal, Juventus were mired due to a succession of well-worked, but hypnotically squandered opportunities.

Marco Pacione was the profligate culprit as he missed chance upon chance laid on for him by Michel Platini and Michael Laudrup.

Trapattoni had set about rejuvenating his European Cup-winning team, alarmed as he was by their disjointed domestic form of 1984/85. In what would be the last season of his first spell in charge of Juventus before a five-year hiatus at Internazionale, Trapattoni would deliver another Serie A title as his parting gift and Pacione was an awkward part of this rejigged squad.

Recruited from Atalanta as a young striker of rich promise, Pacione would become a startling failure as part of an intake that saw Laudrup finally star for the club after a two-year loan with Lazio. Aldo Serena and Lionello Manfredonia were also purchased, while Paolo Rossi, Marco Tardelli, and Zbigniew Boniek were moved on, to Milan, Inter, and Roma, respectively.

Leaders of Serie A from start to finish, it was not beyond the realms of likelihood that Trapattoni would have added a second European Cup success in 1986 before heading off for the fresh challenge of Inter, had Pacione converted at least one of those early opportunities.

Platini squared the scoreline on the night, shortly before half-time, finishing intelligently, after being played through by the impressive Laudrup, yet there was only frustration to be found in the second period.

Disciplined, and unwilling to panic, this was an accomplished display from Venables' team, and when placed alongside their performances against Sparta, Porto, and Göteborg, it is easy to see why it finally felt like destiny was calling out to Barcelona to lift the European Cup.

With the final taking place 620 miles to the south-east of the Camp Nou, Barcelona supporters were in Seville in huge numbers. Conservative estimates put the figure at 50,000, yet it is likely that far more made the journey. Some 300 buses were appropriated, 12 aeroplanes chartered, and six trains put on. That does not even take into account those who climbed into their car to drive.

At the Ramón Sánchez Pizjuán Stadium, give or take the 1,000 or so vetted and state-approved Steaua supporters in attendance, the 70,000 people packed up and into the rafters were there to witness Barcelona make history. History would be made, but it was not the sort that anybody had really expected.

Like a finely tuned mathematician, Steaua had played the percentages all the way to the 1986 European Cup Final, becoming the first eastern European finalists in two decades and only the second in the competition's history. As a club who had never previously made it beyond the first round of the European Cup now heading to Spain to take on Barcelona, absolutely everything seemed to be against the Romanian champions' hopes of success.

Armed with just one player to have made the Romania squad for the 1984 European Championship finals, László Bölöni, who was playing his club football with ASA Târgu Mureş, Steaua were a compelling complexity.

Having shared modern domination of the Romanian game with Dinamo Bucharest, while neither Steaua nor their great rival had existed prior to the Second World War, through footballing reformation, club foundation and merger they were to swiftly become the footballing representations of the Ministry of National Defence, and the Internal Affairs Ministry.

Throughout the first half of the 1980s, Steaua had been stuck in something of a rut, trailing in the wake of not only Dinamo but also a fine Universitatea Craiova side. But 1984 marked a turning point and using nothing more than footballing gravity, and the stubborn vision of Emerich Jenei, footballing chemistry began to work its magic.

Not only had Steaua's players been massively marginalised at international level, but they also had to watch on as Dinamo reached the 1983/84 European Cup semi-final before falling to Liverpool. Within a year, they had, however, won their first Divizia A title in seven years.

Jenei, in the third of his six spells in charge of Steaua, had also been a player of purpose for the club. A defensive midfielder by trade, pragmatism was something of an art form for him and it was the only way he could make a concerted assault on the European Cup.

Arguably the least likely of European champions, much of the Steaua squad had been involved with the club during their years of toil and struggle. Emboldened by the arrival of Bölöni and the blossoming of Marius Lăcătuş, Jenei could also rely upon the prolific Victor Piţurcă and the adaptable Gavril Balint, who could operate in a variety of attacking positions, all offset by the more textbook approach of Mihail Majearu.

Wonderfully unknown across western Europe, it was upon Jenei's defence that their success was built. Helmuth Duckadam had replaced Vasile Iordache in goal, the only

Steaua player to have made Romania's Euro '84 squad, while Miodrag Belodedici's defensive qualities would go on to earn him a second unexpected European Cup-winners' medal five years later with Red Star Belgrade. Stunningly disciplined, Ştefan Iovan, Ilie Bărbulescu, Adrian Bumbescu, and Lucian Bălan anchored the side perfectly. Yet also looming upon the touchline was a 36-year-old Anghel Iordănescu.

Iordănescu, a legend of the Romanian game as both player and coach, had returned to the club in 1984 as assistant to Jenei after a two-year spell with Crete-based club OFI. Keeping up his registration as a player, he was named among the substitutes in Seville perhaps with sentimentality in mind, but conversely maybe with his experience and guile at the forefront of Jenei's thinking.

Another ingredient against Steaua going into the final, was the suspension of Tudorel Stoica, the talismanic captain of Jenei's team. Such a huge blow, this too might have precipitated the idea of Iordănescu's involvement being more than a mere token one.

Minimalist on the road, Steaua had been frugal in their approach to away legs despite being blessed with a relatively easy route to the semi-final. Vejle Boldklub, Budapest Honvéd, and Kuusysi Lahti created a dream combination of games, although the quarter-final against the Finnish side almost tuned into a nightmare.

Erring towards safety, Steaua were happy to accept a draw in Denmark and a narrow low-scoring defeat in Hungary during the first legs of the first two rounds before going a little more freestyle in the return games at the Stadionul Steaua, winning both 4-1.

Lahti proved to be infinitely more problematic, however. With Steaua thrown the curveball of hosting the first leg they recorded a goalless draw, leaving Jenei with the headache of needing to be that little more expansive on foreign soil in order to reach the last four.

After what had been 176 minutes of deadlock, Pițurcă snatched the only goal of the game. It was to be Steaua's second, and last, goal on their travels in the 1985/86 European Cup during regulation play.

Fully expected to be readily dispatched by Anderlecht in the semi-final, Steaua opted for flatpack frustration in Brussels and left with only a 1-0 deficit plus plans to pounce in the second leg. Having played their cards close to their chest, Jenei's men launched themselves into the Belgian champions from the very outset.

Fast, intelligent, and devastatingly incisive, when added to by the ambiance of a gloriously intimidating Bucharest atmosphere, Steaua swept Anderlecht aside with a template performance of the ones they had visited upon Vejle and Honvéd earlier in the competition. It was as simple and bludgeoning as it was beautiful. Score early and overwhelm with movement.

What was doubly impressive was the scriptures by which Jenei's defence operated. Giving no ground and no quarter, Stoica was particularly imperious and focused, a player who knew from the fifth minute that should his team reach the final then he would not be joining his team-mates on the pitch for it.

Sadly this was not the Steaua who headed to Seville. It was back to the percentage-playing version for the final. A prototype for Red Star Belgrade's success five years later, the thinking was that no matter what Jenei's team was capable of, it was too much of a risk to stand in the centre of the pitch and dance it out with a star-studded Barcelona. For Red Star, this was repeated word for word with Olympique de Marseille, in 1991.

A battle plan was carved, and it would involve as little risk and invited peril as possible. A deep-lying and disciplined back line, protected by two defensive midfielders, would help the team absorb pressure and hit on the counter, but never with the company of rampaging full-backs. All missions on the front foot would be undertaken with the pace of Lăcătuş, and Piţurcă, supported by occasional breaks from midfield by Bölöni, and Balint.

Tactics designed to win the trophy, rather than friends, worked to perfection. Barcelona were constantly repelled, and when both the half-fit Schuster, and the hastily recalled Archibald ran out of steam, Venables' side were swiftly out of ideas and heart.

With his team accused of playing for penalties, Duckadam was to be the hero for Steaua as much for ending the torture of the game for its viewers as for winning his club the European Cup. Given how Barcelona had excelled from the spot in the semi-final the way they disintegrated in the final was spectacular.

They missed all four of their kicks, while Steaua even had the good grace to miss their own first two kicks. It was almost an apology of a finish to what could have been a wonderful occasion.

This was Steaua in the form of a team having watched AS Saint-Étienne, and Borussia Mönchengladbach fall short of the prize the previous decade, despite playing some of the most entertaining and evocative football imaginable.

A pattern for success had been created by Steaua, and it would be one that was to be regularly recycled in the years ahead. Not only would Red Star use the Steaua method of winning the European Cup, but you could also see it within Greece's success at the 2004 European Championship. Even Brazil opted for pragmatism and the fear of defeat in the style with which they won the 1994 World Cup Final. A whole new phenomenon had been born into football: playing and prevailing through a fear of defeat, rather than setting out to win by fluid means.

Within two years, PSV Eindhoven had become the third Eredivisie team to lift the European Cup, in another penalty shoot-out, after not only 120 goalless minutes of football but on the back of narrow away goals successes in the quarter-final and the semi-final. Over the course of the final five games on the route to glory for Guus Hiddink's side, they scored only two goals in regulation time.

It was a success that was hard-earned but there was also an element in which it seemed like they had done it without making eye contact with any opponents who were a clear and present danger. PSV edged past the Real Madrid of Emilio Butragueño in the last four in 1988 and deprived the world of Los Blancos going up against Benfica in what would have been an evocative duel, at least on paper, and a repeat of the 1962 final.

Added to this, Benfica were owed a debt of gratitude, as they had unseated the holders, Steaua, in the semi-final. Surely, they had done enough to blow away the curse of Béla Guttmann? Clearly not, as PSV took the prize with a team that belied the manner of their measured march to success.

Despite the sale of Ruud Gullit to Milan, Hiddink's PSV were a well-respected entity, thought to be a long-awaited heir to the throne of Total Football and suppliers of a quarter of Rinus Michels' Netherlands squad that went on to win the 1988 European Championship.

Equipped with a spine of Hans van Breukelen, Ronald Koeman, Søren Lerby and Wim Kieft, PSV were the favourites going into the 1988 final. In response, Benfica largely pinned their hopes on a plan that revolved around the wonderfully talented Diamantino, only for him to damage knee ligaments four days prior to the game.

Plan B for the Portuguese champions was to be a pragmatic one. Contain and suppress, then hit on the break or pounce from a set piece. This was all while the iconic Eusébio sat watching from the sidelines as assistant coach to Toni. It all seemed so out of sync with what Benfica had been about as a five-time finalist throughout the 1960s.

Two hours of negative and occasionally cynical ball play by both teams was followed by 11 converted penalties, and finally the failure of António Veloso. At Stuttgart's Neckarstadion, roughly 40,000 PSV supporters quite rightly celebrated wildly after a game that went without a shot on target until eight minutes before the interval.

As telling as the winners of the first three post-Heysel finals were, so too were the identity of the losers. Barcelona, Bayern Munich, and Benfica had each either represented the favourites going into those games, or at the very least one of the historical owners of the tournament. Be it right or wrong to think in such ways, it felt considerably more 'comfortable' to see some of the beaten teams in the final of the European Cup than it did the winners at that point in time.

Porto did offer drama within their 1987 success, however. Another team to rise unsettlingly, they had reached and lost the 1984 Cup Winners' Cup Final to Juventus in what had been the first occasion they had ventured to the business end of a major European competition.

Porto were undoubtedly a growing force, yet in need for something familiar and comforting in the European Cup, what 1987 needed was a ruthless and efficient Bavarian success. What it did not need was the turbulence of another first-time winner.

Reassuringly brutal in their journey to the 1987 European Cup Final, and with Udo Lattek back at the helm, Bayern had dismissed PSV with nonchalance and Austria Wien without breaking sweat, all before the winter hiatus.

With their home legs first for both the quarter-final and the semi-final, Bayern went for shock and awe against Anderlecht and Real Madrid, respectively, to the tune of nine goals combined.

At the Santiago Bernabéu in the return game, so incensed and frustrated by events were the locals that a barrage of missiles, inclusive of golf balls, rained on to the pitch, bringing with it a ten-minute delay to proceedings and ultimately Madrid's next European game being played behind closed doors. Ironically, this would be the first leg of those 1987/88 first-round games against Napoli, and Diego Maradona, that went such a long way in conspiring to alter the whole landscape of not only the European Cup but the broader spectrum of the European club game.

Formulaic in terms of seeing themselves into the final, having been in possession of a three-goal advantage Bayern suffered a costly body blow in Madrid with a harsh red card flashed at their influential captain, Klaus Augenthaler. Joining the Bayern sweeper on the sidelines, however, was Porto's prolific striker Fernando Gomes, who broke his leg just days before the final.

Porto, meanwhile, had enjoyed target practice against the Maltese champions Rabat Ajax before easing past MFK Vítkovice and sneaking beyond Brøndby IF. Given only half a chance of prevailing in their semi-final against Valeriy Lobanovskyi's wondrous Dynamo Kyiv, winners of the Cup Winners' Cup the previous season, in two games that were witnessed by a combined 190,000 spectators Jorge's team pulled off a 2-1 victory in both.

A Kyiv boasting the attacking talent of Igor Belanov, Oleh Blokhin, Oleksandr Zavarov, Vasyl Rats, and Oleksiy

Mykhaylychenko, this was one of the greatest teams not to have won the European Cup. That Porto managed to work past a potentially damaging narrow home win while conceding an away goal was massively impressive.

Cursed to have lost a cluster of its most impressive ingredients, the 1987 European Cup Final took place also without Bayern striker Roland Wohlfarth and midfielder Hans Dorfner. Depleted but determined, Lattek's players were wanting to bring their coach the most glorious of parting gifts, with this to be his last game in charge of the club.

Despite Porto being without Gomes, they still had a plentiful supply of attacking options, including the Algerian international Rabah Madjer, Paulo Futre, plus Brazilian pair Wálter Casagrande and Juary. At the Praterstadion in Vienna, Porto coach Artur Jorge opted for Madjer and Futre.

Lattek's riposte was a front three of Michael Rummenigge and Dieter Hoeneß, supplemented by Ludwig Kögl, who was pushed up from midfield to cover the loss of Wohlfarth. Behind this triumvirate sat a midfield of Hansi Flick and Andres Brehme, himself stepping forward from defence, both of whom orbited the metronomic Lothar Matthäus.

The final had all the makings of an understated classic, which is exactly what it was.

Porto did not shy away from the physical side of the game, instead embracing it. Expertly combining no shortfall in skill with the dark arts, they succeeded in keeping Bayern vulnerable even when the Germans approached the last 13 minutes with a slender 1-0 lead that they had guarded for 52 minutes.

Bayern's makeshift striker, Kögl, had opened the scoring with an excellent diving header in the 25th minute, and for a long time it looked as if the final would prove to be a bridge too far for Porto, despite their appetite to attack.

With Celso, Porto's Brazilian centre-half, in an uncom-promising frame of mind, Bayern were constantly up against a brick wall of defenders, and they were made to pay a heavy cost for not taking as many of the half-chances they did create, none more so than when Rummenigge put a shot wide of the post when clean through.

Maybe Lattek's team would have prospered had Celso received a deserved red card during the second half when launching a thigh-high challenge on Kögl. Bizarrely, Porto were awarded a free kick instead, in one of an eccentric set of decisions for both teams, by the Belgian referee Alexis Ponnet, which included Porto's Jaime Magalhães being ordered to move back ten yards for the throw-in that led to Bayern's goal.

It was with just 13 minutes remaining that Madjer saved the day.

As much as misfortune befell Bayern in the 1987 European Cup Final, bringing with it a certain sense of symmetry to their 1982 defeat to Aston Villa, and almost a degree of karma, arguably, for the way both lady luck and the match officials had smiled upon them between 1974 and 1976, it was difficult not to enjoy Porto's success. This was despite the shades of violent intent that Jorge's side had displayed.

Madjer, a goalscorer for Algeria in their iconic victory against West Germany at the 1982 World Cup, had also had to suffer elimination from the tournament on a back of the result of convenience between their vanquished opponents and Austria in the group-ending game. It was an incident christened as the 'Disgrace of Gijón', and still to this day it is used as the barometer of all Machiavellian collective team actions in major international tournaments. Madjer must have harboured at least a subconscious desire for a touch of revenge when confronted by a West German team in the biggest game of his club career.

With a magnificently calm and collected back-heel, Madjer levelled the scores, and three minutes later his determination and skill set up the winning goal for substitute Juary.

After a decade of finals that at best had been intriguing tactical duels, and at worst abject disappointments, the European Cup at last had a wonderfully layered showpiece of fine football, and drama, all with an undercurrent of needle.

Typically, British viewers were the only ones across the length and breadth of the continent not to see the game broadcast live, with ITV not taking up its option to do so, instead marginalising the occasion to late-night highlights. This would be a repeated pattern by both ITV and the BBC until 1991.

This insular practice might have spared the UK the pain of a wasted evening watching the 1988 final, but it also deprived them of seeing the more panoramic view of the European Cup rebirth of Arrigo Saachi's Milan too. With an Italian-flavoured World Cup looming, it was a missed opportunity.

Turning the decade on its head, Milan had begun the 1980s by being demoted to Serie B for their role in the Totonero scandal. Returning at the first time of asking, they were then relegated on the pitch in 1981/82.

After bouncing straight back up again, for the next four seasons Milan were steady if unspectacular; never higher than fifth, never lower than seventh, with a Coppa Italia Final lost in 1985 for good measure. This status of footballing water-treading was massaged further by an unremarkable run to the last 16 of the UEFA Cup the following campaign.

Change was coming, however. After three years of methodically yet valuably pacing themselves, under the Milan legend Nils Liedholm, the touch paper was then lit by the arrival of Saachi, and a new Dutch influence. First came Ruud Gullit and Marco van Basten in the summer of 1987, and a year later arrived Frank Rijkaard. They provided a quite different foreign flavour to that of England's Ray Wilkins and Mark Hateley.

With Serie A won in Saachi's very first season in charge of I Rossoneri, he swiftly took the strongest elements of the squad he inherited and blended them with an unerring ability to recruit the perfect player.

Blessed to be bestowed with an international goalkeeper in the shape of Giovanni Galli, the defensive security of the team was very much in the safest of hands. Franco Baresi, Paolo Maldini, and Mauro Tassotti were soon joined by Alessandro Costacurta, whom Saachi recognised as the perfect central defensive partner for the genius that was Baresi.

It was in midfield and attack where Milan needed new impetus and only Roberto Donadoni would survive the cull. In terms of reinforcements, along with the Dutch influx, Carlo Ancelotti was purchased from Roma.

The end of the 1988/89 season was set to mark the 20th anniversary of Milan's last European Cup success, yet there would be a new glory to celebrate too. It is strange to consider now, but their opponents were the ones who had all the experience and knowhow going into the 1989 European Cup Final.

Winners in 1986 and beaten semi-finalists in 1988, Steaua came with one last great European Cup run, in 1988/89, and just as with the previous campaign they were armed with Gheorghe Hagi. Added to this, they also boasted Tudorel Stoica, their captain, who had missed the 1986 final through suspension.

Still with the dangerous strike partnership of Lăcătuș and Pițurcă, and now under the management of Iordănescu, who succeeded Jenei after he took the Romania national team job immediately after leading Steaua to glory in Seville, this was now a grown-up Steaua who were not quite as wary as they once were. Still studious and suspicious, yet with an added layer of vision and selective expansion, they were expected to be a close match for the re-emerging Milan. The Italians had all the style and substance while the Romanians had the power and the experience.

Devastating at home but now bolder on the road, Steaua had won 5-1 at Sparta Prague in the first round and would pick off another victory at Spartak Moscow next. With no sign of the percentage playing of 1985/86, Lăcătuş and Hagi were in electric form, scoring 13 goals between them on their way to the Camp Nou. Another star performer was the future Tottenham Hotspur player Ilie Dumitrescu, who would later be suspended for the final.

Ruthlessly taking apart the talented IFK Göteborg in the quarter-final, this was the performance that spoke most loudly of a new Steaua. They were then far too strong for the surprise semi-finalists Galatasaray, with whom Hagi would go on to win the UEFA Cup just over a decade later.

In turn, Milan's route to the final had been a little more precarious. A convincing passage beyond Vitosha Sofia in the first round was followed by a close call against Red Star Belgrade in which Saachi's side were held to a 1-1 draw in the first leg at the San Siro. In the return, amid an encircling fog, the game was called off with 25 minutes remaining and the Yugoslav champions leading 1-0.

Enjoying a narrow escape from elimination when the game was replayed the following afternoon, Milan progressed on penalties to a closely contested and low-scoring quarter-final against Werder Bremen.

Having arguably percentage-played themselves into the last four, Milan finally let loose against Real Madrid. An intelligent 1-1 draw at the Santiago Bernabéu, thanks to Van

Basten cancelling out a goal from Hugo Sánchez, set up the San Siro stage perfectly for the second leg.

This is where the true level of shock and awe that Saachi's Milan were capable of was unveiled to an unsuspecting world. They were 5-0 up in under an hour to leave Leo Beenhakker's side dumbstruck.

Ancelotti from distance, Rijkaard with a towering header, and Gullit with a beautifully directed header of his own, all coming before the interval, left Madrid with an impossible task. Any vaguely held notions that the game could be turned around were obliterated within 15 minutes of the restart as Van Basten powered the fourth Milan goal into the top-right corner of Paco Buyo's net, while Donadoni completed the demolition job on the hour, low to the Madrid goalkeeper's left.

The one downside for Saachi's team was the loss of Gullit to a damaging cartilage tear, which left his involvement in the final open to question.

For the team in all white, it was a sobering moment for Beenhakker and a talented Madrid side that had now lost a third successive European Cup semi-final. In pursuit of what had become their holy grail, it was not long before they were usurped domestically, by Johan Cruyff and his Barcelona 'Dream Team'.

Powered by a cluster of early-1980s Madrid youth products who went by the nickname of 'La Quinta del Buitre', this moniker was a derivative of Butragueño's own nickname, 'El Buitre', 'The Vulture', a goalscorer of majestic grace. Joined by the stylish Míchel, the marvellously rampant Rafael Martín Vázquez and the aggression and intelligence of Manolo Sanchís, this was a Madrid generation that seemed destined to win a European Cup and to end a drought that had now stretched to almost a quarter of a century.

Winners of five successive La Liga titles between 1985/86 and 1989/90, a run that was built upon back-to-back UEFA

Cup successes in 1985 and 1986, it would have been a natural progression to lift Madrid's long-awaited seventh European Cup towards the end of the decade.

Having allowed the fifth member of La Quinta del Buitre, Miguel Pardeza, to spread his wings at Real Zaragoza, Beenhakker had taken advantage of Barcelona discord in the summer of 1988 to recruit the imperious yet volatile Bernd Schuster. Meanwhile, in tandem with Butragueño was the Mexican icon Sánchez, another player dispossessed from a bitter rival three years earlier, on that occasion Atlético Madrid. Combining homegrown products with cleverly identified imports, this was a wondrous Madrid vintage.

Yet it was as if this numbing defeat to Milan broke the resolve of the club. Taking domestic dominance for granted, although John Toshack would lead them to another La Liga title in 1989/90 as Beehakker's replacement, Los Blancos would soon unravel. They went on to suffer a five-year hiatus between league titles, thus denied the opportunity for another assault on the European Cup beyond an early exit in 1990/91. By the time of their return to the competition in 1995/96, it was now the Champions League.

Arguably fragile by the time they faced Milan, Madrid's lost opportunity 12 months earlier, when defeated by PSV on away goals, would have left them braced for the pain of further torture. Losing to Milan must have broken their heart, and it would be a decade before they were crowned as the champions of Europe once more.

Victorious, Milan headed off to the Camp Nou for their date with Steaua. With rumours abounding that Van Basten had signed an agreement to become a Barcelona player in the summer of 1990, there was an eventually unrequited poignancy to the build-up to the game. It was even felt that it was a projected transfer that might have been brought forward a year.

Within a style and verve that was as comparable to that with which Milan would dismantle Cruyff's Barcelona five years later, Saachi's side were a visage of perfection in the final with two goals each for Gullit and Van Basten. For the former it completed a stunning return to fitness, and for the latter, rather than act as the perfect way to bid farewell to I Rossoneri and to signal an introduction to what would be his new playground in Catalonia, it instead served to convince him that he could not depart what was now the undisputed best team on the face of the planet, which played its football in the greatest league in the world, no matter what bonds linked him to Cruyff.

Steaua started the game well, yet by the interval they had been destroyed in what was the most dominant European Cup Final display since Madrid's zenith against Eintracht Frankfurt 29 years earlier.

With Milan pressing and harrying high up the pitch, apart from the early exchanges when Steaua seemed to be the fastest to settle into their task, Saachi's team soon seized the initiative and never relinquished it.

They were determined to make it difficult for Steaua to get Hagi on the ball, meaning that Lăcătuş and Piţurcă were isolated to such an extent that Baresi was able to roam forward at will as if one of the traditional sweepers of the 1950s, and 1960s. With Maldini and Tassotti given the freedom to join Donadoni and Angelo Colombo in attacking down the flanks, and Rijkaard pulling the strings in central midfield alongside Ancelotti, the ball was magnetically drawn to Gullit and Van Basten.

Gullit, with only 35 minutes of football played since the operation to his cartilage, played within a remit of being told he had an hour to win the European Cup.

When a player is rushed back from injury for a game of huge significance, it rarely works well. Steve Archibald in 1986 was the most recent example of this, yet for Saachi with Gullit it was a calculated and measured approach.

Should Gullit have been named among the substitutes, to be thrown on in case of emergency, it could have been counterproductive. Theoretically, the player who deputises is already on alert that his evening might end prematurely, while the half-fit hero struggles to make an impact when introduced, targeted by markers who will be aiming to play on the injury. It is a way of sleepwalking to defeat.

Instead, Saachi was able to start the game with Gullit on the pitch, the Milan number ten enthused by the adrenalin of playing in the biggest club game of his career so far, likely within the knowledge that he would be replaced on the hour. It is the art of dealing with players like the adults that they are.

Gullit played like a man possessed; scorer of the first and third Milan goals, he set the tempo and the energy at a Camp Nou that had at least 80,000 red-and-black-clad supporters within. A gloriously disorientating landscape, both on and off the pitch, it was perhaps the one and only occasion in which the Barcelona faithful watching on their television sets were given a lesson in just what their stadium could look and sound like when cranked up to 11 on the amplifier.

With a touch of fortune to the opening goal, a fine downward header by Van Basten added the second, but the third took the breath away. Gullit's mastery of the ball was exquisite; controlled when coming to him at waist height from Rijkaard, he made it look all so effortless as he cushioned the ball with the inside of his right foot. Directing it on to his knee, he then volleyed it past Silviu Lung from just inside the penalty area. It was a goal that could have been lifted from the pages of the Cruyff footballing manual.

Within a minute of the start of the second half, Van Basten had beautifully guided in the fourth. Yet Steaua had done little wrong. This was an evening when no team could have lived with the mood that Milan were in. To end their 1988/89 European Cup campaign with nine goals in two games against Madrid and an under-celebrated Steaua side was phenomenal.

It was a performance that was the springboard for the regeneration of the European Cup; it was a performance that evoked the spirit of Hampden Park and 1960, on an evening when the attendance was the highest for a European Cup Final since Alfredo Di Stéfano, and Ferenc Puskás lit up Glasgow. In this respect it restored the legends of the past, who had been left to seem so inconsequential in the aftermath of Heysel.

A year later, Milan retained their European Cup with a sense of authority, although within an infinitely more prosaic final against Sven-Göran Eriksson's Benfica in Vienna, to complete a hat-trick of European successes for Serie A clubs in 1989/90.

In a game of few clear-cut chances, a moment of magic between Van Basten and Rijkaard settled the outcome midway through the second half. Gullit, largely a pedestrian, had suffered for his efforts in the 1989 final and missed almost the entirety of the 1989/90 season.

Riding a wave of supreme confidence after dispensing with HJK Helsinki easily enough in the first round, Milan drifted through a series of narrow victories on their way to the final, fending off a trio of significant opponents as Real Madrid were followed by Mechelen and Bayern. The latter two obstacles had required extra time, and it was obvious that despite their technical gifts, Milan had missed the imagination and power of Gullit.

Going through some impressive motions nonetheless, had Milan instead faced the skill and adventure of an Olympique de Marseille side who had lost the other semi-final to the Portuguese champions despite the presence of talents such as

Enzo Francescoli, Jean-Pierre Papin, and Chris Waddle, then the 1990 European Cup Final might have been one of the greatest of the lot.

With the ban on English teams set to end, the European Cup would still have one further season without a First Division element given Liverpool's 1989/90 domestic title success. The four-times champions had initially been handed an extra three years to serve, which would eventually be commuted to one. How English teams might have fared between 1985/86 and 1990/91 will always be open to conjecture, none more so than Everton in 1985/86.

For the rest of the continent, it is questionable whether European football missed the English clubs or not, but it did open the door for other compelling heroes who might have succeeded regardless of whether a First Division representative was there or not.

Steaua's rise was not an accidental one, and they evolved throughout those years of the ban; Porto gave us the best European Cup Final for a decade. PSV were part of a wider wave of Dutch endeavour, while Milan's European rebirth could not have been stopped by anyone.

The European Cup proved many times over that trends were there to be changed, be it the drift of southern Europe from the mid-1960s after their early domination through the rise of the north of the continent, via pockets of success in Scotland, England, the Netherlands, West Germany, and England once more.

Ban or no ban, that English hegemony was on borrowed time, and Saachi's Milan would have risen to the top, to mark a new era. Unbeknown to most people, however, the European Cup was on borrowed time of its own.

14

Belgrade Calling

BELGRADE IS inextricably linked to the European Cup. It is a relationship which is utterly unique when compared with that of other cities. Home to one European Cup-winning team and the location of another beaten finalist, it is also the place in which too many fine players kicked their last ball.

On 6 February 1958, an Airspeed Ambassador bound for Manchester crashed in treacherous conditions on its third unsuccessful attempt take off from Munich-Riem Airport. Of the 44 people on board, only 23 survived the initial impact. Frank Swift, journalist and former England international goalkeeper, died on his way to hospital, while one further victim would succumb to his injuries 15 days later. Duncan Edwards became the predominant symbol of loss at the Munich air disaster.

The death toll eventually rested at 23, and while this was a tragedy that was played out in another city, in another country, Belgrade was forever cast in a degree of shadow which would only darken further over three decades later.

Manchester United were returning home from a successful European Cup quarter-final second leg against Red Star

Belgrade; an eventful 3-3 draw had been enough to send Matt Busby's side through to the semi-finals. They had been in Munich only to refuel before continuing their homeward journey.

Just over eight years later, Busby and his team returned to Belgrade to play in the European Cup, this time in the semi-finals and this time against Partizan. The team from Old Trafford were viewed in some quarters as the best team in Europe at the time and the outcome was touted to be a formality, especially given the fact that United had systematically dismantled the mighty Benfica in the previous round, clocking up a 5-1 victory in the second leg at the Estádio da Luz.

Partizan, meanwhile, were labouring in sixth position in the Yugoslav First League as the first leg of the semi-final rolled into view, and at the end of the campaign they would eventually trail in 11th. It is within these impossible circumstances that Partizan defied logic in reaching the 1966 European Cup Final.

In many respects it should not have been a shock, however. While Partizan had watched on from the wings as their great rivals Red Star had dominated much of Yugoslav football during the 1950s, the black and whites had emerged from the Belgrade periphery during the early 1960s to dramatic effect. Not only had they won the Yugoslav First League in 1964/65, but they had also completed a hat-trick of title successes between 1960/61 and 1962/63.

These glories for Partizan had come during a strong era of both Yugoslav club football and for a national team, who had reached the final of the 1960 European Championship and the semi-finals of the 1962 World Cup. Indeed, while those involved with Partizan publicly played down their chances of defeating Manchester United, there was at least a mild degree of skepticism from Busby and the British press.

Despite these reservations, given that Real Madrid and Internazionale were contesting the other semi-final, United's path to the final was the easiest route. Conversely, although Partizan were struggling domestically, they went into the semi-final on the crest of a European Cup wave.

Just as United had done, Partizan also scored five goals in the second leg of their quarter-final. In the case of Partizan, however, rather than a result-validating masterclass, as had been the circumstances of United's win in Benfica, Partizan's was as part of one of the greatest second-leg comebacks in European football history.

Defeated 4-1 in the first leg by Sparta Prague, Partizan were given little hope of overturning the deficit back in Belgrade, yet with a hypnotic and forceful style of play and a belligerence towards what was the expected outcome they swept to a 5-0 victory, this being inclusive of scoring one of the greatest disallowed goals of all-time. Within just 35 minutes, Partizan had overhauled Sparta to the incredulity of their own stunned supporters. It was the type of occurrence you took lightly at your peril.

At a packed-out JNA Stadium against Manchester United, Partizan were initially on the back foot, however. Denis Law hit the bar and David Herd missed the rebound from point-blank range. Law also missed another golden opportunity when through one-on-one with the Partizan goalkeeper Milutin Šoškić.

Whether by design or good fortune, Partizan drew the early sting of their opponents and hit them with a counterpunch at the very beginning of the second half when Mustafa Hasanagić broke the deadlock. A disallowed John Connelly effort and a second Partizan goal later, from Radoslav Bečejac, left United to lament the flagrant disregard that the Yugoslavs had shown for the script.

Busby had undeniably got his biggest call wrong when fielding the half-fit George Best. Best had been at his most artistically destructive in Lisbon against Benfica and instead of erring toward caution during the first leg against Partizan, Busby threw Best into the thick of it, and while remaining as United's most dangerous player, the effort and physical expenditure he displayed was ultimately for scant return. It also ruled him out of the return game.

Partizan's dissection of United's hopes had been so all-encompassing that they had even come close to a third goal. Chants of 'Slavie, Slavie' reverberated from the stands of the JNA Stadium, followed by a shower of confetti and bottles. It was a classically trained intimidating home crowd that sent their opponents, and the 100 or so intrepid supporters they arrived with, back to England with the noise of klaxons and whistles ringing in their ears.

A week later, at Old Trafford, Partizan finished the job off as they escaped with a 1-0 reversal having withstood a late onslaught. Their coach, Abdulah Gegić, had essentially set up with a flat back nine, and they were were awarded an ungracious response from the United faithful at full time. The concept of Belgrade pragmatism prospering in the European Cup would surface again a quarter of a century later.

In the Brussels final against Madrid, Partizan were brave and bold, opting for expansion over pragmatism. Adopting the adventurous approach which they had taken into the second leg of the quarter-final and the first leg of the semi-final, with 20 minutes remaining Partizan still led thanks to a 55th-minute goal from the magnificent Velibor Vasović. From there, Los Blancos came on strong and the trophy once again returned to Madrid, albeit for the last time for 32 years.

Those 20 minutes were landscape-altering ones for Partizan and their coach. Legend has it that Gegić had been promised the

Madrid job in the event of a win for the Yugoslavs. He would indeed depart Belgrade that summer, but instead for Fenerbahçe, where he began a long association with Turkish football.

Gegić's on-pitch successes were relatively modest in Turkey, but he went on to be credited as a major influence on an entire generation of coaches who would lead the country's game from the shadows at both club and international levels. Mustafa Denizli, Şenol Güneş and Fatih Terim were notable students.

Partizan's run to the final and brave defeat to Madrid came with unfortunate side-effects. Swiftly, Gegić was followed out of the club by Vasović, who went on to captain Ajax to their first European Cup success, in 1971.

Gegić and Vasović were not the only ones making their departures from Partizan either, as Šoškić also joined the exodus, heading to 1. FC Köln, while Fahrudin Jusufi, Vladimir Kovačević and Milan Galić left for Eintracht Frankfurt, Nantes and Standard Liège, respectively. With Yugoslavia far less controlling of its footballing borders than other eastern European nations, the dismantling of Partizan was startling. The 1966 European Cup Final was the perfect shop window and it would take the club a decade to recover.

A quarter of a century later, the increasingly troubled city of Belgrade finally claimed its European Cup success. It came just weeks after a brave mass public demonstration against the Serbian president Slobodan Milošević, in which up to 150,000 people took to the streets and independent media was placed under a government-ordered black-out to suppress news of the protests. The circling backdrop of the Yugoslav Wars made for a dysfunctional undercurrent to what was, on the surface at least, almost the perfect team.

On this occasion it was Red Star who were in the ascendancy and just as when Partizan went close in 1966, they too were wind-assisted by a strong Yugoslav international team, who were being heavily tipped to win the 1992 European Championship. Four members of Red Star's 1991 European Cup Final side went to the 1990 World Cup finals.

In Italy, the hypnotic Dejan Savićević, Robert Prosinečki and Darko Pančev were joined by the steely determination of Refik Šabanadžović. Also, in the squad for Italia '90 was their then-Red Star team-mate, Dragan Stojković.

Stojković would play a part in the 1991 European Cup Final but in the all-white of Olympique de Marseille, having moved to the French giants on the back of his displays at the World Cup, particularly in being the driving force in the elimination of Spain. Criminally, he would be restricted to just eight minutes in Bari against his old team-mates, and would not get the chance to take a penalty in the shoot-out to decide the outcome.

This was all unfolding within the weeks in which Croatia was upon the brink of proclaiming independence from Yugoslavia after the initial tensions of the Log Revolution, the precursor to the Croatian War of Independence.

Red Star's 1991 line-up was an eclectic collection of elements, drawn from the many splintering fragments of the rapidly exploding Socialist Federal Republic of Yugoslavia.

The success that the club achieved, despite the complexities of their squad, was astounding. Beyond the obvious presence of Serbian players, it was a side inhabited by a defecting Romanian, a Kosovan, three Montenegrins, two Macedonians, and a Bosnian. There was also the thorny relationship between Prosinečki and Siniša Mihajlović.

Prosinečki, who was born in West Germany to a Serbian mother and a Croatian father, would go on to play in the red and white of Croatia, while the polarising Mihajlović was born in the incendiary city of Vukovar, on Croatian soil, to a Croatian mother and a Serbian father.

Mihajlović would instead embrace his Serbian roots, playing on for what remained of Yugoslavia and eventually becoming the coach of the Serbian national team. For Red Star to be unified, while their surroundings were anything but, made little in the way of sense.

Red Star's run to the semi-final was a relatively sedate one as Grasshopper Club Zürich, Rangers, and Dynamo Dresden all struggled to match the speed and fluidity of Ljupko Petrović's impressive side.

There was a compelling sense of destiny about the Red Star of 1990/91, having previously been a club who had come so close to European glory only to fall agonisingly short.

Red Star had reached the European Cup semi-final as far back as 1957, while in 1971 they contrived to self-destruct at the same hurdle when they threw away a 4-1 first-leg advantage against Ferenc Puskás's Panathinaikos. They lost out in heartbreaking circumstances on the away goals rule, thus missing out on facing the Ajax of Rinus Michels and Johan Cruyff at Wembley.

There had been further Inter-Cities Fairs Cup and European Cup Winners' Cup semi-final losses in 1962 and 1975, respectively, along with a run to the 1979 UEFA Cup Final, where they were narrowly defeated by Borussia Mönchengladbach. Having been so close on so many occasions, there was a wonderful stubbornness not to be denied in 1991, which simply seeped from Red Star's performances on their way to the semi-final showdown with Bayern Munich.

When Red Star travelled to the Olympiastadion for the first leg, they embraced the occasion with a sense of bravado, coming back from 1-0 down to claim a 2-1 victory which shocked Europe. With Marseilles having dislodged the holders, Milan, in the quarter-final, it now meant that one of the continent's great pretenders appeared set to finally reach the promised land.

A wild night in Belgrade during the second leg put Red Star's part in that scenario under mortal danger, however, when with heavy shades of 1971 in the air and the scoreline at 2-1 to the visitors, the home side found themselves just seconds away from being forced into extra time by Bayern. A calamitous injury-time own goal from the usually calm and dependable Klaus Augenthaler put Red Star into the 1991 European Cup Final.

Guaranteeing a new name upon the trophy, Red Star would be up against a Marseille side who had risen swiftly throughout the second half of the 1980s to become the dominant force of French football.

It was a team who had evolved impressively, never standing still, always shape-shifting and lifting trophies at the behest of the sometimes-questionable puppeteering of Bernard Tapie. At great expense, Stojković had arrived as the heir apparent to Enzo Francescoli, only to suffer a serious knee injury that meant he missed much of the 1990/91 campaign and was only fit enough to take up a place among the substitutes in Bari.

This was offset by the belated blossoming of Abedi Pele, however, and he formed a dangerous front three alongside Jean-Pierre Papin and Chris Waddle. In the absence of Stojković, however, Marseille's midfield made for a much more workmanlike unit, and it would be this reduction in creativity that stifled their hopes in the final.

Led by the storied Raymond Goethals, who had stepped in after the turn of the year when Franz Beckenbauer struggled with the realities of full-time management and the demands of Tapie compared to the more part-time aspect of the international game, the former Belgian national manager was hoping to add European Cup glory to the Cup Winners' Cup he had previously led Anderlecht to in 1978.

Beckenbauer had helped ease Marseille into the quarter-final largely thanks to powerplay performances at the Stade

Vélodrome against Dinamo Tirana and Lech Poznań, assisted along the way by a skilled but erratic Eric Cantona.

In the last eight, both Marseille and Red Star were involved in volatile situations from which they would be awarded 3-0 second-leg victories in games that never reached their natural conclusion. Red Star's match away to Dynamo Dresden was disrupted by objects being thrown on to the pitch as Prosinečki attempted to take a corner, while for Marseille it centred on Milan's refusal to return to the pitch after a late floodlight failure.

Both Dynamo and Milan were subsequently banned from European competition for the following season. In the case of Dynamo, when added to the reunification of the German club game, it meant the end of their endeavours in European competition completely.

No matter how Marseille's quarter-final ended against Milan, the French champions had undeniably been the better side, and there was a feeling that it had been an evening upon which the power of the European game had definitively tipped toward the south of France.

Like several other teams before them, Marseille suddenly felt like the heir apparent to the dethroned Milan. Yet becoming favourites brings with it a new pressure. Expectancy can rest heavily, and like Barcelona in 1986 or Hamburger SV in 1980, that last step to what many presume to be destiny can be the biggest and hardest one of all.

Red Star being bold and brave on their way to the final, combined with the beauty with which Marseille played, meant the 1991 European Cup Final was an eagerly anticipated one. However Petrović's side would play rope-a-dope with their opponents, playing the percentages or simply aiming for penalties, while Goethals' team struggled to land a punch. It was with a heavy sense of déjà vu and 1986 that the 1991 final dragged itself to its conclusion.

The affront to footballing decency that the final was mattered not to a delirious Red Star. Petrović had countenanced that he could not go toe to toe with Goethals' artistic Marseille front three. In essence, Petrović seriously underestimated the capabilities of his own side, yet he walked away with the spoils regardless.

Defying the odds once more and having been shorn of their coach and many of their European Cup-winning team, Red Star came close to reaching the final again 12 months later. This was despite them being required by UEFA to play their home matches away from their own troubled country, along with the systematic dismantling of the Yugoslav First League, throughout the 1991/92 season.

Red Star's victory through pragmatism was a fascinating contrast to the approach of Partizan, who lost their shot at a European Cup Final when playing in a more expansive style than their Belgrade rivals did in winning theirs. Belgrade as a city was a seemingly more unified place at the time of Partizan's run in 1966, while Red Star's ultimate glory came at a time when the city was consuming itself.

Within a year of their success, the entirety of Red Star's European Cup-winning side had departed for safer environments. Eastern Europe as a footballing powerhouse ebbed away, its most promising players spirited away to the west at the first sign of talent. Red Star's success of 1991 was the pinnacle of a footballing movement which was shrouded in mystery and wonderment, at which Belgrade as a city was in the very epicentre.

15

The Holy Grail

THERE ALWAYS seemed to be a mischievous curse at play when it came to Barcelona and the European Cup. Prior to the dawning of the Champions League era the Catalan giants, so often classed as the self-entitled biggest club in the world, were among the participants in only five of the tournament's 37 campaigns. Long goaded by their great nemesis Real Madrid, Barcelona's often dysfunctional domestic difficulties meant that it was a harder task for them to qualify for the European Cup than it was to be a challenger for the trophy once they had gained entry.

Between Barcelona's La Liga title successes of 1959/60 and 1990/91, they prevailed in pursuit of their domestic league title on only two other occasions. One success was in 1973/74, when masterminded by Rinus Michels and powered by Johan Cruyff, while the inexplicable 1984/85 success came on the back of the sale of Diego Maradona to Napoli and the recruitment of Steve Archibald from Tottenham Hotspur, a victory spun for them by Terry Venables.

At best sorely lacking in domestic consistency, while at worst the regular victims of the whims of the enforced political administration of General Francisco Franco, going into the 1991/92 season Barcelona's love affair with the European Cup was still an unrequited one.

It might come as a surprise to millennials, who became accustomed to the sight of the Blaugrana on the winners' podium at the end of finals in the Champions League, but Barcelona used to be a watchword in how not to win the European Cup.

The 1961 final was lost to Benfica a season after they had been brushed aside by Madrid in the semi-finals, and it was not until 1974/75 that Barcelona returned for another attempt at the biggest prize in the European club game. As intelligent as the football was under Michels and as aesthetically pleasing as the vision on the pitch of Cruyff was, they were undone once again in the last four by what would be their mid-1970s Achilles' heel, the English barbarians, and their perceived Anglo-Saxon version of the game.

Leeds United were the insurmountable barrier between Barcelona and Cruyff facing Beckenbauer and Bayern Munich in the 1975 European Cup Final. A year later, Bob Paisley's Liverpool defeated them in the semi-final of the UEFA Cup.

When Barcelona finally came back for another go at the European Cup in 1985/86, their grief and humiliation was complete when beaten on penalties at the end of 120 torturous minutes of football against Steaua Bucharest in the final at the Ramón Sánchez Pizjuán in Seville, on a night when Helmuth Duckadam scorched his name into the history books of the tournament.

Failing to fully recover from that loss, Venables hung on to his job until the early exchanges of the 1987/88 season and his departure, rather than galvanising the club, set it on the road to further rancour as the Camp Nou fell into what was akin to a status of civil war.

A squad in mutinous mood and an increasingly unpopular president in need of getting indifferent supporters on his side was the environment that Cruyff walked into when asked to take the helm in the summer of 1988. A precarious peace descended as the Dutch master swept out 17 players and began a revolution that is still felt at the Camp Nou well over three decades later.

In the summer of 1988, suspicions abounded to such an extent that not even Cruyff was fully trusted by the Barcelona faithful, feared by some to be a puppet of the president Josep Lluís Núñez, the man whose standoff with the players over the culpability of tax demands led to the infamous Hesperia Mutiny.

While Barcelona burned, Madrid prospered and won five successive La Liga titles between 1985/86 and 1989/90, only to see this offset by European Cup frustration with three semi-finals lost within the same period. To add insult to Catalan injury, the last of those two title wins had been facilitated by the addition to their ranks of Camp Nou hero Bernd Schuster.

Within a year of Cruyff's arrival, Barcelona had won the European Cup Winners' Cup, a tournament that they had seemingly been a kindred spirit of. Finding access to the Cup Winners' Cup easier to stumble across than was the case with the European Cup, by the time of its discontinuation beyond the 1999 final Barcelona had won it on four occasions, twice as many times as any other club. They had also won the predecessor to the UEFA Cup, the Inter-Cities Fairs Cup, three times during the 1960s, even taking permanent possession of the trophy when winning a 1971 play-off against Leeds.

There was certainly nothing wrong with Barcelona's continental pedigree, but the European Cup remained hauntingly out of reach. It wasn't just that it had been so unobtainable, it was the way the torture had been administered:

a semi-final lost to Madrid, two finals lost with one of them on penalties, and a chance of success under Michels and Cruyff appearing, then vanishing, as if it were a mirage.

Barcelona had lost the 1961 final with the incredible forward line of Zoltán Czibor, Luis Suárez, Evaristo, Sándor Kocsis, and László Kubala, while not only had Cruyff been part of the 1974/75 attempt but so too had Johan Neeskens. In 1985/86, Schuster and an ocean of Barcelona support had been expected to crowd surf the European Cup for every single one of the 615 miles north-east back home to the Camp Nou.

As the European Cup launched itself into its very last season prior to its rebranding as the Champions League, it was with a mixture of bemusement and question marks over Catalan mental fragility that learned football watchers scratched their heads over why Barcelona hadn't already won the tournament two or three times. It was one of football's greatest anomalies.

At the 1989 Cup Winners' Cup Final, Cruyff and Barcelona had beaten the rising force of Sampdoria, the team they would face three years later in the 1992 European Cup Final.

Cruyff refused to rest on his laurels and in the summer of 1989 he showed the exit door to another ten players, including Gary Lineker, plus the free-spirited and wildly popular Lobo Carrasco. Among the new recruits were Ronald Koeman and the gifted Michael Laudrup, while from the Barcelona B team into the first team squad came a young student of the game by the name of Pep Guardiola. Within a year, Hristo Stoichkov was in a Barcelona shirt.

In 1990/91, Barcelona took the La Liga title by ten points from Atlético Madrid. Still within the two points for a win era, this was an emphatic endorsement of Cruyff's blueprint for football during a title race they had almost led from start to finish. The only fly in the ointment had been their loss of the Cup Winners' Cup Final to Manchester United on an evening in Rotterdam where Alex Ferguson's pre-match mind games, and Mark Hughes, desire to prove himself against his former employers won the spoils.

Twelve months later, Barcelona would retain their La Liga title, although this time via Real Madrid capitulating on the final day of the season away to Tenerife, a feat they would unerringly repeat a year later against the very same opponents. Madrid had led the race since the end of October, and only relinquished top spot with the trophy set to be handed to them.

Two and a half weeks prior to this unexpected gift, Barcelona had been at Wembley for their long-overdue crowning as champions of Europe, a success that meant so much they eventually purchased the goalposts through which the hoodoo was broken.

Like a test event ahead of the Olympic Games, the 1991/92 European Cup was a dry run for the introduction of the Champions League the following season. Barcelona finally winning the trophy couldn't have been any more fitting, and as the city hosted that summer's Olympics, it was the most prominent sporting location on the planet that year.

Back in October 1991, as Madrid climbed to the top of the La Liga table, Barcelona's domestic season had begun poorly. Meanwhile, in the European Cup, they were nervously edging past 1. FC Kaiserslautern in the second round, the first two rounds of the tournament continuing within the format of two-legged knockout games before group stages replaced the quarter-final and the last four.

Hansa Rostock had been overcome in the first round, East Germany's last participant in the tournament. At the Camp Nou in the first leg, Michael Laudrup weighed in with two goals as part of a 3-0 victory, the first of which was wonderfully set up by the Netherlands international Richard Witschge.

Witschge had been an unfortunate figure. Signed from Ajax, reportedly at a mutually agreed inflated cost as a favour to the Amsterdam club, he was a talented player who had been part of the Netherlands squad at the 1990 World Cup and of great importance at De Meer. However, at Barcelona he was dogged by competition for places and injury problems, one of which would rule him out of contention for a place in Cruyff's team for the 1992 final.

What couldn't be taken from Witschge, though, was that it was his ingenuity that got Barcelona's European Cup-winning ball rolling. Midway through the first half he glided past four Rostock players before cutting it back for Laudrup. The Danish legend dipped his shoulder, evaded the last defender, and sat Daniel Hoffman on the turf when stroking in the opening goal past the helpless visiting goalkeeper.

For purists it was a goal that had the merest hint of a deflection off that last defender as the ball went through his legs. Yet Laudrup had dealt effortlessly with a ball that had hit a sizeable divot halfway between him and Witschge.

Laudrup's adjustment as the ball deviated its way towards him was an almost imperceptible piece of genius, and it was in the back of the Rostock net a split second later. It was typical Laudrup brilliance, but Witschge's part in the build-up was wonderful too. It was so impressive that on initial sighting, you could easily mistake it to be the work of Laudrup himself. It takes multiple viewings to sufficiently convince your brain that it is instead Witschge.

Just two minutes after the restart, Laudrup and Barcelona had their second. A fine team goal, on this occasion it was another Cruyff recruit, Andoni Goikoetxea, who timed his run to perfection and exploited the space Rostock were gifting in the full-back positions before laying on the opportunity for Laudrup, which he gleefully accepted.

In the 62nd minute the compliment was returned via a probing run from the halfway line by Witschge, carrying the ball deep into the Rostock half. Playing a diagonal pass to Laudrup on the left, it was then clipped to Goikoetxea, who was converging on the right-hand side of the penalty area. The Spanish international midfielder was then the recipient of a piece of great fortune as his off-target effort was diverted into the net by the unlucky František Straka.

It was too big a mountain to climb for the last winners of East Germany's top flight and while Rostock won the return game it was only by the single goal, scored by the marvellously named Michael Spies. The result gave East Germany its European Cup send-off, with a vague nod to the subterfuge of Stasi back in 1974/75 when Magdeburg faced Bayern Munich.

More German opponents came in the second round after Kaiserslautern had stunned everybody but themselves when winning the 1990/91 Bundesliga. Their coach, Karl-Heinz Feldkamp, had been roundly laughed at when suggesting his team was more than capable of winning the title before going on to prove the doubters wrong, holding their nerve to edge out a stunned Bayern Munich.

When Barcelona won the first leg, 2-0 at the Camp Nou, they did so with a Txiki Begiristain double. He was first to the rebound just before half-time when a Witschge effort from distance bounced back off the Kaiserslautern goalkeeper Gerald Ehrmann, while Barcelona's second also came from some excellent penalty box opportunism. Shortly after the hour the ball landed invitingly at Begiristain's feet, central to goal, around seven yards out, after Stoichkov was bundled out of the way by Wolfgang Funkel with Witschge again involved in the build-up. It wasn't Funkel's evening and, as it had for Barcelona's first, the ball seemed to touch him last before crossing the line.

A fortnight later, any notions that the game was already over as a contest vanished swiftly at the Fritz-Walter-Stadion. With a desperate rearguard action in operation, Barcelona did well to delay Kaiserslautern's first goal until the 35th minute, when Demir Hotić got a deft touch on an in-swinging corner to make it 1-0. Caught, or possibly dragged badly out of position, a furious Andoni Zubizarreta protested foul play to no avail.

Three minutes into the second half, Hotić levelled the aggregate scoreline and sent Catalan anxieties through the roof, the visitors undone with another corner. Yet worse was to come and, with 14 minutes left, Kaiserslautern hit Barcelona on the break and the future Chelsea and Fulham midfielder Bjarne Goldbæk, drove home what threatened to be the goal to send Cruyff's team out before the new group stages had the opportunity to begin.

These were events that seemed entirely in keeping with Barcelona's relationship with the European Cup; yet another promising situation allowed to slip from their grasp. It couldn't have been any more 'Barcelona' of them.

Then came the 89th minute and José María Bakero with the goal that simultaneously set his club on the path to history and a new future. Rising high on the angle of the six-yard box, only he will know if he intended to direct his header towards the far corner of the net or across the goalmouth for others to potentially prosper, but when the ball looped in it mattered not a jot. The celebrations were wild, with Guardiola running from the touchline to join in.

As points of footballing eureka go, Barcelona's playing of a European Cup get-out-of-jail-free card was incredible. Between there and Madrid gift-wrapping them the La Liga title on the final day of the season, Cruyff's side lost just five games.

In the group stages, Barcelona were able to observe the 1992 European Cup Final magnetically draw towards them from a distance. In Group B alongside Benfica, Dynamo Kyiv and Sparta Prague, the main challenge surprisingly came from Sparta.

Sparta were always a step or two behind Cruyff's side, however, even when they inflicted Barcelona's only defeat of the group stages, in the penultimate game, at the atmospheric Letná Stadium. It was a result that kept the group alive until the final night but still left Sparta with a mountain to climb. They were ultimately foiled by their struggle for results on the road.

Yet back on the opening night of the group stages, Barcelona had been stringently tested by Sparta at the Camp Nou in a game where the home side were down to ten men from the 17th minute after Guillermo Amor was the recipient of a straight red for a stunningly cynical professional foul on Martin Frýdek. Amazingly, this red mist moment came just 60 seconds after Amor had given his team the lead; Petr Vrabec promptly scored from the resultant free kick.

Frantic for a spell in the immediacy of conceding the equaliser and losing Amor, Barcelona eventually found their stride once more and reclaimed the lead in the 34th minute when Laudrup drove the ball low past the exposed Petr Kouba.

With Barcelona rejuvenated, Sparta were losing their composure and Koeman was at the centre of the home side's performance. He continued to influence the game as the second half began, rattling the crossbar from distance with a free kick shortly before Bakero extended their lead, almost stumbling the ball over the line at the end of a swift counter-attack.

Barcelona only managed to hold on to their two-goal advantage for three minutes before Václav Němeček reduced the deficit, setting up a nervous last 25 minutes for Cruyff's players. In the great scheme of Group B it was a result that heavily influenced what was to come.

A group format in which second place really was nowhere had the winners of the two groups progressing directly to the final. After this initial victory for Barcelona, over the course of the next four games it was Sparta who took marginally more points, emboldened by three of those four matches being at home, including victory on the penultimate night against Barça.

Armed with a far superior goal difference, realistically a draw at home to Benfica in the last round of games would be enough to see Barcelona through to the final. Meanwhile, Sparta would need to win away to a Kyiv side who had lost every game since a victory on the opening night.

Sparta fell to a frustrating 1-0 defeat in Kyiv with Oleg Salenko scoring the late winner. By the time that goal went in, Barcelona were cruising to a 2-1 victory at the Camp Nou, fittingly against Benfica, the team who defeated them in the 1961 European Cup Final.

Stoichkov opened the scoring in the 12th minute, taking advantage when Benfica right-back José Carlos failed to control a long pass played out of defence by Koeman. The Barcelona number eight drifted in from the left to ruthlessly claim the ball and plant it past a startled Neno.

Midway through the first half it was 2-0, Bakero doubling Barcelona's lead with Stoichkov the provider when reaching the byline and cutting the ball back for a thunderous effort to be dispatched into the roof of Neno's net.

From there Barcelona took their foot off the gas, conceding just four minutes later when César Brito powered through on goal, placing the ball low and to Zubizaretta's right. Never in any true sense of jeopardy, however, Cruyff's team were able to saunter to their place in the final.

In the opposite corner at Wembley, Sampdoria had followed in the Serie A footsteps of Fiorentina, Milan, Internazionale,

Juventus, and Roma by becoming the sixth Italian team to reach the continent's biggest club game.

A team who hold a special connotation for those who grew up on Channel 4's magnificent helpings of *Football Italia*, in terms of the wider breadth of Italian football Sampdoria were something of an interloper, just as Napoli and Verona were, ruining a meticulous party that was meant to be dominated by Arrigo Sacchi's Milan, Giovanni Trapattoni's Inter, and a Juventus who were spending hand over fist in their failed bid to climb back to top spot.

An amalgamation of a collection of various clubs, Sampdoria as we know them were the result of a 1946 merger of Andrea Doria and Sampierdarenese, the latter of these two component parts having previously absorbed other smaller teams. It made them something of a patchwork quilt of a club that flew in the face of the city of Genoa's other iconic team, named after its home location.

Whereas Genoa had cultivated a rich history, being crowned as Italian champions nine times long before Sampdoria had been born, these comparative upstarts in blue had had to wait until 1985 to get their hands on a first major trophy when defeating Milan in the final of the Coppa Italia.

Apart from two relegations into Serie B, the second of those being a prolonged five-season exile that bridged the end of the 1970s and the start of the 1980s, Sampdoria had at least made themselves a staple of the Italian top flight despite never threatening honours prior to the rise to the presidency of the club of Paolo Mantovani.

Mantovani, having made his money in oil, was Roman by birth and an adopted son of the city of Genoa. Having grown up a Lazio supporter, after his arrival in Genoa it was in watching Sampdoria's city rivals that he initially got his surrogate football kicks.

He was invested enough to sign up for a two-year subscription to Genoa in the mid-1960s as part of a scheme that was created to ensure the club's retention of their star player, the ultimately tragic Gigi Meroni. This was a campaign formulated when their president Giacomo Berrino cited financial difficulties and a need to cash in, only to state that if the supporters wanted to fund Meroni's continued presence in a Genoa shirt then they could feel free to mobilise.

Despite this meticulously organised uprising, Meroni was still controversially sold to Torino, and in protest Mantovani withdrew his support of the club, continuing to pitch up at the Stadio Luigi Ferraris, except to watch Sampdoria instead. By 1973 he had taken on the role of press secretary, a position he filled alongside overseeing the growth of his oil business.

In the right place at the right time to take advantage of the 1979 Oil Crisis, Mantovani hit the financial mother lode and before the year was over he was the Sampdoria president. Via gradual improvement, the club was back in Serie A by 1982, complementing their promotion with a run to the semi-final of the Coppa Italia.

Measured within his recruitment of coaches and players alike, Mantovani proved to be a unique president. Ill health eventually required him to make a choice of relinquishing control of either his oil concerns or his position at Sampdoria. It was oil that he elected to sideline.

Whereas many club presidents took to their positions out of a thirst for greater personal power, Mantovani was in for the love of it and for footballing glory. Engendering a family atmosphere at the club, the breakthrough was made with that 1985 Coppa Italia success under the guidance of the former Internazionale coach Eugenio Bersellini, leading a team laced with a British flavour in the shape of Graeme Souness and Trevor Francis, offset by a collective of talented young domestic talent and one or two with a point to prove to former employers.

Another Coppa Italia Final was reached in 1986, but this time they fell short, losing out to Roma with the outcome put beyond any lingering doubts in the last few seconds of the second leg by future Sampdoria midfielder Toninho Cerezo.

Despite that, Sampdoria's league form had been inconsistent and when Bersellini accepted the offer of taking over at Fiorentina in the summer of 1986, Mantovani made the bold move for Vujadin Boškov.

With the concept of employing a foreign coach still seen as an unusual, even esoteric move, Boškov at least arrived at the Stadio Luigi Ferraris as a former Sampdoria player, having spent the 1961/62 season in Liguria.

Brought in from Ascoli, who Boškov had just led to the Serie B title, the Yugoslav was handed a job that was one of the most intriguing in Italian football. On one hand, to be the successor to the man who had recently delivered the club its first piece of major silverware might have been a foreboding prospect, but on the other he was in a no-lose situation.

Essentially, Boškov had all the ingredients at his disposal to build upon Bersellini's previous efforts, yet he also had the added insurance policy that if his time in Genoa did not work out then there would be no shortage of offers to work the same magic he had propelled at Ascoli.

Boškov had joined Ascoli in November 1984 with the club struggling at the foot of a ruthless 16-team Serie A, where any weakness would be taken advantage of. While it took a prolonged period to earn a first victory, he had swiftly made the team difficult to beat, mirroring what he had done when in charge of Sporting Gijón.

Unable to stave off relegation despite an impressive attempt, it would have been no stain on Boškov's character to have moved on from Ascoli in the summer of 1985, yet he elected to stay in a bid to return the club to Serie A at the first time of asking.

This Boškov did with his side not only winning promotion but doing so as champions, in a campaign when former Serie A winners Lazio, Cagliari, Bologna, and Genoa were water-treading in the second tier of the Italian game.

A man who dealt in loyalty, as a player Boškov had been wholly committed to FK Vojvodina, even returning to the club as technical director in the mid-1960s to oversee the levels of success that had been unattainable to them when he played. Within this, his actions with Ascoli should have come as no surprise, and it also made him the perfect foil for Mantovani at Sampdoria.

With Real Madrid also on his CV, Boškov was not only a La Liga-winning coach, but he had also led Los Blancos to their only European Cup Final between their successes of 1966 and 1998. Prior to this, he had made Real Zaragoza one of the most entertaining and perplexing teams in Spanish football, capable of brilliance on home soil yet barely able to pick up the occasional point on their travels.

Arriving as a flawed visionary perhaps, Boškov essentially had a free swing at the upper reaches of Serie A and European club competition beyond with Sampdoria. Inheriting many of the components of the team he would field at Wembley, when he arrived in the summer of 1986 he was blessed by the presence of a strong defence and a potent strike partnership.

Of those players he was met by, Pietro Vierchowod was the cornerstone of the defence, Moreno Mannini would travel the distance at right-back, while Marco Lanna would be brought through the ranks by Boškov, firstly as a left-back before switching to central defence. Fausto Pari would be the man around whom the midfield chemistry was perpetually spun, with Cerezo arriving the same summer as Boškov to complement Pari, and at the peak of this, there was Gianluca Vialli and Roberto Mancini.

It meant that throughout his six-year tenure, Boškov was never in a situation where revolution was required. It was more a case of him seasoning the recipe. The recruitments of Gianluca Pagliuca, Srečko Katanec, and Attilio Lombardo were the prime examples of this.

At the end of Boškov's second season at Sampdoria he led them to their second Coppa Italia success, going on to retain it in 1988/89. Alongside this they also reached the 1989 Cup Winners' Cup Final, where they were overpowered by Cruyff's Barcelona. Undeterred by this disappointment, Boškov and his team simply returned to the final 12 months later and defeated Anderlecht. It was this success that prompted Mantovani to proclaim that his team was ready to challenge for the Serie A title.

With a supreme sense of the impossible being nothing, Sampdoria didn't just challenge for the 1990/91 Serie A title, they won it. Outthinking and outmuscling the Milan of Sacchi and the Inter of Trapattoni, Boškov also left in his slipstream a Roberto Baggio-powered Juventus, the fast-maturing Parma, a self-destructing Diego Maradona at Napoli, and their Stadio Luigi Ferraris bedfellows Genoa, who themselves enjoyed a campaign that brought them UEFA Cup qualification.

Given that Sacchi and Trapattoni had seen and done it all, and that both Milanese giants had at multiple points led the 1990/91 Serie A title race, the achievement was nothing short of remarkable.

This was close to top-level Italian football being able to offer up a family club able to outwit the upper classes. In a battle of Vierchowod, Cerezo, Lombardo, Vialli, and Mancini, up against Maldini, Baresi, Rijkaard, Gullit, and Van Basten, plus the threat of Zenga, Bergomi, Brehme, Matthäus, and Klinsmann, then Boškov and Sampdoria should have had no chance whatsoever. Yet succeed they did, and with no shortage of counter-attacking swagger, taking not just the Scudetto but also a place in the 1991/92 European Cup.

After breezing past Rosenborg at the first hurdle, Budapest Honvéd had proved tougher opponents in the second round. Sampdoria narrowly lost the first leg but emerged with a valuable away goal scored by the veteran Brazilian midfielder Cerezo, who had been part of the Roma side that lost the 1984 European Cup Final.

Sampdoria seemed set to sweep to a sedate comeback when Lombardo opened the scoring within ten minutes of the start of the return game, supported by a brace from Vialli either side of the interval. Yet, when Pari contrived to score an own goal with 25 minutes still to play, it left I Blucerchiati teetering on a knife edge. Concede again and Honvéd, such an iconic name of the pioneering pre-European Cup floodlit friendlies of the early-to-mid-1950s, would gain themselves a place in the group stages. Boškov and his players were most relieved to hear the final whistle.

Drawn into Group A with the holders Red Star Belgrade, Anderlecht and Panathinaikos, Sampdoria's fortunes fluctuated throughout their first four games. From a crucial opening-night victory at home to Red Star to a goalless stalemate in Athens, Boškov then absorbed the body blow of a numbing 3-2 defeat away to Anderlecht on an evening when his team had led twice, before succumbing to an 88th-minute winner. While it was a damaging loss, it was one they reversed at the Stadio Luigi Ferraris a fortnight later to set up huge clash with Red Star in Sofia.

With Yugoslavia tearing itself apart, Red Star were forced to defend their European Cup exclusively on the road. After earlier homes games had taken place in Szeged and Budapest, they had finally rested in Sofia, where a narrow win had been earned against Panathinaikos. It was the third of three successive victories and an impressive response to their loss to Sampdoria on the opening night. It all meant that by the time Boškov and his team headed to Sofia to take on Red Star in the penultimate round of group games, a win for the holders would send them through to the final with a match to spare.

When Siniša Mihajlović arrowed in a beautifully arced free kick with less than 20 minutes on the clock at an atmospheric Stadion Balgarska Armia, the writing seemed to be on the wall for Sampdoria. Yet it was entirely symbolic when Katanec proved to be the identity of the scorer of the equaliser, with a less aesthetically pleasing but no less valuable strike 15 minutes later.

Before half-time, disaster had struck Red Star when Goran Vasilijević guided a lovely lob just beyond the reach of his own goalkeeper, Zvonko Milojević, after beating Vialli to a Mancini knock-down. It was then Mancini himself who cemented the outcome when he netted Sampdoria's third with just under 15 minutes remaining.

Armed with a one-point advantage when heading into the last round of games, a draw at home to Panathinaikos seemed likely to be enough to send Sampdoria to the final. Given that Red Star slipped to a 3-2 defeat at Anderlecht, Boškov's side ultimately could have lost and still attained their target, although they wouldn't have felt quite so blasé midway through the first half when trailing their Greek opponents at the same time that Red Star were level in Brussels.

By half-time Mancini had equalised for Sampdoria, while Red Star trailed to Anderlecht. It meant that the second half meandered to an inevitable conclusion rather than offering any discernible drama. It was a huge night for Sampdoria yet it barely registers amid a litany of iconic European Cup moments when teams were sat upon the cusp of the final.

To Wembley Barcelona and Sampdoria went, for the famous old stadium's fifth European Cup Final. For Cruyff, it was 21 years on from him playing there in his second final, and prevailing for the first time, against the Ferenc Puskás-led Panathinaikos.

In some ways the competition had indeed gone full circle. Although not in at the ground floor with Real Madrid, Puskás had been part of their 1960 winning team, scoring four times in their iconic success against Eintracht Frankfurt at Hampden Park. The 1971 final offered a sensory passing of the baton from Puskás to Cruyff in the same way that Cruyff fielding Guardiola in the 1992 final had reverberations that are still felt by football to this very day.

For Sampdoria, there was a defined ending to an era being played out. While there remained one Serie A match still to be played beyond the final, this was very much a case of the club having scaled the impossible mountain. It symbolically marked the end of the line.

Boškov had dragged Sampdoria as far as humanly possible, and on the table was a lucrative offer from Roma that he simply could not refuse, while Vialli's time at the club was also about to come to an end with Juventus waiting in the wings with an exorbitant fee. Cerezo was set to return to Brazil, and Pari was casting an eye to the exit door too.

It seems strange to suggest it now, but going into the game there were also doubts about Cruyff's future at Barcelona. Although they would go on to snatch the La Liga title on the final day two and a half weeks later, as things stood they looked set to be dethroned domestically and hadn't topped the table at all throughout the campaign.

So much was hinging on the outcome of the European Cup Final for Barcelona, and given their dysfunctional relationship with the tournament and the constantly volatile political undercurrent at the Camp Nou, it meant that Cruyff's position wasn't as stable as the outside world would have expected it to be.

With muted hopes of a more entertaining final than had been the case 12 months previously, Barcelona and Sampdoria indulged in a first half that was largely one where both teams probed for weaknesses without landing a goalscoring punch.

For Sampdoria, Lombardo forced Zubizarreta into a smart save, while at the other end, always keen to show off his impeccable reflexes, Pagliuca had produced a selection of stops that leaned more towards style than true substance. Other than this, Mannini earned himself a yellow card for a late challenge on Laudrup as the game meandered towards the interval.

The first 45 minutes had revolved around Barcelona enjoying the greater possession yet Sampdoria seemed happy enough to let them have it, content to pick off the occasional counter-attack, particularly down the right via Lombardo.

With Barcelona throwing themselves forward with increased intent at the beginning of the second half, Salinas and Eusebio rigorously tested Pagliuca with early efforts that drew two fine reactionary saves, almost one after the other. Sensing the swiftly escalating threat, the Sampdoria goalkeeper remained grounded after his second stop, bringing the physio needlessly into play in a clever bid to dampen the spark with which Cruyff's side had returned to the pitch.

This proved to be the ignition to a fascinating second half in which Barcelona's fine passing game constantly stemmed from Koeman bringing the ball out of defence to link with the deeper-lying Laudrup, who in turn sought to supply the effusive Stoichkov and the determined Salinas.

In response to this, Sampdoria's defence was calmness personified, while on the front foot they burst forward with a wonderfully dangerous counter-attacking vibrancy that really stretched the nervous disposition of a Barcelona defence that sometimes posed more questions than answers.

For the Catalans, it was a battle of their dreams of the ultimate success in attaining football's holy grail against the recurring nightmares of the unrequited finals of 1961 and 1986. The scars of Seville in particular, when they had been the hottest favourites ever going into a European Cup Final, were only six years old at this point.

These fears would have been at their apex when one of Lombardo's bursts down the right led to a golden opportunity for Vialli, who then wasted the chance. It would be the first of three gilt-edged sights on goal for the Sampdoria number nine, and they arguably should have won his team the final. Yet rather than freezing, Barcelona continued to do the simple things well, and Laudrup soon sent Stoichkov free only to see his sweetly struck effort hit the post and be cleared to safety.

Being bold with the situation, Cruyff's answer to Sampdoria's increasing threat was to withdraw Salinas midway through the second half, replacing him with Andoni Goikoetxea and pushing Laudrup alongside Stoichkov, thus handing Vierchowod new concerns.

Still the next dangers were posed by Sampdoria as Vialli forced Zubizarreta into a fine save before moments later chipping one just wide of the post. It was an opportunity that seemed a certain goal for a normally lethal marksman who would for a short time during the summer of 1992 be the most expensive footballer on the face of the planet.

With the game finely poised, Giovanni Invernizzi was then introduced in place of Ivano Bonetti with 17 minutes to play and suddenly proceedings became that little bit more combative, as the fear of being the team to make the mistake that lost the European Cup began to kick in.

Both teams subconsciously eased off as extra time loomed, although Stoichkov did manage to hit one that Pagliuca dealt untidily with, while for Sampdoria, Katanec headed over the bar when gifted the time and space to do better.

Goalless it might have been after 90 minutes, but it was an absorbing enough of an encounter to make an extra period a welcome addition. Extra time was dominated by Barcelona as they took a stranglehold on possession. As is so often the case with an added 30 minutes in a cup final, the game begins to focus on a specific duel, and in this one it was most definitely Vierchowod's with Laudrup.

With Sampdoria offering little going forward, Boškov made the ultimate sacrifice by sending Renato Buso on for Vialli just as the clocked ticked to 100 minutes. This seemed a bold concession that his team's most realistic route to victory in the remaining 20 minutes perhaps lay within a set piece or an aerial attack from deep positions.

Fatigue was also taking hold. Even Cruyff had been mindful enough to replace the youthful Guardiola with the veteran José Ramón Alexanko, a man who had almost 15 years extra wisdom on the future Barcelona, Bayern Munich, and Manchester City coach.

The best chance of the first period of extra time fell to Bakero, with a low shot that was straight at Pagliuca. Meanwhile, Sampdoria's best opportunity was an early Mannini header that he couldn't control.

With an understandable slowing down of proceedings during the second half of extra time, there was little further to note until the German referee Aron Schmidhuber awarded Barcelona a generous free kick just outside the D with nine minutes left to play. It stemmed from a tangled battle for possession between Invernizzi and Eusebio that should have really resulted in a drop ball, with even some of Barcelona's players seemingly nonplussed at being gifted a free kick.

Refusing to look the gift horse in the mouth, Stoichkov and Bakero neatly teed the ball up for Koeman to power home past the outstretched hand of Pagliuca and through the forest of Sampdoria legs that had splintered from the defensive wall in a bid to close the shot down.

Wembley erupted; Barcelona players, officials, and supporters in the joy of the moment that was set to end their long wait for European Cup glory, and their Sampdoria counterparts in protest at the unjust nature of the awarding of the free kick that had presented Cruyff and his players the biggest prize in European club football.

With Sampdoria now having no option but to stretch their shape, this offered Barcelona more room to operate. Stoichkov forced Pagliuca into a fine save, and the hero Koeman sent Laudrup away in the final seconds for the Danish maestro to square to Stoichkov, who failed to capitalise.

It should have been a second Barcelona goal, but thankfully for them, although Sampdoria piled on the pressure, they were unable to cultivate a clear sight of Zubizarreta and the endgame was eventually played out towards Sampdoria's right-hand corner flag.

Given that Barcelona had been tortured for so long by the European Cup, when their moment finally came it seemed almost surreal. Whereas László Kubala, Evaristo, Sándor Kocsis, Zoltán Czibor, Luis Suárez, and Bernd Schuster had fallen short, Koeman, Laudrup, Stoichkov, Bakero, and Guardiola had succeeded on what was the European Cup's last night.

Afterword

A Super League of Their Own

IN APRIL 2021, amid a lingering global pandemic, the most affluent football clubs on the face of the planet announced their intentions to form a breakaway Super League, detaching themselves from the apron strings of UEFA, while with expert calculation the word 'European' was left out of the equation, indicating that the future involvement of teams from other parts of the world was not entirely out of the question. This being an added prospect that offered the possible encroachment upon vaguely floated FIFA ambitions of creating an enlarged version of the Club World Cup, battle lines were drawn and gauntlets were thrown down by those involved and those looking on from the outside.

Causing a general state of discontent and uproar, within not much more than 72 hours this house of cards had toppled. Supporters took against the owners of their own clubs, players mobilised to voice their disapproval, and certain managers planted their flags of defiance on the centre spot in post-match interviews after hollow games were played out in empty stadiums on a West Yorkshire Monday evening. Tellingly, Sky Sports' on-camera employees were allowed free rein to campaign against the Super League, something that arguably spoke just as much of a television channel that hadn't been offered a sniff of an opportunity of being awarded broadcast partner status than it did the genuine outrage of former Liverpool and Manchester United players.

In a situation where nobody other than the game's holy trinity of supporters, players, and managers had the right to claim the moral high ground, the status quo at least temporarily won the day, drained by the knowledge that this is unlikely to be the definitive end of the threat to European football's governing body and its associated domestic leagues. Yet UEFA was essentially complicit in the advent of the Super League that never was. Everything it has done across the span of the last three decades has provided a series of stepping stones to the biggest clubs craving more of a say, more autonomy, and more money. The COVID-19 pandemic then escalated the situation swiftly.

The telling moment was the 1987/88 first-round encounter between the Napoli of Diego Maradona and Careca, and the La Quinta del Buitre-powered Real Madrid. From that point onwards, European club football's power brokers unilaterally decided that what was needed was an increase in the biggest head-to-heads.

Without UEFA saying so much out loud for all to hear, the weakest became an enemy to be eliminated. This concept was then enabled further by the fall of the Iron Curtain, with eastern Europe's most talented players free to flood west for the riches on offer, soon followed by the sweeping away of rules restricting teams to fielding only three foreign players per game. Then came the cherry on the cake and the advent of the Bosman rule, which permitted players complete freedom of choice upon the expiry of their club contracts.

Football has a repetitive history of substantive landscaping once every 30 years or so, from the formation of the Football

Association in the early 1870s and then FIFA in 1904, onward to the birth of the World Cup in 1930, the dawning of UEFA in the mid-1950s along with its requisite European club and international tournaments, and then the dawn of the Champions League in 1992, the very same year of the launch of the Premier League. Three decades later came the attempts to force through the Super League. I shudder to think of what plans might bubble to the surface by the time the 2050s roll on to the radar.

Some of the Super League's structural ideas were not all that terrible to be honest, and certainly would have offered a more interesting group stage compared to what the Champions League serves up. But, as a behemoth to making money for a select cartel of football clubs who would play one another on a near constant loop, and would be inoculated against relegation, it was quite rightly viewed as an overindulgence in an entirely new type of cake by those who already siphon off the biggest slices of the existing one.

Whereas the Champions League largely helped in killing off the romance of football, the Super League itself might have been no more than a Champions League 2.0, except within the control of its founding clubs rather than UEFA. Yet the Super League shop would have been one that was firmly closed to all but football's contemporary elite, with historical giants cast into the ether left behind. There would certainly be no hope for those clubs who shoot for the stars temporarily before returning to their natural resting position, and nor could the perceived minnows be allowed the chance to dream of crossing paths with these members of European royalty. There would essentially be the installation of a glass ceiling, that the teams cocooned above would skate across.

With smoke and mirrors arguably at play, UEFA has methodically herded the Champions League towards Super

League status anyway. As much as I rolled my eyes at the idea and excesses of a Super League, I cannot claim for one minute that any instincts to protect the Champions League kicked in. It just smacked of one bloated edifice that wanted to protect its interests, fighting off another projected and even more bloated structure.

How can UEFA claim to be saving football from a fate worse than death, when its alternative is more games, and the introduction of wildcard entries for the giants who fail to qualify via their domestic league position?

On top of the completely needless and convoluted UEFA Nations League at international level, and the advent of the Europa Conference League club competition, the expanding universe of European football will reach a breaking point. Yet I still foresee a time when a European Super League takes place, perhaps under the banner of UEFA and resembling the format the renegade 12 clubs unveiled, to be run alongside smaller domestic top-flight leagues of no more than 16 or 18 teams, and one domestic cup competition. An increase in European fixtures would offset a balancing of domestic duties.

When group stages were trialled in the 1991/92 European Cup, in preparation of the following season's rebrand to the Champions League, it was at least for a tournament that was still contested solely by teams who were their nation's reigning domestic league champions. Change came in 1997/98 when multiple teams from the strongest European leagues were allowed admittance, firstly with one extra place and soon followed by another two.

Within those first five seasons of the Champions League, with most western European domestic leagues maintaining a certain degree of strength, it was no surprise to see the 1980s Swedish powerhouse IFK Göteborg be the main threat to Milan reaching the 1993 final, or to see them only narrowly miss out on a semi-final spot two years later, nor that Panathinaikos put a run together in 1995/96 that took them to the last four.

By 1997/98, that first season of multiple participants from the biggest leagues, Göteborg had just reached the Champions League group stages for the last time. Meanwhile, it took Red Star Belgrade until 2018/19 before they reached the group stages for the first time since the 1992 rechristening, despite winning the European Cup in 1991. The upheaval of football during the 1990s was outdone only by the political and geographical landscape of Europe being redrawn due to the fall of the Iron Curtain.

When Real Madrid finally ended their 32-year hoodoo by defeating Juventus in the 1998 Champions League Final, it was fitting that the showpiece was contested by the previous season's Spanish and Italian domestic champions, in spite of it being the first campaign where teams no longer had to go to the trouble of winning La Liga or Serie A to gain entry to the tournament. It felt like a heart-warming riposte to change, but it was now only a matter of time before we were confronted by champions of Europe who attained their goal by the road less travelled.

We did not have to wait long, as 12 months later Manchester United, the 1997/98 Premier League runners-up, completed an unlikely looking late comeback at the Camp Nou against a stunningly profligate Bayern Munich. The team from Old Trafford had been largely outplayed, but Alex Ferguson's players struck with great ruthlessness to upturn the suspected outcome.

It was a turn of events that gave the Champions League its essence of drama. A new unwritten strapline to be replayed over and again, with 'Zadok the Priest' as the accompanying soundtrack, while simultaneously being coerced towards which tyre manufacturer, credit card, beer, and gaming console you should subscribe to.

A year later, Valencia were contesting the first of two successive Champions League Finals despite not having won La Liga since 1970/71, while in 2002 Bayer Leverkusen reached the final regardless of the fact they had never won the Bundesliga. In 2005 Liverpool took the honours, 15 years since their last domestic league title and 15 years from their next one. A sixth European Cup/Champions League was won by the Anfield club in 2019, almost three decades since they had been the champions of England. They reached the mark by defeating another English side, Tottenham Hotspur, who themselves have not won a league title since 1960/61.

Yes, the trophy that Jordan Henderson lifted into the Madrid night sky at the Wanda Metropolitano in early June 2019 looked like the one that Emlyn Hughes, Phil Thompson, and Graeme Souness had hoisted high in 1977, '78, '81, and '84, but the tournament and the route to glory was unrecognisable to what it had been. It was still good, but it was a vastly different type of good.

If 1992 was not a defined marker, it certainly represented a starting pistol being fired, not only for the European Cup but in the whole tilting of football's vaguely balanced playing field. It was there, prompted by the escalation of television rights, that the elite clubs strapped on the rocket boosters and put themselves out of the league of clubs not only such as Red Star and Göteborg but also the likes of Steaua Bucharest, Malmö, and Partizan.

When the Premier League was launched in 1992, underpinned by a huge cash injection from the entrance to the market for television rights of Sky, a template was cast for other leagues and competitions to follow.

In early 1986, halfway into a 1985/86 campaign that had begun without a television contract in place for English football, a belated deal was struck for an uneasy alliance between the Football League, the Football Association, and what was deemed to be a cartel of the BBC and ITV. It amounted to £6.3m for a season and a half of football coverage, while talk of an English Super League raged on. This was a scheme that was being pushed by Liverpool, Everton, Manchester United, Arsenal, and Tottenham Hotspur, a collective of agitators who were labelled the 'Big Five'.

In a familiar-sounding set of events, ITV was on board with the plan, and English football stood at a crossroads until a temporary accord was reached to keep the 92-team Football League intact for the duration of a £44m, four-year contract with ITV, for exclusive coverage of league football and the League Cup. In response the BBC and the yet-to-launch BSB signed a separate contract with the FA for coverage of the FA Cup and England games.

For towing the collective party line, the Big Five and their fellow First Division clubs were given greater voting rights by the Football League. It left the biggest-hitting teams unsatisfied, despite the increase in money and the voting concessions.

Rancour continued to regularly bubble to the surface, and by 1992 the Premier League was born, a concept that again operated as a bargaining collective rather than clubs either individually or in smaller collectives striking their own bespoke deals. A 22-team collective, as opposed to 92 teams, these breakaway clubs shared the ballast of a television bounty that rocketed up to £304m just over six years after the football powers that be had laboured their way that £6.3m.

It really was a whole new ball game, and the prices that Sky and others had to pay to obtain and retain their rights to broadcast the Premier League went stratospheric. Within this, the teams at the top counted their piles of money and thought for themselves that it still was not enough.

Of the 12 prospective breakaway teams for the Super League, it was no surprise to see that six were members of the Premier League. There has always been a sense of injustice harboured by the biggest clubs in English football, that the perceived smaller clubs are riding on the back of their coat tails. This will not simply vanish. Within the failure to float the Super League, the next avenue of agitation will likely be the right for clubs to strike their own bespoke television deals.

Three decades of the Champions League shapeshifting helped morph this unpalatable present-day situation. By 1994/95, if your team were the national champions of a lower-ranked European nation then you were no longer guaranteed a crack at the continent's biggest prize; by 1997/98 you did not have to be the domestic champions of Europe's biggest leagues to procure a shot at the Champions League. Since then, various tweaks have increased the number of guaranteed group stage berths allotted to the biggest teams, while the eye of the needle for the lesser lights to be able to join the party has shrunk dramatically.

Part of me felt that the 2021 rebellion against greed was mistimed by 30 years.

Since the inception of the Champions League, the final has been contested by teams from just seven different nations. Among them you will find the Netherlands, with its two appearances being in the last millennium, plus Portugal starring once, an appearance that now resides comfortably over a decade and a half ago. Then you have France and its dysfunctional relationship with European club competition: three very isolated finals in 1993, 2004, and 2020.

This leaves us with the more usual suspects from La Liga, Serie A, the Premier League, and the Bundesliga. Yet, when you come to look at Italian clubs, you must go back to 2010 for the last Serie A team to succeed in a Champions League Final. Once the definitive high plateau of European club football, Serie A has regressed markedly, decade on decade, pretty much since Channel Four stopped covering the league in 2002.

We seem to have reached an age whereby using a simple process of elimination, before a ball has been kicked in anger you can whittle down the Champions League's runners and riders to identify a select cluster of teams likely to be at the business end of the tournament. Even some traditional heavy hitters can be excluded at this stage. Barcelona's relationship with the tournament has soured after a series of epic capitulations, for instance, to the point of them being psychologically scarred. They almost seem as unlikely a Champions League winner as a Serie A team is.

Real Madrid dominated the second half of the 2010s, Liverpool and Bayern Munich have been fixtures, while try as football might, the riches of Paris Saint-Germain and Manchester City will not be repelled forever.

It is almost as if these supersonic clubs could do with a league of their own, while it is a situation that is not improved domestically either. Monopolies prevail. Juventus have just been dethroned after winning nine successive Serie A titles, every La Liga title bar two since 2004 has been won by Real Madrid or Barcelona, and PSG have won seven Ligue 1 titles in the last nine seasons.

Strangely, the Premier League has bucked this trend in recent years, as while Manchester City have every advantage to dominate profusely, four different teams have won the title in the last six seasons, including Liverpool ending their 30-year drought and Leicester City's shock success of 2015/16. All this at a time when Manchester United's last title win drifts into an ever-distant past as they struggle to find a place for themselves in a footballing life beyond Sir Alex Ferguson.

Yet this more competitive Premier League era has been entirely out of character for an entity where it took 20 years for it to summon up a fifth different winner, when in comparison the last three First Division titles were won by three different teams.

Elsewhere, we have recently passed the 30th anniversary of Sampdoria's 1990/91 Serie A title success, a period in which only twice has the Scudetto not ended up in the possession of either Juventus or one of the two Milan giants. Yet even those two occasions when the Serie A title instead went to Rome are now sat a distant two decades ago, while within the Juventus, Internazionale, and Milan hegemony, AC have become a significantly reduced threat.

We're heading into 'no shit Sherlock' territory here, but top-level football has long been driven by money, and the cost of that ever-escalating lust has been the erosion of hope. Whereas once upon a time anything seemed possible in a sport where a team like Nottingham Forest could narrowly climb out of the second tier of English football and become champions of Europe two years later, now we have an environment where the impossible is no longer possible.

It is as if those who roused themselves to do battle with the greed of 2021 had not been paying any attention to the last 30 years whatsoever.

Back to the European Cup and 13 different nations were represented in its 37 finals, including teams from Scotland, Greece, Belgium, Sweden, Romania, and what is now Serbia. Armed with a revolutionary coach and a set of players who were caught within the eye of a beautiful storm, impossible was nothing if not conquerable for any team. Even the smallest of participants were able to dream, if not of realistically achieving the most ultimate of European club glories then certainly of pitting their wits against the most legendary of teams and players in the earlier rounds. It was a special brand of magic that could touch anybody.

Up against this embedded streak within me, which is defiantly against modern football, battles the tribal romantic who is lucky enough to support a team that is still capable of the impossible. I was present at Anfield on the evening Liverpool overturned a 3-0 first-leg deficit against Barcelona, in May 2019, from where they went on to Madrid to become champions of Europe for the sixth time.

Notice the wording I used there. It is all in the wording. It is never about winning the Champions League; it is instead all about belligerently continuing to refer to the competition as the European Cup or stating the prevailing team to be the champions of Europe. It is akin to walking into a shop and asking for a Marathon or a packet of Opal Fruits, as opposed to a Snickers or a packet of Starburst. Which I also insist upon doing whenever the want arises.

That incredible victory over Barcelona has been classed by many long-standing Liverpool supporters as the club's greatest European night, outdoing Internazionale in 1965 and AS Saint-Étienne 12 years later. I was not around for the former, while for the latter I was still roughly eight months away from my dad taking me along to Anfield for the first time, so I cannot compare them. I do know that Barcelona 2019 was the greatest night I have ever experienced in that electric old but heavily restructured stadium.

There have been other great contemporary occasions. I was also in attendance on the 2005 evening when Luis García scored his ghost goal against Chelsea, and Eiður Guðjohnsen flashed one past the Kop end goalpost deep into injury time. Exiting Anfield, I immediately dispensed hugs to anybody who required one and met up with friends to begin plans that took us to Istanbul for 'that' final against Milan. It was to be the trip of a footballing lifetime.

There have been other incredible days and nights, and other wild trips. I went to Athens in 2007 and completed some stunning road trips to Kyiv and Madrid in 2018 and 2019 that were both tests of physical and mental endurance, and something akin to *The Cannonball Run*.

Modern football can still be good from time to time, but I would class it as a different type of good. It is now a case of embracing anything that stirs the soul of the inner child and letting those rare moments of passion envelop you: those moments when all of football's extremes melt away, reduced to its basic core brilliance, be that a last-gasp goal-line clearance that earns a mid-table point on an afternoon when you are sharing something you love with people you adore, or responding to Trent Alexander-Arnold's corner-kick subterfuge in a European Cup semi-final and embracing a multitude of people you have never met before, and quite possibly never will again.

Football is all about that era when you were at your most impressionable. The point of genesis, to roughly the age you are first handed bills to pay. From there it is about chasing anything that makes you feel like a child again. Change is frowned upon because these alterations happen to something precious that you embrace as your own.

We are all hardwired to the football of our youth, and in writing this trilogy I most certainly have been, as due to a head injury I sustained in my early 20s, it means there is a part of my brain that is perpetually locked in 1992. Putting this labour of love together, I have learned that that is not such a bad thing. I thank everybody who has picked one of these books up and taken the time to come along for the ride.

Also available at all good book stores

9781785315534

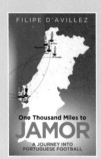

9781785316258

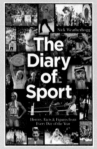

9781785316289

9781785316654

9781785316791

9781785317194